T0332265

Why am I like this?

Why am I like this?

my brain isn't broken
(and neither is yours)

GEMMA STYLES

Andrews McMeel
PUBLISHING®

First published in Great Britain in 2024 by Bantam, an imprint of Transworld Publishers.

Andrews McMeel Publishing
a division of Andrews McMeel Universal
1130 Walnut Street, Kansas City, Missouri 64106

www.andrewsmcmeel.com

25 26 27 28 29 LAK 10 9 8 7 6 5 4 3 2 1

ISBN: 979-8-8816-0016-7

Library of Congress Control Number: 2024943103

Editor: Danys Mares
Art Director: Julie Barnes
Production Editor: Kayla Overbey
Production Manager: Chuck Harper

ATTENTION: SCHOOLS AND BUSINESSES
Andrews McMeel books are available at quantity discounts with bulk purchase for educational, business, or sales promotional use. For information, please email the Andrews McMeel Publishing Special Sales Department: sales@amuniversal.com.

For all the overthinkers who feel too much and
not enough

Contents

"We don't even understand the brain of a worm."

CHRISTOF KOCH, PHD, CHIEF SCIENTIST
AND PRESIDENT OF THE ALLEN INSTITUTE
FOR BRAIN SCIENCE

Introduction

WHY AM I LIKE THIS? How many times have you asked yourself this very question over the past week? Did you leave a coffee on top of your car? Forget to text someone back? Or did you get lost in a spiral of over-thinking about all the ways you don't like yourself, don't like how you think, don't like how your brain works?

Some of you might be thinking, "Eesh, bit dramatic, Gemma" . . . and some of you will be wondering how I knew that. We're all different! That will always be true and should be celebrated, but whether or not you're feel-ing exasperated with or just curious about the way your brain works, there are some elements of our wiring that are pretty universal. Knowing more about them, in my experience, is both empowering and exhilarating.

For a very long time, I felt trapped and limited by what was going on inside my head. I didn't understand why I was struggling and felt like everyone else was getting along just fine while I was falling, internally, at the first hurdle. The thing that has always made the most differ-ence to how I feel is information. Getting an answer. For me, a lot of those answers were to questions relating to poor mental health or, as I would later find out, ADHD. This isn't a memoir, but I am going to be talking about my own experience with mental health issues and the struggles I've faced since my late teens (specifically, depression and anxiety). This is partly so you can see where I'm coming from, in the spirit of being open and honest about things a lot of people face at certain times in their life, and also because the best place to start is often with the things you know most about. My questions might not all be the same as your questions but, for each of us, the way we feel about ourselves is deeply entangled with how we navigate the world we live in.

Let's face it, there are always going to be new things we notice and more idiosyncrasies we'd like explained. It would take a thousand books to try to sum up every little experience of any one person. We might not all relate to exactly the *same* things, but we'll all relate to some. The beauty of examining how we process the world in such a universal sense is that the things you learn about yourself, you can apply to others too. Maybe you're most frustrated with yourself, or maybe with other people. *Why are they reacting like that? Why aren't they listening to me?*

But far from feeling resigned to the more exasperating ways in which our brains work (and make us feel), I want us to see the method in the madness, as well as realize that there are things we can change. Your brain isn't working against you—even when it feels like that—it's often trying to keep you safe. The world in which we live has changed so much and so fast. The things we feel threatened or angered by aren't the same as they were when we evolved to spot the tiger lurking outside the cave, and yet our brain chemistry can't always tell the difference.

There are people who spend their lives studying neuro-science, psychology, and anthropology in order to better understand humans. I'm not an expert in any of these fields. But I don't think you need to be to grasp some information that will give you that vital "Aha!" moment that unlocks something for you. I really love being able to take information and present it in a way that allows people to understand it (which is probably why I did a degree to become a science teacher). There are many ways into a topic as vast and as complex as the human brain and how its functioning affects us. As someone who is baffled, frustrated, and ever fascinated by learning more about how we all tick, I've realized that we have it in our power to understand ourselves a bit better. And, by so doing, to have more compassion for ourselves and those around us, making it a bit easier to live in this complex and challenging world of ours.

I'll be talking a lot about mental health in this book, how it differs from mental illness and how we're collectively affected by life nowadays—with 24/7 news coverage, hits of dopamine (figuratively) in our pockets and more opportunities to compare ourselves than ever before. I want to explore the things we have in common rather than deep-diving into our uniqueness. You know that feeling when you scroll past an infographic and it just so happens to perfectly explain something you do or feel? The satisfaction of understanding yourself just a smidge better? That's what I want you to get from reading this book. If you've been nodding along so far, if you recognize that feeling of being frustrated by your own brain, then I hope there'll be things in here that will help you. At one time or another, we all come up against ourselves and are forced to wonder, "Why am I like this?"

And what then, if we find the answer? Knowing why you do something doesn't necessarily stop you doing it, of course. But being aware of some of the things happening in our own heads, knowing the biases and evolutionary wiring we're working with, can help us to stop wasting so much time being upset with ourselves and, frankly, get on with our lives.

As we'll come on to later: How can you argue against someone when you don't know what their point is? If we don't know what's happening when our brains whisper their jealous thoughts or revert back to a bad habit or can't stop replaying an embarrassing moment, what are we supposed to do about it? That feeling when you're gritting your teeth in exasperation and the person you're arguing with is inside your own head . . . hooo boy.

Here's what I've learned is bad for your mental health, from hard-won personal experience: not being on your own team. I spent so long being annoyed at myself, wondering why I slipped into old habits or thought patterns, why I didn't cope with things like everyone else seemed to, why I cared so much about what other people think.

It's draining. And I've realized that what's worse than any of those tendencies is existing in a state where you think you're weird because of them and it's all your fault. That's time I don't want you to waste anymore!

Essentially, what I've come to understand (through many years of wrestling with my own problems) is that knowing why something happens makes it that much easier to get through the day. It's as simple as that. Plus, is—in my opinion, and hopefully I will convince you of this too—*so* interesting. You really don't have to be a biology or psychology nerd to enjoy feeling sheer awe that we have these amazing brains in our heads that are capable of so much cool stuff.

That's what I'd like to share with you here: an opportunity to step back and appreciate how complicated we are as a species, why that is, and how it's helped us to survive. I want us to break free of the resentment we can feel toward ourselves when we react in anger, when we compare ourselves to others, when we feel numbed by a world on fast-forward—because stopping feeling that way means we can spend less energy on an internal battle and more energy on what we put into the world. Maybe that's campaigning for change in our communities. Maybe that's no longer feeling like an imposter at work. Maybe it's simply being a safe space for your friends. I want you to feel vindicated in the things that you find hard. Comforted that you're not the only one who feels that way. And then empowered to carry on in all your imperfect glory.

1

WHAT'S HAPPENED TO OUR MENTAL HEALTH?

LET'S START WITH THE POSITIVES. There has been quite an obvious shift in the mental health conversation recently, I think most people would agree. It used to be pretty major to start talking about taking antidepressants or having a panic attack, and now that's not so much the case. Being open about our mental health has become far more common, and that's a wonderful thing as far as I'm concerned.

But is talking about mental health the same as talking about mental illness? Are mental health issues and mental illness more widespread these days or is it simply the case that we are hearing more about them as the discussion opens up and the stigma that once came with them recedes? And while it's great to talk openly about things that can go wrong in our brains, what happens then? In an ideal world, we could all see a mental health professional when we need to, but underfunded public health systems and prohibitive private costs, as well as a sheer outweighing of demand versus trained ears, means it's not always an option for everyone. And are the labels that those professionals put on our symptoms always helpful to have, or can there be such a thing as too much diagnosis or too much mental health awareness? When we're struggling, how can we try to make sense of our brains and what's going wrong up there?

Fair warning: depression and anxiety are going to be things I talk about most often in this chapter, purely because they're the things I've experienced myself. I am aware that other mental illnesses are available, but since these two are also the most common, I'm hoping my experiences will be relatable at least for some of you. The specifics of those worst periods become hazy for me as time passes, but I have certainly found that there's a lasting mark that severe depression, and suicidal ideation, have left on me. Not in a way that means I feel closer to going back there, but in a way that leaves a permanent appreciation for feeling good, feeling happy—and a deep, heavy empathy with people who are currently in the trenches.

I am lucky that (at the time of writing) I'm in a good place relative to other times in my life, and that in turn means it's a lot easier to talk about mental health in a general sense, as well as to look back to when times were harder for me. As I've mentioned, I began struggling on and off with my mental health in my late teens. During those earlier years, I'd say anxiety was my main issue, often around the expected stresses like exams, but with the hindsight that experiences since then have given me, I know I was steering into unhealthy territory from that stage.

When I went to university, I began to suffer much more from depression. I was reasonably quick to see a GP about it, but their suggested treatments were mainly group sessions to talk about the pressures of student life, or self-help books—neither of which did much to help and, unfortunately, just didn't suit me as a person at that time. Contrary to how it may seem, given that I'm writing about my mental health in a book, I'm a very private person, and even though they can be so incredibly helpful to lots of people, group therapy or discussion groups just weren't my bag because I didn't want to talk about those things with strangers I might later bump into in the student union. For a long time I've also been acutely aware that talking about my life, or childhood, or family means talking about people who the outside world are, let's just say, very curious about, and being fiercely protective of those people and their privacy meant I was reluctant to trust outsiders with such personal information. This same concern put me off seeing a therapist for years, which in the end turned out to be the best decision I could have made. So if you are someone who feels the same way about talking over your problems with people you don't know, seeing a well-matched therapist may be a much more comfortable experience than you're picturing. Learn from my mistakes.

But before it got better, it unfortunately got worse. I went from experiencing some mild symptoms of depression to going through pretty severe depressive episodes throughout my late teens and well into my mid-twenties. I felt at times so utterly bereft, though I couldn't tell you why. When sad things did happen, I used them to excuse how badly I was doing, because it made sense to me that I should feel terrible. In the worst swamps, I didn't actively want to die . . . but I so badly wanted to opt out of what my life had become that it boiled down to the same longing. Luckily, the shock and fear of realizing that's what I was thinking did prompt me to get help, but I wouldn't have had the strength to do so without the extreme good fortune of having just the right friends around me at just the right moment. Knowing that there are people who experience those low points without the lifelines that I had makes me feel so sad, and even more passionate about mental health care and provision.

During this period, not everything was terrible all the time. Sometimes I'd feel better for a while, only for a low to hit me without warning, or else sneak up gradually as I caught glimpses of its approach in my peripheral vision. Sometimes I thought I was OK and just enjoying my life when what I was really doing was numbing myself and running from it. And, as is so often the way, I'm sure a lot of people wouldn't have necessarily noticed anything was wrong. Yet, for a long time, it felt like my entire adult life had been stretched and scarred by feeling hollow, sad, and unworthy. In its typical cruelty, depression makes you feel both desperately empty and also that it's your own fault, like you somehow just haven't lived your life well enough and now you can't quite find the thread that would help you trace back the route that led you to this miserable place.

I thought for the longest time that I was always going to be at least a bit depressed. Even with medication or when I was in therapy, even if things were generally going well and there were plenty of up moments, I didn't think of myself as a happy person, or someone for whom the day-to-day bits of life were going to be enjoyable. Since being diagnosed with ADHD in my early thirties, I've been able to see that some of those lingering symptoms, like finding it hard to motivate myself or struggling to maintain the admin of friendships, may well stem from the ADHD and not the depression, as I'd (reasonably, I think) assumed.

Neurodivergence and mental illness are often found together; they are what's known as comorbid conditions, but they aren't one and the same. Being neurodivergent doesn't automatically mean there's something wrong with your mental health, but, in reality, existing in a neurotypical society while being different from most people around you often does take an emotional toll that can result in symptoms of mental illness. For the "everyone has ADHD all of a sudden" brigade, it's worth noting that in the UK, the National Institute for Health and Care Excellence (NICE), and therefore the NHS, didn't even recognize that ADHD existed in adults until 2008, and in 2018 went as far as updating its guidance to high-light the chronic issue of under-diagnosis in women and girls.[1] So it's not that everyone's suddenly decided they have ADHD, it's that they've always had it and we're dealing with an enormous backlog of people having no access to support or treatment. Consider me on my soapbox, but as someone personally affected, it really irritates me to read people with zero stake in the game wanging on about how neurodivergence is now "trendy." For women like me who are statistically more likely to be diagnosed later in life than other groups anyway, it's often taken many years of trying and failing to mitigate symptoms of a condition you aren't aware of before that diagnosis is reached, and, fairly obviously, this cycle of feeling like a failure has a big impact on your self-esteem and mental well-being. I'm focusing on ADHD here because I can speak from personal experience on the connection to mental illness, but other neurodivergent conditions, for example autism, Tourette's, or dyslexia, all bring their own challenges that could reasonably and rationally end up affecting someone's mental health—even though these aren't mental illnesses.

All this is to say that, even though I've come a long way in understanding my own mental health issues, and even though they're probably on the less thorny end of the scale, I still have a lot of question marks and unex-plained connections floating around. Like, why did I suffer with anxiety and depression in the first place? Are they linked to each other? Were they caused by my

ADHD or only egged on by it? Why did some medications work and others didn't? We might wish that treating mental illness was as simple as taking a measurement and prescribing a pill to precisely alter that measurement to a place of sunshine and rainbows, but unfortunately (and beautifully) the way our brains function is a heck of a lot more convoluted.

How far have attitudes to mental illness changed?

I've been asked many times when and why I decided to start talking about mental health online and I don't have one concrete answer. I can't remember it ever feeling like a before-and-after kind of decision. I don't think I did any "big reveal" post or introductory explainer to my own mental health landscape. As far as I recall, it was a drip-feed process for me—a mention of anxiety here, sharing a depression meme there. As is the case with most things on social media, these tiny snippets of ourselves that we choose to share, whether overthought or flippant, form a public picture of who we are, and, little by little, I became known as someone who talks openly about mental health. I'm proud of that.

That being said, I am aware that the conditions I have or have experienced are on the more common and "acceptable" end of the spectrum. Acceptable being very deliberately in quote marks there, because I'm talking about acceptability in terms of how well they are tolerated by society at large. In other words, the way people react to me talking about my experience of anxiety and depression is something of a breeze compared to a lot of the narratives encountered by people living with more maligned or misunderstood conditions. Other illnesses such as bipolar disorder, post-traumatic stress disorder (PTSD), premenstrual dysphoric disorder (PMDD), and obsessive-compulsive disorder (OCD) face their own distinct challenges, from general awareness of their existence, to stereotypes about sufferers, to simplified, co-opted ideas about their effects. (Please don't talk about someone who likes to keep a clean house as being "a bit OCD.")

In any given week in England, eight in a hundred people will experience mixed anxiety and depression, whereas bipolar disorder, for example, only affects two in a hundred people across their entire lifetime. Psychotic disorders like schizophrenia will affect fewer than one in a hundred people in any given year.[2] So, while it's understandable that we're plainly, statistically, more likely to have either experienced or come across the more common illnesses, it also means we should be more willing to actively form an awareness of these less prevalent disorders.

Don't get me wrong, many people are still dismissive of depression or anxiety. I don't think it's possible to "not agree" with the concept of individual mental health. If you "don't agree" with mental illness or mental health issues as a reality, it's because you don't understand them. Like climate change. You can be as skeptical as you like about global warming, but the science is the science and the ice caps are melting. And yet, unfortunately, there are still plenty of wilfully uninformed and unsympathetic people out there. In their most boring, tired rantings, the critical and/or dismissive contingent tells us that the youngest generations in particular are just too sensitive, self-obsessed, and quick to seek a diagnosis. Any snowflake-haters who picked up this book by accident will surely by now have put it down again. (I hope they're happier without me.) When we step out of mental health positive spaces, we can be swiftly reminded that years of awareness campaigns and reminders to talk to each other haven't quite reached everyone. And even where we have achieved an increased awareness of mental illnesses, this doesn't automatically equate to a comparable level of sympathy or understanding across all our communities or for everyone struggling.

So what's the truth? Is there any way of measuring general attitudes to mental illness? Well, in a 2019 US survey conducted by the Harris Poll on behalf of the American Psychological Association, 87 percent of respondents somewhat or strongly agreed with the statement that "having a mental health disorder is nothing to be ashamed of." Encouraging! However, in the same poll, an almost equal 86 percent of people somewhat or strongly agreed that "the term 'mental illness' carries a stigma."[3]

Hmm ... OK. Now, it could well be that these respondents disagreed with the stigma while believing it exists (though the first answer suggests that such a stigma ought to be far less prevalent than they seem to assume), but the numbers still seem puzzling to me given such a strong showing of support for removing the associated shame. Is it the small proportion of holdouts who are causing all the issues? Maaaybe. But more likely, I believe, is that this highlights the wide gap between superficial awareness or acceptance of mental illness and practical support or accommodation of sufferers.

While we can logically acknowledge that stigma against mental illness is unfair, we don't live in a perfect world and can see that it often prevails anyway. People are more understanding of depression in the abstract, but that understanding can disappear as soon as someone's symptoms affect *them*. We can get our heads around anxiety but maintain prejudices about people with schizophrenia or OCD. As I'll come back to momentarily, treating mental illness as a one-size-fits-all issue often leads to these head-scratching moments because it's simply too complex to deal with within the scope of one question.

"She's got mental health"

That we have a long way to go when it comes to meaningful awareness and acceptance of mental illness is evident even in how we talk about "mental health" versus "mental illness." These two phrases have become almost synonymous in mainstream conversation. And while we can definitely take a moment to celebrate the progress that is the very existence of a mainstream conversation about mental health, we are still left with the issue that this confusion is not super-helpful in encouraging what we all want: for everyone to be taking care of themselves. You, like me, may have come across people flippantly using sentences like "Oh, she's got mental health" when talking about someone who's experiencing some difficulties. (If you're already thinking, "Well, surely you'd say 'mental health *issues*,'" then gold star for you.) There are myriad reasons why this tone is often, let's say, not quite right . . . but let's just look at two big ones.

Firstly, everyone has mental health. Whether your current mental landscape is good, bad, or somewhere in between, we all go through life with thoughts and feelings, being more or less able to cope with the ups and downs we come across. To use the phrase "mental health" as a diagnosis, a term for something that some people experience negatively and most people aren't affected by whatsoever, does a disservice to everyone, and nothing to educate or encourage people to be aware of that landscape—let alone notice when people are suffering, or to implement steps in their lives that could improve things.

Secondly, to refer vaguely to someone "having mental health" creates a real "us and them" look at emotional well-being, rather than recognizing it as something that ebbs and flows for each of us throughout our lives. Also, for many, a period of mental ill health is just that: a time in their lives that doesn't last forever. Saying someone "has mental health" (even though, see previously, we all do!) seems to carry much more weight than saying someone "has a cold"—and yet, for plenty of people, a period of mental ill health may well be a temporary, curable state of being. Granted, it will most likely take longer than a cold to get over, but in a world where there's still a decent level of stigma against mental illness, the idea that once someone is open about their struggles, they're seen as having issues in perpetuity is not only fairly likely to be inaccurate, but also carries the kind of judgment that makes people worry about seeking help in the first place.

The other important thing to bear in mind here is that, according to the American Psychiatric Association, "mental illnesses are health conditions involving changes in emotion, thinking, or behavior (or a combination of these). Mental illnesses can be associated with distress and/or problems functioning in social, work, or family activities."[4] In other words, it's a big area. Someone experiencing a temporary bout of moderate anxiety and someone living with a severe, lifelong illness aren't going through the same thing, and they will need different approaches when it comes to support. And I hope that if we're talking about someone suffering with mental illness, we're doing so in the context of wanting to help them! Some of the broad categories of mental illnesses include mood disorders like depression, anxiety disorders, psychotic disorders like schizophrenia, trauma-related disorders, substance abuse disorders, and eating disorders. That doesn't cover everything, but hopefully illustrates why using very reductive language when talking about someone's mental health isn't useful.

Indeed, the level of individuality inherent in any one person's mental health can be difficult to understand even for the most open and willing. A group of people who experience the same mental illness are not a monolith, and even when we look at one person, the severity of illness they're experiencing won't always be the same from day to day.

As described by the UK's National Institute for Health and Care Excellence:

> A **mild** mental health problem is when a person has a small number of symptoms that have a limited effect on their daily life.
>
> A **moderate** mental health problem is when a person has more symptoms that can make their daily life much more difficult than usual.
>
> A **severe** mental health problem is when a person has many symptoms that can make their daily life extremely difficult.
>
> A person may experience different levels at different times.[5]

Depression is perhaps one of the most commonly understood examples of a mental illness that can switch between the categories defined above in one individual. Someone who lives with long-term depression often experiences symptoms in cycles and may feel better or worse from one week, month, or year to the next. Recognizing that its impact changes over time can help us to be more accommodating and better able to offer support. Being able to see people as they are and not rigidly clinging to an image of them at their very worst or very best, or to a narrow understanding of a disorder, makes us better listeners and better supporters. Incorporating even this level of nuance is really helpful in furthering conversations about mental illness, which is a good step in ensuring that we do, in fact, understand the difference between mental illness and taking care of our mental health in general, whether we're struggling with it or not.

What if you're sad when you don't have anything to be sad about?

There are definitely some things we do know about what causes poor mental health, and there are a multitude of factors that affect whether someone is impacted by mental illness or not. According to this list from mental health charity Mind, plenty of contributing factors have been identified:

- childhood abuse, trauma, or neglect
- social isolation or loneliness
- experiencing discrimination and stigma, including racism

- social disadvantage, poverty, or debt
- bereavement (losing someone close to you)
- severe or long-term stress
- having a long-term physical health condition
- unemployment or losing your job
- homelessness or poor housing
- being a long-term carer for someone
- drug and alcohol misuse
- domestic violence, bullying, or other abuse as an adult
- significant trauma as an adult, such as military combat, being involved in a serious incident in which you feared for your life, or being the victim of a violent crime
- physical causes—for example, a head injury or a neurological condition such as epilepsy can have an impact on your behavior and mood[6]

However, a confusing and difficult reality for some sufferers of mental illness is that they could look at that list and not really find themselves in it. As I hope we all know by this point, mental health issues don't discriminate, and there are plenty of people who seem both from the outside and to themselves to be in a good position in life and "not have anything to be sad about." That just isn't how it works, though, and brings us on to look at the idea of situational depression versus clinical depression.

Neither one is less real or less serious than the other,

but an understanding of which one you're dealing with can be very helpful in determining the best treatment. Situational depression is otherwise known as an "adjustment disorder with depressed mood,"[7] and tends to result from a change or traumatic event in a person's life. Clinical depression is otherwise known as "major depressive disorder" and is officially classified as a mood disorder.[8] Situational depression is likely to be more short-lived and may resolve itself without treatment, but if that's not the case and adequate help isn't provided, it has the potential to evolve into clinical depression, which is usually more severe.

Globally, major depression in women is 1.7 times more common than in men. While there are many factors that may contribute to this statistic, for example gendered differences in levels of abuse, education, and income (aka the gender pay gap), similar ratios have been observed both globally and in more developed countries where those socio-economic factors are likely to be less impactful. In other words, there doesn't seem to be a big difference between countries where women overall experience a markedly lower status than men, and countries where our status is more even. This seems to suggest that there could be a biological explanation for the higher levels of depression observed in women and girls.

Girls are important to highlight here. According to the Global Burden of Disease Study from 2010, from puberty onward, young women are at higher risk of major depression and mental disorders than any other group globally.

In the ages 14–25 bracket, depression is more than twice as prevalent in young women as it is in young men—but this ratio does decrease with age.[9,10] Over the age of sixty-five, rates of depression decline across the board, and the frequency evens out between genders too.[11]

You would think that, with this being the case, there would have been more emphasis on treating depression in women specifically. Before puberty, the rates of depression are about the same in boys and girls, but the hormonal changes associated with puberty appear to affect mental health hugely. This is echoed in other instances too, as higher rates of depression are consistently observed in women during times of hormonal change, such as before menstruation, after pregnancy, and during perimenopause. However (and prepare to be annoyed), many studies tend to focus on male subjects in order to control for changes in behavior that could be associated with the menstrual cycle.

This isn't to say that we should accept being female as a risk factor for depressive illness and move on. It actually feels quite frustrating to point to a possible hormonal factor, as it seems like that's all society has done for a long time. "Eh, hormones—whatcha gonna do? Have you tried the pill?" But in talking about feeling sad when you don't know why, it seems that, for a lot of young women, hormones could be a part of the puzzle that often fails to be legitimately acknowledged in a way that feels serious or sympathetic, as opposed to reductive and dismissive. Solid data on how pervasive mental health issues are within this demographic can hopefully offer some vindication to young women, who are as a group so often belittled for their feelings.

Is our mental health getting worse?

So, is mental illness really more common these days, among young people or otherwise? To keep it simple, the data says yes. According to the Health Foundation, among children aged six to sixteen in England, rates of probable mental illness rose to one in six in 2021, compared with one in nine back in 2017.[12] (There are, of course, myriad possible factors that could be contributing to declining mental health in young people, and we don't have enough pages to deep-dive into each of them, but we'll swing back to a particularly relevant one later on when we look in more depth at social media.) It's an alarming rise to see in a young population, but this is mirrored in wider data for other demographics too. According to the World Health Organization, mental health conditions are in fact increasing worldwide, with a 13 percent increase in mental health conditions and substance abuse disorders in the decade leading up to 2017—though it notes that this is mainly attributable to demographic changes.[13]

Pointing to changing demographics means that the way people are living now, compared to other points in history, can be seen to correlate with higher incidences of mental illness. In a 2021 study of self-reported mental health conditions in Estonia, researchers were able to illustrate that incidences of stress, depression, overtiredness, and suicidal thoughts were visible on a distinct gradient of socio-economic circumstances.[14] A lower income was associated with a higher incidence of all mental health complaints measured in the study. Lower levels of education were linked to a higher incidence of depressiveness, while lower levels of job skills predicted a higher likelihood of suicidal thoughts. Interestingly, all the mental health complaints examined were reported more frequently in the younger population than in the older group (fifty- to sixty-four-year-olds) as well as in single people (not married or cohabiting).

Looking quite simply at these findings, you can see how these patterns occur. It's well documented that today's younger generations find themselves in a vastly different position to previous generations in terms of cost and standard of living. Even before the acute cost-of-living crisis that began in 2021, there had been decades of shifting trends in, for example, average wages versus the cost of renting or a deposit on a home. This is definitely not attributable to an increased fondness for avocado toast in bougie cafes. With reduced income being linked to mental illness, it's reasonable to assume that for some single people, being solely responsible for household bills, et cetera, is an additional source of stress—some of those people might also be single parents, which makes that financial burden even more pronounced.

So, yes, there is data to show that mental health problems are more common than they used to be, and the reasons for that are numerous, complex, and not simple to fix. What's also true is that public perception and acceptance have changed, at least to the point at which more of us are being open about suffering from a mental illness. This has a compounding effect on our sense of the numbers: when more people are indeed experiencing these issues and a higher proportion of them are willing to discuss it, to anyone observing, the incidence of mental illness understandably looks dramatically higher within a short space of time.

This useful example illustrates why we should interrogate seemingly simple data points or clickbait headlines on mental health (and lots of things, actually). It's all well and good to point out that young people are more likely to report experiencing mental health struggles than older generations, but we have to take into account that the world these young people are growing up in is completely different and, while we've moved forward in a lot of positive ways, modern life can be hard. In a chapter about mental health in a book titled *Why Am I Like This?*, I think it's particularly important I take a moment to pause on that. If you are one of those people who has struggled with their mental health, or is struggling right now, you are very much not alone. It is not your fault and there are much wider issues happening in the world that have contributed to how you feel, even if it's hard to pinpoint them. You're doing great just by keeping going.

It's not a simple case of cause and effect

The truth is that definitive cause and effect can be hard to come by in researching correlations between societal or demographic factors and mental health conditions, not least because of the infinitely interconnected nature of the subjects. It's not like we can point at something and say, "Well, this one thing got worse so that's why people now feel this way." Much as we talk about intersectional feminism, for example, and try to examine the cross section of factors at play when it comes to someone's experience of gender inequality, we have to examine deeper than the top line and interrogate all the possible explanations—which is hard to do when there are so many variables to try to account for! If you'll indulge me, I'll use the example of a headline I found interesting, about a nutritional study conducted in Brazil in 2022, which determined that non-meat eaters are around twice as likely to suffer from depressive episodes than those who eat meat.[15] It's easy to imagine the clickbait headline here: "Being Vegetarian Makes You Depressed, Study Shows." So let's unpack.

We've already mentioned that women and girls are statistically more likely to suffer from depression—women are also typically more likely to be vegetarian than men. Aha! Is that what we're seeing here? The Brazilian study did adjust the data to take this into account, though, as well as correcting for plenty of other possible skewing factors, including alcohol intake, smoker status, and activity level, and still found that vegetarians and vegans were twice as likely to experience depressive episodes as those in the study who included meat in their diet. So, am I about to run off and order a steak to protect my mental health? I am not.

Given that this study was looking at people's intake of particular foods and was adjusted to try to look purely at that one factor, it seems simple to determine cause and effect, right? Are those who eat a meatless diet missing out on particular nutrients, which then causes low mood? The production of serotonin in the body is reliant on a solely diet-derived amino acid called tryptophan—are vegetarians and vegans not getting enough of that? It sounds plausible; however, when analyzing their data, the researchers conducting this study did take into account a wide range of nutritional factors, including calorie intake, levels of micronutrients, level of food processing, and protein intake—which suggests that it isn't actually the nutritional content of a vegetarian diet that causes higher rates of depression. The plot thickens . . . but there are plenty of other possible explanations.

Could there be social causes rather than nutrient-based ones? Are people more likely to be vegetarian or vegan in response to caring about climate change and the effects on the planet of farming meat? Are the same people who care about those things more likely to be depressed in response to concern about the climate? Are those same people more likely to be tuned into and stressed about other issues, like animal welfare?

When *The Conversation* reported on this study, it noted that the cultural climate in Brazil could also be relevant to the findings: Brazil as a nation has a famously meat-heavy diet, and while some data from other surveys has pointed to a sharp rise in the popularity of vegetarianism in recent years, in the study we're looking at, non-meat eaters only accounted for just over 0.5 percent of the 14,000 participants.[16] The rarity of this lifestyle among peers, the article suggests, could mean that vegetarians experience an emotional toll due to being teased or otherwise left out of social activities; for example, if their friends are all going to a restaurant and there's nothing they can eat on the menu. Could this sort of thing contribute to increased rates of depression?

All this is to say, I hope this example illustrates that not only are causation and correlation different things, but that we and our mental health don't exist in a vacuum. There are a multitude of factors that affect whether someone is impacted by mental illness or not. When we read headlines or infographics that report links or patterns between particular lifestyle factors and the incidence of mental illness, that's interesting information and useful to build a fuller picture in understanding how different people experience the world. But reading a headline about your diet or hobbies or relationships isn't typically a good indication that changing one thing is going to make a massive difference to your individual mental health. Not that all those headlines are going to be wrong, per se, or that lifestyle changes don't impact mental health, but when we're stumbling around in the darkness of an illness like depression and suddenly read that it's all down to not eating enough burgers . . . There's more at play here, and it's not your fault if you follow that advice and nothing happens. Health is more complicated than cause and effect.

Social media: Help or hindrance?

If we're talking about how life has changed in the past few years, of course we need to look at the impact of social media. I'm sure teens coming of age right now can't even imagine a time without it. It's so common to hear people talking about how social media is bad for us, or extolling the benefits of online detoxes or at least weekends spent offline. And I'm not disagreeing with this advice—it could certainly be a good idea to take a break. I've definitely needed to myself, more than once. Increased opportunities to compare ourselves with others' seemingly perfect online lives can fuel poor self-esteem or dissatisfaction with our own circumstances. Viewing a constant stream of other people's highlight reels may make it harder to experience the fullness of our own lives. But then again, we know that social media comes with many potential positives too—thee connections, the awareness, the ability to be a global citizen. So often, what's lacking both online and when talking about being online is nuance.

Alongside legitimate questions about the relationship

between social media use and mental well-being, there are reductive, lazy conclusions being drawn. For example, we often hear that it's easy to find other people online who can relate to our struggles because experiencing mental illness is "trendy" now. People even suggest that exposure to conversations about mental health online can encourage teenagers and young people to start faking their own mental illnesses—for the cool points. As we've already seen, mental illness truly is more common than it used to be, it's most common in young women and we talk about it more too, but this sentiment still seems to crop up a lot. Can there be any truth to it at all?

A recent example that was eagerly picked up in the news media is the phenomenon of young people fostering and then developing tics, which is often attributed to TikTok. The idea of young people picking up habits or symptoms from social media isn't especially new and isn't specific to TikTok; Tumblr and Instagram in particular have had their moments—some continuing—in this arena of finger pointing. Many believe that seeing high levels of engagement and attention paid to users who talk about and display their tics has encouraged other young people to copy this behavior in the hopes of eliciting the same attention for themselves.

A more medical theory of "TikTok tics" is that young people, particularly adolescent women and girls, aren't "faking" the tics exactly, but they also aren't caused by an underlying illness like Tourette's or epilepsy. Instead, the high frequency with which users watch videos of influencers exhibiting ticcing behaviors and patterns impacts their brains, so that they unconsciously start to mimic. As explained by neurologist Dr. Omar Danoun, "What these teen girls have are called functional tics—it's a functional neurological disorder. We've seen this before in children who have parents or siblings with seizures. They'll develop functional seizures. The brain imitates what it sees. It's used as an escape mechanism."[17]

According to that logic, in this case, a rise in people seeking help for tics and related disorders since 2021 could be linked to an increase or trend in tic-/Tourette's-related content online. Another theory, posed by Dr. Andrea Giedinghagen, a psychiatry professor at the Washington University School of Medicine in St. Louis, is that the increasing incidence of tics during this period could be related to stress arising from the pandemic. Or, of course, a mixture of both things could be true. Functional neurological disorders often come about in place of healthy coping mechanisms and are associated with trauma, depression, or anxiety, so people with those conditions are likely more susceptible to developing functional tics. Given that teen girls are more likely to experience depression and anxiety than boys, it does line up that the tic phenomenon would be more prominent within their demographic. And even though doing some research shows this makes sense ... most people aren't doing that research. How are they to discern someone with Tourette's from someone faking Tourette's from someone not faking anything but suddenly developing symptoms of Tourette's?

The problem with discussing anything that links social media and mental health is that some folks will always take the opportunity to use rare examples of people actually faking illnesses to discredit whole communities. Those people, I believe, are coming from a closed-minded starting point and are swift to jump to mockery, undermining the validity of any criticism. As is true for most things: there's a subreddit for that. On forums such as r/FakeDisorderCringe, users document examples of what they think are people just plain old making things up, whether that's individuals whom they suspect of faking illnesses, or perhaps people posting about symptoms the users don't think could be related to their disorder. They judge people in their own terms, such as "munchie by internet," which I've assumed derives from the now-outdated term "Munchausen by proxy." (If you weren't aware and would like to be, what was previously known as Munchausen syndrome is "a psychological condition where someone pretends to be ill or deliberately produces symptoms of illness in themselves."[18] The "by proxy" addition means that they exaggerate or imagine the symptoms of someone in their care, rather than their own. This is now clinically referred to as "factitious disorder," or "factitious disorder imposed on another" if it's someone else's illness that they are imagining or exaggerating. The more we know . . . !) In other words, "munchie by internet" is a label bandied about to judge a stranger online. Now, this subreddit is an odd part of the internet for me to find myself in, and you might think it's strange that I'm including it here, but—as I'll talk more about later—there can be real negatives to keeping ourselves too penned up in our own echo chambers. It's often necessary to look at something from a point of view you might find uncomfortable or unpleasant in order to be better able to argue against it, or just try to understand where it's coming from. So consider this foray into mental health naysaying territory an attempt to make sure I'm researching in all directions.

It's a dynamic I find weird and sad, though—people forming a sniggering community based on disbelief in strangers' medical disclosures—but I can also imagine how it happens, especially in people who've been cultured into a mistrust of liberal politics or openness about mental health. Even so, having a scroll through their forum in the name of journalism, there are certainly posts about which even I think, "This can't be real ..." Though, of course, then I immediately feel guilty and question my own assumptions. The point I'm making is that I can see how people come down on either side of the line in these scenarios. But I can also see how this is potentially very dangerous. If the news tells you that TikTok is encouraging teenagers to fake mental illnesses and then your teenager comes to you and talks about feeling anxious, for example, you may well already be primed for disbelief and feel you have the evidence to back it up. Yet the fact is, there are way more real sufferers of those illnesses than there are people mistaking it in themselves under the influence of social media. It's frustrating to say the least.

This is uncomfortable to talk about and I honestly hesitated over including it, because it feels like any admission that people fake things such as mental illnesses or elements of their identity is a potentially huge betrayal, not only of an individual but of whole groups of people: campaigners and awareness movements who've spent so much time and energy bringing their issues into the public consciousness. To acknowledge that any deception exists at all feels like it only hands power back to the people who sought to deny others their experience in the first place, to discredit them and minimize very real problems.

But there's a serious point here that fundamentally underpins how I feel about social platforms and mental health in general. Looking at the idea that social media is influencing mental illness from another angle, rather than ending the blame train there, you have to wonder how this has ended up being the case. People who are already struggling in some capacity and turn to social media for mental health advice because they have no other recourse to support may be more vulnerable to the influence of (even perfectly well-meaning) users who share their own diagnoses or mental health landscapes. A culture of openness about mental health is healthy, in my opinion, but a society in which people become reliant on online communities because they have nowhere else to turn is a breeding ground for misinformation and ultimately exploitation.

The "Munchausen by internet" comparison is used derisively, but the description of factitious disorder states that a patient's main intention is to assume the sick role so that people will care for them and they become the center of attention. What is this behavior actually telling us? If a small number of young people really are using their social media accounts to role-play and impersonate disorders, doesn't that scream something pretty urgent about how well we're looking after their mental health? Or at least how we're allowing social and other forms of media to impact them? A desperate need to feel cared for and find people to relate to, which leads to adopting disordered behavior (intentionally or otherwise), should be a cause for concern, not dismissal and ridicule. This is yet another of those instances in which I believe we must try to overcome our baser instincts, take a step back and actively practice compassion.

Why are we relying on the internet for help when we are struggling?

The reality is that so much of the experience of mental illness is lonely and isolating. We're told that it's OK not to be OK and we shouldn't feel ashamed. But while "talk to someone" remains the blanket advice for anyone struggling, endlessly reshared in simple graphics on dedicated awareness days, that does tend to be easier said than done. And how do you choose the right person? Family? A professional? These are the standard options that we well-meaningly suggest to each other, and often that's great advice . . . but sometimes it's issues at home that are causing someone's isolation to begin with, so family support isn't going to be available in the way we might optimistically expect.

A therapist, then? Seems like the only thing for it. However, in the UK, access to NHS mental health services is, at best, a postcode lottery. At one of my lowest points, when I'd reached out to a GP and started taking antidepressants, I was also referred for talking therapy. The way this worked in the part of London I lived in at the time was that I was asked to speak to a sort of triage service on a weekly basis over the course of four to six weeks, so that they could assess whether I needed support and, if so, what kind. After that period, I was told that, yes, they were 100 percent sure that I urgently needed mental health support . . . and also that they couldn't help me because not only were there no appointments available, the waiting list was so long that they had closed it altogether. This begs questions about the point of all those weekly phone calls, but that's sort of by the by . . .

Even this frustrating experience is, I am certain, nothing compared to what many other folks have to go through in order for it to be understood that they need help. These services are desperately oversubscribed, and the community is under-catered for, whether that's talking therapy or specialized treatments for other illnesses such as PTSD. It's also worth bearing in mind that this was my experience almost a decade ago and things have only gotten worse since then, with more people needing help and the NHS in increasingly dire straits. I work in an ambassador role for a research-based charity called MQ Mental Health, which delivered a letter to Downing Street in July 2023 highlighting the desperate need for actual commitment to mental health services, and asking the government to reinstate its canceled ten-year Mental Health Strategy. The fact that this strategy was canceled in the first place, and mental health vaguely lumped in with parts of other plans, is woefully indicative of how quick the powers-that-be are to talk a good game and then sweep the practicalities of mental health care under the rug. Because it does need individual attention. While, yes, mental health and physical health are connected, backpedaling on even the promise of a plan to make mental health support better is completely short-sighted in terms of improving public health. The frustration! Sometimes I could just scream.

Does it feel better to get a diagnosis?

What are we looking for when we can access these services? For most people, treatment, but for many of those who are struggling with their mental health for the first time, or seeking support for a long-standing problem, it could also be a diagnosis. If you're struggling with depression without knowing that you have it, you can find yourself trying to deal with the inherent issues of low mood, poor self-esteem and hopelessness, without any explanation other than that which your brain has already forced you to suspect: that there's something wrong with you and you're not very good. This is a lonely and terrible place to be, and, while being aware that you have depression probably isn't enough in itself to impact your recovery, having an explanation that takes some of that burden off you as intrinsically flawed and puts it on to an explainable, diagnosable issue can be comforting. The same, of course, applies across a whole spectrum of mental illnesses.

However, according to professor of neuroscience and mental health Bhismadev Chakrabarti, firm diagnostic labels for mental health conditions aren't always useful, even for the professionals trying to treat them.[19] He argues that, especially since early intervention has been shown to be the most effective at treating mental illness, the often lengthy process of obtaining a clinical diagnosis isn't always as useful as simply getting started with behavioral interventions—and in fact, speedier access to nonspecialists could be a far better option for many people, particularly where specialist resources are scarce. Perhaps that would mean more of us being able to speak with a therapist when we start to feel "off," without the need for an official diagnosis and subsequent referral. Or maybe it would just mean not needing a label in order to discuss your mental health with someone qualified. Professor Chakrabarti continues:

> At a time when rates of diagnosis for mental health conditions keep spiraling upward, it is worth imagining a world without diagnostic labels: one where an individual is assessed on his or her functional needs and receives care based on the specific needs rather than a somewhat arbitrary label. A world without stigma due to these labels. And a world where scientists focus their search on understanding the biology of behavior across the entire population, rather than create arbitrary groups of people defined by their labels as "cases" and "controls."

I'm honestly not sure where I stand here. It's not an entirely new idea. In fact, even old Hippocrates himself said: "It's far more important to know what person the disease has than what disease the person has."

As someone who has personally found a lot of comfort in receiving a diagnostic label, it's hard to approach this conversation and land anywhere other than pro-diagnosis. But perhaps the label-less approach to mental illness suggested above supposes a more evolved world in general, and an overall more supportive approach to individual mental health. Maybe in a world in which this was the reality, I wouldn't have suffered so much in not understanding the layers of what was "wrong" with me and therefore wouldn't have needed that label to access the comfort. Right now, I think I'd support this lofty goal for the future of mental health, but, keeping two feet in reality, the current landscape means that finding support and treatment is difficult enough as it is, and at least having a name for our problems is one step on the journey. There's plenty we need to work on in the meantime.

Whether we find diagnostic labels helpful on an individual level or not, their existence and an understanding of the wider symptoms of mental illnesses may lead us to expect that these conditions can be always be identified, clinically tested for, or ruled out in a patient. However, often that is not the case, and on the whole we are still pretty much in the dark when it comes to knowing how mental illness impacts our bodies.

The mind–body relationship

The connection between mental and physical health is an element of the mental health conversation that could do with some serious mainstream expansion. Some of this is relatively simple and other parts are inevitably more complex. There are a lot of ways in which mental health conditions manifest physical symptoms. If we take anxiety as an example: as well as restlessness, feelings of fear or dread and difficulty concentrating, the NHS details palpitations, excessive sweating, stomach ache, and insomnia among a laundry list of physical presentations. I've certainly found this to be the case, having experienced many of these symptoms myself. However, as someone with a history of mental illness, I've also had the mental–physical connection used to dismiss me.

Several years ago, I was experiencing pains in my chest and trotted off to the GP, who was swift to attribute it to anxiety. I felt that as soon as he'd glanced at my notes and read the word "anxiety," he immediately latched on to it and that was the only explanation he needed. No further questions. Luckily, I was confident that I knew myself and my usual anxiety symptoms well enough to push back on his conclusion, insisted on some tests and—long story short—found out I had a pretty urgent vitamin deficiency. If I hadn't been feeling up to challenging his assessment or able to advocate for myself in that moment, I wouldn't have been treated immediately and could even have suffered long-lasting damage. As was the case in this one example, which happened to crop up in my life, doctors can sometimes jump to the wrong conclusion and blame an existing mental illness for all sorts of other issues, physical or otherwise. (I hasten to acknowledge that doctors are only human and most are trying their best with the limited time they have; we all make assumptions to fill the gaps in our knowledge, as we'll discuss later on.) Fortunately for me, it all turned out fine in the end. But it's still an example of how links between mental and physical health can be both dismissed unjustly and used to discredit patients.

As well as coming with their own physical symptoms,

mental health conditions can impact sufferers physiologically, as stigma or assumptions mean they are treated differently by health professionals. According to UK charity Mental Health Foundation, people with a mental illness are less likely to be offered routine health screenings,[20] such as blood pressure and cholesterol checks, as (in line with my experience!) health professionals may assume physical symptoms can be attributed to mental illness without investigating them any further.

Doctors may also let their own biases affect the advice they give to patients; if they assume you are incapable of implementing changes due to your mental illness, they may be less likely to offer support for issues such as quitting smoking, a habit which has a plethora of well-documented ill effects on the body. On a broader level, research has shown that people who suffer from a mental health condition are more likely to have a preventable physical health condition, such as coronary heart disease.[21] Taking into account these serious physical impacts as well as the implications for the quality of life of our population as a whole, treating mental health conditions with the respect and seriousness they deserve is crucially important for our overall health.

A lack of serotonin . . .

For many years, I understood the popular "serotonin theory" explanation for depression: that my depression was caused by a lack of serotonin and hence my mood could be improved or corrected with antidepressants. More serotonin = happier. This theory of depression, a link between low levels of serotonin and low mood, was first proposed around sixty years ago and became more well known from the 1990s, with the advent of SSRI (selective serotonin reuptake inhibitor) antidepressants. As we'll see in more detail later, serotonin is a neuro-transmitter, a chemical which carries messages throughout the body. Once it has fulfilled this role, it is reabsorbed by our cells (reuptake), but, as the name suggests, SSRI drugs work by preventing that reabsorption, thus increasing the amount of free serotonin in the body and meaning more is available for further use.

Surveys suggest that over 80 percent of the general public now believe that depression is caused by a "chemical imbalance."[22,23] In practice, plenty of our GPs and psychiatrists explain poor mental health this way too. Neurotransmitters like serotonin and dopamine have made it into our everyday lexicon; we kind of understand what they're for and the feelings they're supposed to give us. Serotonin, our "feel-good" chemical, regulates mood, so a lack of serotonin, or an incorrect balance, was an explanation that I found really comforting at certain points over the years—it did seem to offer some concrete reason for why I was struggling. We see this crop up in encouraging mental health conversation all the time, where comparisons are made between people who take drugs like antidepressants or anxiety medications and folks who require drugs like insulin to regulate their blood sugar due to diabetes. It's all just regulating chemicals, right? You wouldn't shame a diabetic for it!

In July 2022, a systematic review of the evidence on serotonin and depression was published in the journal *Molecular Psychiatry*, entitled "The serotonin theory of depression: a systematic umbrella review of the evidence." (For context, umbrella reviews provide an overview of all the major existing research, making them among the highest levels of evidence currently available in medicine.) It found that: "The main areas of serotonin research provide no consistent evidence of there being an association between serotonin and depression, and no support for the hypothesis that depression is caused by lowered serotonin activity or concentrations."[24]

I was thrown for a loop on reading this, and I wasn't even taking SSRIs anymore. Maybe "upset" isn't quite the right word, but I felt a real swirl of emotions about it, like the comforting blanket of explanation had been ripped away from me. I'd hazard a guess that lots of people reading this will also have heard about the findings in the press: a scientific study that says a type of medication taken by millions of people is all based on false information? The paper was downloaded over a million times.

I want to delve into this because it felt like a big event in mental health news and it was covered so extensively. I certainly believed in its credibility from the stories I saw! Relying on outrage, as is so often effective, headlines such as "Justice for Millions of Americans

Prescribed Antidepressants for a Chemical Imbalance of the Brain that Doesn't Exist?"[25] ran with the suggestion that patients had been misled and overmedicated by their doctors—leaning on the idea that individuals had been lied to and tapping into readers' fear. They talked about "fraudulent promotion of the unproven theory" and even grounds for a class action lawsuit. It all sounds quite alarming, doesn't it? In an article titled "The serotonin theory of depression: how the media got it all wrong," senior data journalist Julia Robinson of the *Pharmaceutical Journal* examined concerns that the intense coverage by media outlets might actually cause significant numbers of patients to stop taking their medications, either against or without medical advice. As an aside, in case it's relevant to anyone reading, SSRIs are not a family of medication you should decide to stop taking on your own, or come off cold turkey. Having done it myself, sometimes by accident, on multiple occasions, I can attest to the unpleasantness of the withdrawal symptoms that may follow. Whatever the reasoning—please discuss with your doctor if it's something you're considering!

By the summer of the following year, the scientific community was responding. In June 2023, a new article was published in the same journal as the original review, entitled "A leaky umbrella has little value: evidence clearly indicates the serotonin system is implicated in depression."[26] (Because the original was an "umbrella review," get it? This is like the *Real Housewives* reunion show for science. Snark for days.) Led by researchers from King's College London, this response article explains that "the serotonin theory of depression was not proposed to suggest that people experience the condition because of an imbalance in a single chemical in the brain (serotonin), but rather as an example of brain changes that are present in depression that could help explain how some antidepressants work."[27]

What seems to have gone wrong here is that calling it the "serotonin theory" was a little bit too simple. In the *New York Times*, health and science writer Dana G. Smith highlighted that the response to the umbrella review had exposed a great divide between how the public understood depression and how experts in the field viewed it.[28] So, what are the experts thinking that we don't get?

To make a long story as simple as I can, there are lots of mechanisms related to serotonin, so we have to look at way more than just its quantity: how it's made in our cells, the chemicals it's made from, the processes it helps to facilitate, how serotonin itself is transported by the body, the types of messages it helps to communicate throughout the brain.[29] The thing is, though, research continues into how each of these aspects, and many more, affect depression—we're just not sure yet exactly how it works. Even though the simple explanation of simply "not having enough" is one that's easy to grasp for those of us without neuropharmacology degrees, it's not quite true . . . but that doesn't mean we've been sold a lie.

Whether or not the scientific community continues its back-and-forth on the specifics of low serotonin levels, we do know that serotonin and other neurotransmitters impact brain function and mood. For the majority of researchers and doctors working in this field, whether SSRIs are effective or not was never in question, as succinctly explained by Dr. Michael Bloomfield, professor of psychiatric neuroscience and head of a University College London research team: "Many of us know that taking paracetamol can be helpful for headaches and I don't think anyone believes that headaches are caused by not enough paracetamol in the brain. The same logic applies to depression and medicines used to treat depression. There is consistent evidence that antidepressant medicines can be helpful in the treatment of depression and can be life-saving."[30] Well, alrighty, then. Even though there are a percentage of people who suffer from so-called "treatment resistant depression," for whom finding an effective drug is difficult, we're still looking to affect serotonin as a method of treatment through emerging research into psychedelic drugs such as psilocybin (magic mushrooms), LSD, or even ketamine.[31] To my mind, the issue with antidepressants mainly arises if they are prescribed in place of other treatments that could be more beneficial, or presented as the only option, which they are not.

Anyway, I wanted to talk about this because unfortunately the extensive coverage afforded to the 2022 review doesn't seem to have been replicated for the criticisms of it. When I started writing this book, I thought the findings of the review must be true, and by the time I finished it, the work seemed to have been pretty firmly debunked. But I didn't hear that in the press, even though I went looking for it. I wonder how many of the people encouraged by inflammatory media coverage to stop taking their medication have seen the critical responses? How many have gone back on their meds? How many have been negatively affected?

Where do we start with improving our mental health?

What this whole story tells us is that aside from the important work we've collectively done on awareness around mental health and mental illness, investing in science and research continues to be vitally important . . . but so is how we communicate that information to the general public. People deserve to be told about emerging research in a way that's accessible, that we can all understand, but oversimplified conclusions and headlines can really be harmful. There's a balance to be found.

I know it can feel like there are always too many draws on resources and it's hard when there are already too many people in urgent need of treatment and support, so we invest our energies into trying to have the most immediate impact on people's lives. We need more emergency helpline services. We need more therapists being trained. The drawback of this reactive approach is that it only really tackles the short term and doesn't leave space to facilitate a better future. Without investing in the big picture of understanding mental illness on a deeper level—the reasons why people become ill, why certain treatments work for certain people, right down to the key pillars of our knowledge, like the functioning of our brain chemistry—we approach long-term solutions to actually improving our mental health on much shakier ground.

If you are struggling right now, or someone you care about is, know that it can and will get better. When I was in the depths of depression, I thought I was just shit at being a person, that I was fundamentally Not Good Enough. That was not true. I needed to talk to someone. I needed to try some antidepressants and to understand that what was going on in my head was important enough to do something about. That I was important enough. It was part of my life but it wasn't who I was. There are resources online and communities that can help, in my experience, but there are, of course, dark corners of the internet that should be avoided. Sharing Insta-art and relatable memes (as is in my wheelhouse) is no substitute for getting help. That said, I do sometimes feel like the right sentiment can present itself to you right when you need it. I find it endlessly gratifying when I share something that has resonated with me that day and end up with an inbox of people describing that very feeling of being found at the right moment. The experience of mental illness is isolating. So these small moments of connection—while they may not heal you—can remind you that you are not broken, you are not "wrong," and, most importantly, you are not alone.

2

WHY ARE WE LIKE THIS?

WHAT WOULD BE GREAT IS a brain manual. A simple list of parts, how they fit together, which buttons to press when and a troubleshooting guide at the end. *Feel sad? Insert custard creams x 2. Repeat until issue resolves.* You know that meme where a person talks about how we humans think we're so intricate and mysterious . . . and then we feel happy in the sunshine and realize we're just a big leaf? It's comforting to find those simple things that actually do make us feel better, whether it's the great outdoors, drinking more water, or a good night's sleep—but that can make it all the more frustrating when those quick fixes don't seem to work, or we're faced with negative feelings that are much harder to solve.

Fortunately for the species (and sometimes unfortunately for us as individuals), we really are much more complicated than a boiler or washing machine or, indeed, a leaf. And even though that makes us too messy to be covered in a simple handbook, any additional knowledge we can soak up about the way our brains work can only be a helpful piece of the puzzle. Thanks to my experiences of anxiety, depression, and a late diagnosis of neurodivergence, I have, at various points, been sad and angry with my brain because I have felt on some level that it is "wrong" or not good at things other people's brains seem to tackle with comparative ease. But learning a bit more about neuroscience, psychology, and myself has made me think about this incredible, perplexing organ in a different way.

There are so many factors that come together to make you *you*. You're a product of your genes, your upbringing, your environment, your culture—even your brain chemistry and your diet, to an extent. And that's ignoring all the millions of random chances in human evolution that had to occur to make us *us*. It's completely mind-boggling. Sort of ironically. But some things are the same for all of us *Homo sapiens*. With all our individual differences, most of us are walking around with the same basic machinery in our heads.

I know I'll never understand the half of it and yet I'm always keen for any new snippets of knowledge. How is this dense, squidgy organ that ticks along unseen inside our skulls capable of such complicated processing, and how the hell did it get to be like this? Because in one simple sense, our brain is just another organ like our kidneys or pancreas, but those parts of our bodies don't have a major say in who we are as people.

While there's much that the scientific community still

doesn't know about the brain, there are plenty of things we have discovered that can both inform how we take care of ourselves and provide an insight into who we are. So whether you feel like you're a weirdo or are fairly sure everyone else is, let's begin with a quick tour of the brain. Think of it as first-day orientation, or a factory tour if you like.

One of these animals is not like the others

Human brains are pretty special compared to those of the rest of the animal kingdom. We have impressive language skills, use reason and logic to make decisions, can process emotions, and do a whole lot of other things that other species can't, or can't do nearly so well. Along with some handy (ha!) opposable thumbs, our highly developed mammal brains have made us evolutionary outliers and allowed us to hugely change the world we live in. So you would think that there must be something that makes our brains physically different to other animals'—even chimps, our closest relatives, right? Well, not really.

Our brains are proportionally larger than you would expect for an animal our size, around three times bigger relative to our body mass when compared to other primates. But it can't just come down to how much brain you physically have in your head, or animals like whales and elephants would be much smarter than we are. And if it were just about the ratio of brain to body size, the capuchin monkey would be cleverer than a gorilla.[1] But that's not the case either.

Aside from plain size, another theory is that intelligence could correlate to how many neurons we have within our brains. A neuron is a type of nerve cell that passes chemical and electrical signals all around the body and thus allows us to do everything from walking to thinking to talking. Even the things we don't think about, like heartbeats, sweating, sneezes—they're all controlled by the nervous system, this network of neurons. Neurons receive and transmit information, making up neural pathways that connect one part of the nervous system to another, so presumably it would be better intelligence-wise to have as many neurons as possible at our disposal. But when a neuroscientist called Suzana Herculano-Houzel came up with a new way of counting them, by dissolving brain tissue into a kind of brain soup—which sounds gross and efficient in equal measure—she concluded that the number of neurons we humans have relative to the size of our brains is not that different to apes, therefore suggesting that it isn't being generously endowed with neurons that gives human beings their intellect after all.[2] Basically—and I'm paraphrasing the science here—humans are peculiar as well as brilliant. (We certainly seem to be the only ones using our brains to study other brains, as Professor Herculano-Houzel points out.)

The average adult human brain weighs about 1.5 kilograms. If you make two fists and put them together, that will give you a rough idea of its size. Admittedly, this is far from scientific, but I do enjoy that it looks sort of like the two hemispheres of the brain, with those finger grooves lending a delightful brain-wrinkly quality to the whole visual. Unlike your hands, your brain is about 60 percent fat and 40 percent water, protein, carbohydrates, and salts.[3] It isn't a muscle, although we sometimes talk about it like it is, when we say things like "a brain workout" or "training your brain." It's made up of what's known as white matter and gray matter. Though it's kind of pinky-gray, if you want to know the actual color . . .

Sidebar: I actually once helped with the dissection of a brain. My grandad, Brian, suffered from Parkinson's, a disease which I'm sure many of you will have encountered, and over the last several years our family has done various fundraising activities in aid of the charity Parkinson's UK. (I find myself wondering what new feat my mum will have signed herself up for by the time this goes to print.) We were honored to be invited by the amazing team there to look round one of their research labs and see what sort of work is being funded by the donations they receive, which included seeing how donated brains are carefully examined and studied. An interesting thing I learned through this experience is that lots of people are generous enough to donate their brains to Parkinson's research. This is absolutely essential to investigation into the disease. Understandably, though, most people who sign up to donate their brains want to help because they have Parkinson's, so what the team is always short of are non-affected organs to compare them to, as science demands. Most people have the luxury of not considering it, I suppose. It's a point about medical research that really stuck with me, and maybe will stick with you, if you've ever thought about being an organ donor.

Anyway, when I say I "helped" with the dissection, I mean I was handed small pieces of brain tissue that had already been expertly sliced and placed into labeled cases, so that the researchers could tell exactly which part of the brain they came from. I put the lids on and carefully placed them into a larger container. Just to reassure everyone, this was thoroughly supervised and my untrained hands did not touch a scalpel.

There's something about seeing a human brain in the flesh, if you will, that makes it all the more mystifying. Seeing one in this context, preserved and sterile, is, I know, a little different to what it's like in our heads, but it's as close as I'm ever going to get. To think about all the unfathomably elaborate processes that our brains can carry out, to know that each person is different and we each have memories and personalities and preferences, and it all comes from within this ... bouncy, lumpy thing. It doesn't look like much. And then finding that even with all the medical know-how and scientific genius and technology we have at our disposal, the starting point for examining and gleaning answers from this mysterious mesh of cells is, essentially, slicing it up with a bread knife. (It wasn't a bread knife, but it wasn't *unlike* one. And that's as graphic as I'll get, I promise.) That's not to underplay the skill involved in this research—quite the opposite, in fact. It gave me a new respect for the whole process of trying to understand previously unknown things about our bodies, trying to research diseases and symptoms and cures.

I think there's a tendency to feel very removed from the world of science if you're not in it—but break-throughs are all discovered by people, just like you or me. I think not feeling like part of the "world" is some-times our problem. While we might not have the training or be on the path for making ground-breaking medical developments, it doesn't mean we can't understand *any-thing*, and we're still allowed to ask questions. It's the same way I feel about politics. The fear of not knowing enough makes people scared to get involved at all, lest they look stupid. And who does that help? Luckily, I am more than willing to ask questions and risk looking stupid on your behalf, and so: on with our layman's guide to brain exploration.

A map of your brain

While from the outside a brain looks very similar through-out, we know there are certain areas of the mass that do different things. At the highest level, the brain is divided into three main bits: the cerebrum, the cerebellum, and the brain stem. The brain stem connects the brain itself to the spinal cord. The cerebellum is just above that, a smaller section of brain located roughly behind the nape of your neck. The cerebrum is the largest part and what you're probably picturing when you think of what a brain looks like. For our purposes, as we try to understand more about why we are wired the way we are, we want to look at the cerebrum and specifically the cerebral cortex, which does most of the thinky-feely stuff—problem-solving, learning, communication, reasoning, emotional response, etc.[4] This is the gray matter we hear so much about. And, going back to the question of how our brains differ from those of primates, it's worth noting that this part of the human brain contains twice as many cells as our ape cousins'.[5] I don't want to spend too much time hyper-focusing on brain anatomy here, because I've got a feeling that if that's what you were looking for you'd have picked up a different book, but if this does grab your interest then do feel free to go and lose some hours on the internet to this subject, as I have.

The cerebrum is located at the top and front of your skull and is divided into two hemispheres—the left brain and the right brain. Have you heard the terms "right-brain thinker" and "left-brain thinker," meaning those whose right hemisphere is dominant are creative free-thinkers and those whose left brain takes charge are analytical and rational? It's based on research that started in the late 1960s and was popularized by some books in the 1970s, for example, *Drawing on the Right*

Side of the Brain by Betty Edwards, which instructs readers to access the right side of their brain in order to become better artists. I remember a poster, which I think was on one of the classroom walls when I was at school, where the left side of the brain was pretty blandly decorated with calculators and graphs and the right side was an explosion of color and paintbrushes and the sort of hats that only a poet would wear. As someone who'd always been thought of as more of a "left brain" person, it made me feel pretty dull, to be honest. The popularity of this theory is a good example of how much we love an easily understood concept that explains something about who we are and how we work. We'll learn more about why we love a convenient phrase or neat explainer later, and when that can be a good thing and a bad thing. But in scientific terms, this one at least is a massive oversimplification and unfortunately doesn't hold up.[6]

It is true that some functions appear to be concentrated more on one side of the brain than the other—for example, language seems to be a left-brain function. (Although, for those of you who are left-handed, about one in four of you will have your language function on the right side of your brain.[7] Why? No one knows!) And we know that different areas of the brain do take charge of different areas of life, partly through how injuries to specific parts of the brain impair specific abilities—for example, causing amnesia or reducing the fear response. But the two hemispheres work together and are connected by a thick band of neural fibers called the corpus callosum. As I said, no real evidence has been found to support the idea that one side of your brain dictates what you are good at, or whether you are a creative type or an analytical person.

There are a number of other parts of the brain that all have their own specialism but work together to get you through your day, decide how you feel about things, make decisions about what to cook for dinner, etc. One explainer I read likened it to a panel of experts.[8] I can't help but imagine the set-up from the film *Inside Out*. For the purposes of this discussion, and because I watch a lot of television, I'm going to describe these areas as a cast of sitcom characters. So, in this analogy, some of the lead roles are:

The prefrontal cortex

This part of the brain—located at the front, not shockingly—is kind of like the leader. It deals with a lot of the input and suggestions from the other parts of the brain. It's responsible for complex decision-making and motivation—as in, not just to get up and go for a run first thing, but anything that influences you to do something. If someone sustains damage to this part of their brain, they can become apathetic and unmotivated to do anything. So, a lot of your personality and how you interact with other people comes from your prefrontal cortex.[9] There's a good chance that ADHD, particularly difficulties with focus, could be related to an issue with this part of the brain. Thanks, prefrontal cortex.

The amygdala

This little guy has some important jobs, a lot of which relate to fear and emotions. Many different studies have indicated that the amygdala can stimulate action without the information going via our prefrontal cortex first for vetting. In other words, you don't have to consciously think about a scary thing before the amygdala tells you to react to it. As someone who is very arachnophobic, this makes perfect sense. If out of the corner of my eye I see something black and scuttly, my body is off and reacting before I'm aware of having had the thought "Oh no, is that a spider?"

As you probably know already, the "fight, flight, or freeze" mechanism, in which the amygdala plays a big part, is there to keep us safe from danger. But, as with my spider fear, it can be prone to overreaction. Unsurprisingly, anxiety disorders could be related to an issue here, as our mind and body make us feel we are in danger when there is nothing actually threatening us.

The hippocampus

Included here partly on the strength of its name, the hippocampus is part of the limbic system,[10] along with the amygdala. It is responsible for our awareness of space and how we navigate around. Although, one of its big jobs is dealing with episodic memory—our ability to remember past events and "reexperience" them in our heads as memories—and informing how we respond emotionally. It acts as temporary storage, transferring what it considers the important stuff into our long-term memory. It's quite associative too—when you smell cloves and cinnamon and immediately think of Christmas, that's your hippocampus's work. Rather sweetly, it is often described as being shaped like a seahorse. Not a hippo.

The thalamus

In our brain sitcom, the thalamus is the well-connected character who knows everyone and drives the plot forward. A real Monica. One of its main jobs is to act as a sort of hub or relay station—it picks up signals received from your senses and sends them to other parts of the brain for processing. And it coordinates all this inbound info to help you make sense of it. Say, you hear someone scream. Your thalamus will process the signal from the auditory nerve. When your brain sends a signal to your muscles to turn you around to the source of the scream, the scene in front of you will be relayed via the optic nerve to the thalamus. The thalamus will communicate all this to the prefrontal cortex for review; the prefrontal cortex will make the assessment as to whether this is a scary thing or not—is someone in trouble or just messing about with their friends? And, of course, the amygdala will be there too, getting a bit jumpy, wondering if any quick action is going to be needed.

The idea that different parts of the brain control different things has been floating around for a long time. Before we knew anything about our sitcom character functions, we theorized that discrete sections of our brains must be responsible for various parts of our personalities; phrenology, the pseudoscience of reading the bumps on someone's head to determine their character traits, was popular in the early nineteenth century. Phrenologists thought that the brain was formed of muscles and the bits that were used the most would bulk up and push on the skull, causing lumps.[11] This "science" of visible traits would commonly be pedaled as a novelty, with practitioners carrying out "skull readings" on people, which were often little more than veiled flattery ("Ooh, madam, what a well-developed benevolence lump you have") but would eventually be co-opted in far more sinister contexts, to justify slavery as well as other racist assaults on Black and Jewish people.[12,13] While most of us wouldn't like to draw from such a problematic practice, whispers of phrenology linger to this day. This idea of visible brain size is actually how the terms "highbrow" and "lowbrow" entered our vocabulary, the theory being that an individual with a large brain, and therefore more intelligence, would have a higher forehead to accommodate this impressive organ.[14] It's another example of how these misconceptions get into language and culture and sort of . . . hang about there.

Humans may not have a brain that is radically different from other mammals' in terms of its relative size or how it's organized, but we do have a proportionally larger cerebral cortex—the processing bit—than other mammals, and our brains use around 20 percent of our energy, despite accounting for only 2 percent of our body mass. And it seems that as we've evolved, a lot has been sacrificed for this.

Why do our brains take so long to develop?

If you've ever wondered why a baby giraffe can be born, fall from a great height, then stand up and walk, or a lamb will be springing around in a field twenty-four hours after its birth, but human infants are entirely dependent on their caregivers for years ... well, our brains are a large part of the answer. That baby humans have a pre-ambulatory adjustment phase—i.e., if you put them down, they won't go anywhere—before they can independently wander off and get themselves into all sorts of trouble seems like something of a positive, quite frankly, but the time it takes is unusual compared to many other species. How can being so defenseless possibly have been an evolutionary advantage? If it wasn't, we wouldn't have ended up this way—as we know from natural selection (aka survival of the fittest). So why does our species spend so much time in the helpless phase?

For decades, evolutionary biologists have theorized that the brain, and the size of our brains specifically, is an important factor here. Casting aside the wonders of modern medicine and cesarean sections, the route out into the world for a human infant is, to put it mildly, a tight squeeze. It's crucial for the safety of both parent and child to have an adequate exit point. This is through the mother's pelvic bones. During female puberty, one outcome of an increase in estrogen is a widening of the hips. In pregnancy, at around ten to twelve weeks, the ovaries and placenta increase their production of a hormone called relaxin, which loosens muscles, joints, and ligaments to allow the body to literally stretch to accommodate a growing fetus and, eventually, better accommodate its passage out into the world. (Side note: I do love how some of these things are named. Relaxin. Relaxes ligaments. Sometimes science is complicated; sometimes less so.) But even with all the hormonal help available, a bone is a solid thing. And so here is where the size of the child's head (read: brain) versus the size of the space through the middle of the pelvis becomes important. It has been estimated that if a human baby was born at the same stage of neurological and cognitive development as a baby chimp is at when it arrives in the world, the gestation period would be around eighteen to twenty-one months. It's not just that being pregnant for that long would be a horror show, or that the strain it would put on the mother's body wouldn't be great for the success of the species, but women would have to give birth to children already the size of toddlers. Which quite clearly wouldn't work. So our helpless infants seem to be a compromise.

Or are they? There's one theory that the rapid development our brains undergo after we are born actually puts us at an advantage,[15] making us really good at learning and adapting to our environments. Yes, an infant's survival relies on it being cared for and protected in its first few years, but not having a lot of information hardwired into our brains makes us potentially more mentally flexible. Humans are not the strongest or fastest—there are plenty of things we are pretty poor at as a species, compared to other animals—but we are curious and very resourceful. Let's think about bats for a minute. (Yes, bats.) As a group, they are very successful—there are many of them and they are found all over the world. But to be so successful they have had to physically adapt to the different places in which they live, with the result that there are something like 1,400 species of bat.[16] Humans also live all over the world, but there is only one type of us: *Homo sapiens*. In the simplest terms, it is our brains that have allowed us to survive in the different environments in which we have found ourselves.

How did we end up like this?

One key thing I think is super-interesting is that, despite the fact that our large brains require a lot of energy to power them, as brains got larger, our guts got smaller. Our earliest ancestor, who came up with the idea of living on the ground rather than in the trees with the other apes, was *Australopithecus*, who lived between 3.85 and 2.95 million years ago.[17] *Australopithecus* had big flat teeth for grinding up plants, a large gut for digesting them and—you've guessed it—a small brain. *Homo erectus*, who later pioneered the uniquely human two-legged approach to life, was a meat eater who no longer needed the plant-digesting gut. Crucially, it seems that these guys were the ones who learned to cook, a very useful way of cutting down on the energy needed for digestion and increasing how many calories they could easily consume. There's been an increased interest in gut health in recent years, and how it impacts our brains—I'm sure you've heard the gut referred to as our "second brain." So it's quite incredible that science is talking about a connection that goes back this far. In fact, according to Peter Wheeler and Leslie Aiello from Liverpool John Moores University, the amount our brains grew at that point in our evolution mirrors how much our guts shrank—20 percent.[18] Hmmm.

There are many theories as to how evolution delivered our species to the point where we have these large, complex brains. It's likely that it was a combination of myriad environmental and social factors, only part-fueled by our enjoyment of campfire cooking. So I will step back from this potential rabbit hole in just a moment, but before I do, I have to share one of those factors, partly because it conjures up some fun mental images. It's known as the Stoned Ape hypothesis and, happily, is pretty much exactly what it sounds like. It was first proposed by American ethnobotanist Terence McKenna in the 1990s—ethnobotany being the study of the relationships between people and plants. The theory goes that at some point soon after humans had evolved that upright swagger and started to travel longer distances, they came across some magic mushrooms. In his 1992 book *Food of the Gods*, McKenna suggests that what enabled *Homo erectus* to evolve into *Homo sapiens* (us) was exposure to and consumption of psilocybin,[19] the psychedelic compound responsible for the mushrooms' effects, which changed our brains and accelerated the development of things like language and cooperation—maybe even spirituality.

It's important to note that this is something of a fringe idea, which has been widely criticized for a lack of evidence. However, I still think the idea sounds interesting if only because it reminds me of what we were looking at just now regarding the gut–brain connection. There are clearly things in our species' dim and distant past, as well as our better-understood present, that science is only just now asking questions about. Much more attention is starting to be paid to the study of psychoactive compounds, after it has long been stunted by the whims and prejudices of drug lobbyists. You might even have already learned a bit about psilocybin's effect on the brain and how it could potentially be used to treat different conditions, as this conversation has expanded out of online forums and into the mainstream, for example in Netflix's 2022 documentary series *How to Change Your Mind*.

How to grow a brain

OK, enough evolutionary theory for the moment. Let's come back to how our *Homo sapiens* brains are organized now and how we come to "grow" them, as it were. In pregnancy, the first makings of a brain start developing early, at around three weeks after fertilization. It's not yet a brain as we know it, capable of feelings or thoughts, but the precursor—an oval-shaped disk of tissue called a "neural plate" in the very tadpole-esque fetus. Over the course of a week, this oval plate folds its edges together to form a "neural tube" that will then become the spine and brain. By the end of Week Six, the tube is closed at both ends and the brain is already made up of three distinct parts: the forebrain, midbrain, and hindbrain.[20] From here, there's still a lot of work to do, of course—just the casual task of developing an entire nervous system—and it's in the last few weeks of gestation that this really skyrockets. Between twenty-eight and thirty-nine weeks, the brain triples in size to become around a quarter (27 percent, ish) of its eventual adult size.[21] Then, knock knock, it's eviction time.

In the first year of a child's life, its brain doubles in size, and then continues this rapid growth to reach around 90 percent of its adult size by age five. Now, if you needed any further real-world confirmation that a bigger brain doesn't precisely correlate to intelligence levels, then there you have it. Most of us would like to think we've become more than 10 percent more intelligent since we were five years old. I mean, no offense, five-year-olds, your potential is boundless, but your precious little minds are not done yet.

Interestingly, opinion seems split in neuroscience about whether a person has all the neurons (brain cells) they're ever going to have by the time they are this age. Many think we do, but there is some evidence that we can grow new ones in the hippocampus—remember that guy?[22] If we can, there are some interesting implications for how we treat epilepsy, PTSD, and Alzheimer's, among others. But I digress. It's actually the connections between those cells that go toward all that development.

We'll come back to this, but neural connections—synapses—are fundamental to our brains as they are how we learn and retain knowledge and skills. They also play a significant role in how we relate to others and develop empathy. And they underpin pretty much everything, really. Simply put, they are one brain cell talking to another, through neurotransmitters and electricity, but on a massive (though also minuscule) scale, branching off, creating this intricate network, allowing the transfer of information. And that, brain fans, is how we get consciousness.[23] Whoa.

In the womb and for the first few years of their lives, children are forming neural connections at a rate of one million per second.[24] My fully grown brain and I can't fathom that one. After the age of five,[25] our brains keep ticking on in their growth much more slowly, reaching their fully grown size somewhere in early adolescence.

And here we arrive at a piece of brain information that I think we all should be aware of. The brain stops *physically growing* when we are in our early teens, but it doesn't finish *developing* until we are around twenty-five years old. That's right. Puts some of those questionable decisions you made when you were in your late teens and early twenties into a slightly gentler light, doesn't it?

Again, it comes back to those neural connections and the different parts of the brain we met earlier being able to communicate effectively with one another. They may be working great individually—for example, your average fifteen-year-old can assess hypothetical risk as well as a grown-up. However, if the line between the hippocampus, amygdala, and prefrontal context is working at the capacity of dial-up internet rather than fiber-optic broadband, then those messages are not getting through so well. The part of the brain that is responsible for self-control isn't on the same page as the part of the brain that controls the fight-or-flight response.[26]

It stands to reason, then, that these ongoing developments in the teenaged brain, along with all the other fun stuff you go through in a few short years around this time (Puberty! Exams! Burgeoning sexuality! The crushing weight of expectation! Etc., etc.), make young people more likely to experience mental health problems. So whether it's current you or your teenaged inner child who needs to hear this: your developing brain is resilient and your prefrontal cortex will get there in the end.[27] Go easy on yourself.

Eighty-six billion neurons

I hope you've enjoyed this very abridged tour of the inside of our skulls and some of the theories about how it came to look like that. It does fascinate me that we all have the same basic machinery and yet how we see the world can vary so much from individual to individual. It's just one more thing that makes our species so weird. Presumably snails don't have different views on the color of the leaf they are sitting on and dolphins don't argue about what kind of fish tastes better.

If you were crossing your fingers that this chapter was going to be that brain manual I mentioned wishing for, I hope you're not disappointed. I expect that you are as keen to get your hands on one for your brain as I am for mine. But if we do want to understand ourselves better, I think this isn't a bad place to start. Though there is, of course, so much more to the story, which we will take a look at in the next chapters.

There is a lot we don't know about the brain, but that just makes me excited for the discoveries that are surely going to come about in my lifetime. Maybe you rolled your eyes when I mentioned how Victorian phrenologists believed that overdeveloped bits of brain "muscle" caused bumps that could be "read" to determine personality. OK, yes, that does seem silly now. But it makes me think about all the things we accept as scientific fact nowadays, and wonder which of them people will look back on and roll their eyes at in years to come.

It's hardly surprising that we're going to get it wrong, though. You have to start somewhere, and a working theory is better than shrugging our collective shoulders and not bothering to look into it. After all, your brain is made up of around eighty-six billion neurons—that's comparable to the number of stars in the Milky Way—and when we look at counting synapses (the connections between those neurons), that's somewhere in the region of one quadrillion. That's one followed by fifteen zeros. To make it even more complex, those neurons and synapses aren't all the same. There are likely hundreds of different types of neurons *and* they're not even the only type of cell in the brain.[28] Given the mammoth scale of the numbers involved, is it any wonder that this wondrous organ is so confounding?

As a species, our intelligence, our curiosity, and our highly developed social skills have made us very successful. While also, of course, causing huge problems—for ourselves and for the planet on which we live. There is so much that can't be explained just by looking at the machinery in our heads. Why are people so quick to judge each other? Why do we often find it easy to act against our own best interests? How can we know so much about the environmental damage we are doing to the planet and still not make those "green" choices? Why can our brains sometimes recover from physical damage yet we still struggle with our mental health? All these questions lead straight to the top, but also can't be answered by looking at a slice of brain under a microscope. So, let's continue to look around in some other areas to try to make sense of us . . .

3

WHAT WAS I THINKING?

WHEN WE TALK ABOUT MAINTAINING good mental health, we're often referring to the way we feel. But when it comes to treating symptoms of poor mental health, or specific mental illness, whether it's in a therapy session or through mindfulness exercises, we're suddenly referring more to the way we think. While I believe conscious thoughts and feelings can be separate (I often feel anxious or exasperated without specific thoughts about why), looking at patterns of thought can be very helpful in identifying where our feelings are coming from. How you think, in other words. For example, do you have a voice in your head? By which I mean, do you ever "hear" your thoughts as you have them and, if you do, is it your voice or someone else's?

Say you suddenly remember that you need to get the washing out of the machine—is there a voice in your head telling you to do that? And, if so, how is it speaking to you? Is it saying, "You need to unload the machine,"

"I need to," or even "We need to"? Or do you see a picture of the washing machine in your mind or imagine yourself getting the clothes out and hanging them up to dry? The crux of the question is: Can you articulate how you experience that thought?

It's hard, isn't it? In everyday life, we speak a lot about our subconscious, an inner voice, positive or negative self-talk. We can sometimes struggle to understand our own thoughts or flounder as we try to put them into words for the benefit of someone else, because we want to be understood. But what actually is a thought? Though we throw these terms around like we understand them, how is it all actually working in there? How is that brain machinery we met in Chapter Two providing us with this inner experience?

We have thousands upon thousands of thoughts every day. "I think, therefore I am," said Descartes . . . thoughtfully. To have this inner life is a big part of what makes us human, though sometimes we can feel overwhelmed by our thoughts or spend time with meditation apps trying to get them to leave us in peace for five minutes. And yet to explain to someone, or even to ourselves, the form a thought takes in our brain is weirdly tricky.

That voice in your head

The idea of an inner monologue is one that I see pinging around online on a regular basis and that never gets old, which seems to speak to our fascination with all this. I find it riveting to read the comments on these posts, as they're always filled with people describing in great detail the way in which they experience thought, the voice inside their head. I don't feel able to do that at all, so taking in other people's experiences in order to say, "No, that doesn't sound right for me," is pretty helpful too. Process of elimination! Rather than feeling strongly about the way I experience a train of thought inside my own head, I really find it a challenge to pick out whether there's an actual, discernible voice in there, so having read other people's explanations of hearing thoughts "out loud," I'm left thinking I don't have an inner voice at all. I just know what my thoughts are, or rather know what I think about things instead of those thoughts feeling like an actual conversation in my brain.

But many people have reported having a very different experience. A curious *Guardian* article from 2021 quotes a woman simply identified as "Claudia," who says that she hears two people in her head—a passionate, flamboyant, rather stereotypical Italian couple who begin arguing the two sides whenever she has a decision to make. Claudia doesn't have Italian family or friends and says she has no idea where this couple have come from; in fact: "It's probably offensive to Italians." This sounds distracting (and quite possibly stressful) to me, but she says that she finds it relaxing; as the Italians fight it out, she can sit back and listen and then come to her decision: "I let them do the work, so I don't get stressed out by it."[1]

Maybe your inner voice takes different forms depending on the situation—for example, if it looks like it's

going to rain, perhaps you hear a parental voice reminding you to take an umbrella with you. Deaf people have
given scientists important insights into how the inner
voice might work. Some people who are profoundly deaf
report thinking in sign language, printed words, lip-
reading, or images (I got completely absorbed by a Quora
thread in which people with different levels of hearing
discuss their experience of an inner "voice," which I
totally recommend looking up if you are interested in
knowing more about this).[2]

So much of how we interact with the world is through
language and communication, and, perhaps logically, it
seems that whatever "mode" of communication we are
used to is likely to be the way we experience our inner
voice. In a study that used neuroimaging, allowing visu-
alization of brain activity in real time, when signers were
imagining sign language—or, in other words, internally
signing to themselves—the same areas of the brain were
activated as in hearing people when they were experiencing inner speech, even though signing is a physical
thing that requires the input of different (visuospatial)
areas of the brain. This suggests that thinking in any
kind of language—i.e., talking to yourself in your head—
shares a common neural pathway, no matter how you
do it.[3,4]

The idea of an inner voice is something that plenty of
people have attempted to study—even though it's inherently difficult to do so. This shows how central we see it
to understanding how we as individuals experience the

world. After all, even with all the scans, equipment, and medical know-how out there, none of us can peer into someone else's brain and see exactly what they're thinking or how they experience that thought. This hasn't stopped people trying, though, and researchers have come up with multiple different ways to try to measure a subject's inner monologue. One of these is known as descriptive experience sampling. Developed by Russell T. Hurlburt, a clinical psychologist and professor of psychology at the University of Nevada, Las Vegas, it requires subjects to report on their "inner experience" at random times throughout the day. A buzzer will go off (or a notification will pop up on their phone) and the idea is that they stop what they are doing and immediately record what they were thinking and/or feeling at the time. One of the key advantages is the immediacy— if someone asks you how you feel or what you think about something that happened yesterday, then you'll have processed that to an extent and you'll be relying on your memory of it. This method is all about real time, and when lots of data is gathered from many different subjects, psychologists can analyze it for patterns and insights into the way we think.

By using data from descriptive experience sampling, Hurlburt estimates that between 30 and 50 percent of people experience an inner monologue on a regular basis, but that some don't have this at all and not many people have it going on all the time.[5,6] However, other researchers using alternative methods have come up with different results, with one study suggesting that people generally experience the monologue as much as 75 percent of the time. One problem seems to be that it depends on how researchers frame the questions when conducting the study. And it all goes to show that however far we have come in neuroscience, and no matter how much we put people in functional magnetic resonance imaging (fMRI) scanners to measure blood flow to the different areas of the brain, the human consciousness is a strange and elusive thing. It's really hard to quantify or explain what the hell is going on in there. But, as with lots of things we will encounter here, that doesn't mean we should stop asking the questions. The only way to learn more about ourselves, after all, even just on a personal level, is to keep asking: Why? What is that like? Is this the same for you? (I'm asking, anyway, even though for me it's bloody hard to describe!) That's whether we are scientists working in the field or just regular, curious humans wondering about it and filling in "inner monologue" polls on Instagram.

As you're here reading this book, I expect you share some of my fascination with this. It sort of goes back to that point I mentioned earlier, which was made by neuroscientist Professor Herculano-Houzel: that, as far as we know, we are the only animals using our brains to study . . . our brains. It might be impossible to fully articulate what we are thinking and exactly how it's playing out for us, but that doesn't stop us seizing on topics like the idea of an inner monologue or inner voice to attempt to make some sort of sense of it. And wanting to share that with others. We know our thoughts are very powerful, that what we think in a large part defines who we are and the choices we make, and questions like "Do you hear your thoughts as a voice in your head?" are just one way of exploring that.

Imagine an apple

Another thought exercise I find captivating in this area is the concept of a "mind's eye." If your inner monologue is, in a way, how you might "hear" your thoughts, your mind's eye is about how you can "see" things that are not in front of you. Some people have an intensely vivid visual imagination—for example, they report having dreams in which they have visualized whole scenes that they don't believe they have actually seen in their waking lives—while other people say they have no mind's eye at all and cannot conjure images in their heads, a condition that has been named aphantasia. I think I might have it. When I think of dreams I've had, maybe when I try to describe them to someone in the morning, I can recall events that happened but, even then, it doesn't often feel like I can see them, I just know what happened.

Reading descriptions of aphantasia, which is when you can't form mental pictures, feels like a useful reference point for me then to imagine the inverse, which is what most people do experience. Aphantasia isn't a medical condition or a disability and, according to the Cleveland

Clinic, experts estimate it affects somewhere between 2 and 4 percent of people. It could be congenital, aka present from birth; people with congenital aphantasia may not realize they have it, since they don't know other people are seeing mental images. Maybe you're about to realize you're one of those people! Acquired aphantasia, which sets in later in life, usually has an identifiable cause, such as a brain injury, illness, or mental health condition. There are also varying degrees of aphantasia; some people could still see flashes of images, or only struggle to form pictures when they're actively trying.

It blows my mind slightly to think how much our experiences could be differing. There's a classic example when talking about the "mind's eye" in which you try to imagine an apple, if you'd like to have a go. Let's say it's a red one. Below is a scale to try to rate what you can "see."

1. You can see the apple as you would if it were there, perfectly realistic.

2. It's realistic and reasonably vivid.

3. It's a moderately clear image, maybe more blurred.

4. You can see a dim and vague shape, perhaps more of an outline.

5. There's no image, you just "know" you're thinking of an apple.

If you're a solid five, like me, you might have aphantasia. Where do you fall? Can you picture the apple? Does it have some dents or bruises, or is it smooth and shiny? Are you seeing it on its own or in an apple tree—do you see the branches as well? Is the color vivid, as in real life, or more faded? If I close my eyes, it's just black—I don't feel like I am really seeing that apple, I just . . . know what an apple looks like. Is it the same for you, or do our brains work differently? (Send me a message and let me know, if you like!) I think it can be hard to pin down your own experience even when we boil it down to such a simple example, let alone trying to understand how someone *else* is experiencing their mind's eye, or inner monologue.

I'm off again with a quick sidebar: I may have learned something about myself in working on this chapter. As I was rereading this, I was trying it out, shutting my eyes and trying over and over again to picture a red apple. And then a pink elephant, just in case. (Which is because repeatedly reading the word "aphantasia" made me think of Disney's *Fantasia*.) I still couldn't picture anything. But when I opened my eyes to carry on reading, I realized I felt more like I could picture an apple. I still can't *see* it in my mind's eye, but it's a bit different, maybe what I would call a faint mental image. On the previous scale, I've moved from my solid five to a possible four. Think I'm being silly? Hop on to Google, type in "aphantasia eyes closed," and *bam*—"A small percentage of people with aphantasia only experience it with closed eyes. A little over 15 percent of people with aphantasia can 'see' mental images if they open their eyes. Why this happens is unknown."[7] Interestingly, aphantasia may also affect the way people store or access memories. For example, they may have difficulties with autobiographical memory, i.e., recalling things they have personally experienced, because they can't visualize them. This rings very true for me: I have an absolutely terrible memory for my own life. Plus, it could be linked to neurodivergence, which . . . hello. A little journey I've just been on in real time—thanks for the company.

Thinking about thoughts is a strange sensation. Of all the amazing things our brains can do, when I try to process how we are actually doing them, it feels a tad overwhelming.

The unconscious mind

When we look at the power of thoughts, how they affect the choices we make and how we feel, you can't really avoid one man—Sigmund Freud, the inventor of psychoanalysis and a figure who casts a long shadow over modern psychology. I find it kind of bonkers to think that one person and their theories could have such an enormous impact on a field like that. Like Darwin and evolution, I suppose. It makes me wonder about who is currently out there working on a game-changing scientific hypothesis.

There are plenty of criticisms of Freud's theories. As detailed by the British Psychological Society, his views on women were controversial, seeing us essentially as "men, without the penises." He thought that women's lives, problems, and behaviors were mostly influenced by sexual reproductive functions.[8] Take your pick of the issues in those last couple of sentences alone—but we'll push forward for now. We have sort of moved on from Freud's founding theories in many ways, but his writings still influence a lot of discussion and how psychologists come at certain questions.

Freud published his famous paper "The Ego and the Id" in 1923. In it, he laid out the concept of the id—the primitive and instinctive part of the mind, which he called the "dark, inaccessible part of our personality"—and the ego—the learned, social, rational part of the mind. The ego, he said, mediates between the id and the superego, which is our moral center and responsible for our sense of right and wrong.

Say, you're driving and someone cuts you off dangerously. Your superego may feel horrified that someone would drive like that, as they are putting other people's lives at risk, while your id, feeling afraid and angry, might want you to jump out of the car and scream at them. Your ego (who is aware that shouting and screaming in the street isn't socially approved behavior) considers the information and decides what to do, talking your id down from its instinctive response and taking a course of action, like giving the terrible driver a wide berth if you come up to them at the next light, for example.[9]

Though he didn't come up with it—it had been bothering scientists and philosophers for quite a while—the idea of the conscious and unconscious mind is at the center of Freud's theories. The ego, id, and superego connect to this, although they don't map on to it directly—basically, the id operates unconsciously, the ego is the conscious mind and the superego is both. Freud famously used the metaphor of an iceberg to explain how he saw the "layers" of the mind. The bit of the iceberg that you can see poking out above the water represents the conscious mind. This is what we are focused on, what we know we think. Just below the waterline is the preconscious—memories, basically. You are not thinking about this stuff all the time but it can be retrieved and thought about if you want. For example, what was the color of the front door of the house you grew up in? It was (probably!) lurking somewhere in your preconscious until I asked you to think about it, at which point it became a conscious thought. Finally, at the very bottom, deeply submersed, is the unconscious. Freud believed that this is where all your primal desires, motivations, fears, and impulses live. He also believed that this is by far the most important part of the mind.[10]

Freud was interested in the idea that unconsciousness is a dynamic process, whereby certain thoughts are almost forced out of the conscious mind because we've repressed them. This sort of "buried thoughts" theory—particularly focused on suppressed childhood memories—may have formed the basis for psychoanalysis, but in modern psychology and psychotherapy, most professionals would agree that repressed memories are rarely the sole cause of any and all psychological issues that someone might present with. Although, many would say they can still play a role in the more complex overview of an individual's psyche. One possible argument against repressed traumatic experiences (as in, ones we don't remember having) being very significant for us is that when something frightening is happening, the amygdala grabs the controls and the hippocampus—responsible for making memories—tends to get out of the way, with the result that we often don't have a clear recall of the event. It's not that we repressed the memory, per se—just our brain wasn't recording in high definition.[11] You know when you hear someone who has been in an accident say, "I don't know what happened . . ."? That. But then, some people have a vivid recall of a very bad experience (it's not repressed at all), so it's obviously not clear-cut.

Whatever you think about the significance (or not) of repressed memories, it's interesting that this hundred-year-old theory still influences what some people imagine when they picture what therapy is like—the stereotypical "tell me about your childhood" kind of therapeutic exploration where you work with a professional to try to figure out how experiences in your past manifest in your current feelings or behavior. I've never really done that sort of therapy myself and so can't say I have a strong opinion on it, but I'll mention here for anyone to whom it might be relevant that there are lots of other kinds of therapy that focus much more on the here and now, and on current thought processes. Many times, I've heard of a younger person talking about going to therapy and a parent immediately reacting with, "Oh, well, I suppose all your problems are going to be my fault, then!" I think this cliché of therapy that we see on TV and in the media can put people off going to seek support, because they feel they're going to have to immediately reel off their life story, and that generally isn't the case.

Open tabs

It's not going to be a major newsflash that our subconscious does have a big impact, however. It's just not all about how you buried the memory of your childhood goldfish's tragic passing. (Me, recalling the kitchen fish tank massacre circa 1998. That was one intelligent cat.) There is, by necessity, a whole lot going on in our heads that we are not aware of. Have you heard people say that we only use 10 percent of our brain? Well, that's not really true. We may well be using all of it, most of the time, in one way or another.[12] But we obviously aren't consciously aware of that much of what our brain is up to, even if we can override some of the "'automation"—for example, we breathe without consciously thinking about it but can decide to hold our breath underwater.

Over the course of several decades, there has been a lot of research carried out to try to assess just how aware we are of the subconscious thoughts and influences that affect our decision-making and behavior patterns, concluding that our unconscious mind does indeed have a very powerful, though not always strictly rational, influence on our higher cognitive levels of thought.[13] Which probably doesn't come as a massive surprise. So, even though holes have been poked in a lot of Freud's theories on consciousness, cognitive and social psychological experiments have continued to support his notion of subconscious levels of thinking and their enormous potential to impact upon our judgments and behaviors.

Besides a possible vault of repressed memories, our subconscious mind is also responsible for more helpful things—for example, it can be a valuable tool in problem-solving if you know how to hack it a tiny bit. Your subconscious brain continues to solve problems in the background even when you're not consciously focused on the task—and, in fact, going away and taking a break from thinking about a problem can actually be beneficial in solving it. For example, one of my favorite daily habits is (attempting) the *New York Times* crossword. (Shout out to the Spelling Bee-ers.) I know that there's a pattern whereby I can stare and stare at all the answers I'm stuck on and come up with absolutely nothing—no ideas, no clue. But if I close the app, go away and don't think about it for a few hours, often when I return to it new things will jump out at me or suddenly I can think of an answer to a clue that completely baffled me earlier. It turns out I'm in good company with this one, as Ernest Hemingway happened to notice the same thing: "I learned not to think about anything that I was writing from the time I stopped writing until I started again the next day. That way my subconscious would be working on it."[14]

I'm sure you can think of your own example of this phenomenon too. Scientific research seems to support what I'll affectionately term the "open tabs" theory. Neuroscientist David Creswell of Carnegie Mellon University conducted an experiment to investigate this phenomenon, exploring what happens in the brain when people tackle problems that are too big or too convoluted for their conscious minds to solve. He compared groups of people who were asked to solve a problem around choosing the right car according to some given parameters. Groups were either told to complete the decision-based task immediately, allowed some time to sit and solve the problem, or given the information but then instructed to go away and do a "distractor task"—something that held their attention but allowed their subconscious to keep working away behind the scenes. This third group did significantly better than the others when it came to making their final decision. When investigating these findings further using fMRI scans (we mentioned those earlier; they allow doctors to measure brain activity by looking at images of blood flow in different areas of the brain in real time), Creswell was able to show that the regions of the brain that were active when the problem was initially presented continued to be active even when the subject was distracted with another task.[15] In their paper describing the experiment and their findings,

Creswell and his team use the term "unconscious neural reactivation" to describe this kind of background processing, "neural reactivation" meaning the process by which neural patterns formed by or associated with a previous experience or memory are stimulated during subsequent related activities or rest periods.

I love this concept, and reading that it's been backed up by an experiment, as I definitely feel like my brain benefits from "unconscious neural reactivation." I will very often say something like, "I need to step away and let this percolate for a while." Especially with my ADHD, I try to be flexible with myself when I know that I've reached the limits of my concentration span for a particular task. Now I know that processing and decision-making does carry on in an open tab in the background, I feel a bit better about doing that! Staring endlessly at a blank page or seemingly impossible problem rarely does much to help solve it and feels more like punishment than productivity to me. Any authors I've ever spoken to or read advice from all say the same: that forcing yourself into writing when your brain isn't firing in that mode doesn't work. I know this is something of a luxury, getting to move tasks around to when they suit me better because my boss is me (blessing and curse though that is), but I've certainly used this in the past too, even as far back as at school. Having a couple of options when it comes to tasks that need to get done can be really helpful. If I hit a wall with one, I can try to switch to another task rather than bang my head against the table with something I simply can't finish right now, or just give up entirely on getting anything done and feel a bit shit about it. It's yet another way that snippets of information about how our brains work can help us get through the day, berating ourselves just a little bit less![16]

Habits

Another area in which it's very useful to be aware of how our unconscious mind works, so we can hack it/not beat ourselves up when we don't meet our intentions, is habit forming. We're going to see this pop up in lots of different forms, but what is perhaps the surprising thing about our amazing, powerful brains is that you could say they are naturally a bit . . . lazy. Though there is an element of efficiency in here too, to be fair to them.

From an evolutionary standpoint, our bodies are generally programmed to conserve energy. Energy is expensive; the more we use, the more time and resources it requires in making sure we have enough to eat and drink. Especially in our cave-dwelling past, we didn't have unlimited energy, so we had to use it in the best way to ensure our survival. This could help us to understand why it feels so difficult to form positive habits that require us to expend energy, put in a bit more effort. Harvard evolutionary biologist Daniel E. Lieberman wrote a book about this, specifically relating to physical exercise. In conversation with the *Harvard Gazette*, he explained: "All in all, humans have these deep-rooted instincts to avoid unnecessary physical activity, because until recently it was beneficial to avoid it. Now, we judge people as lazy if they don't exercise. But they're not lazy. They're just being normal."[17]

Well, I certainly feel better about myself. Now, the point of Lieberman's book, and indeed this discussion right here, wasn't to let us off the hook but more to explain the behavior so that we're able to recognize and reap the benefits of overcoming it. There's no point wasting time being angry at yourself that you don't feel like going for a run or journaling or making your bed— whichever positive habit you're trying to pick up at the moment. But we're not in the Stone Age anymore, and it's great to try to incorporate into our lives those habits that do impact us positively, whether that's for physical or mental benefit.

In terms of energy conservation, our brains are no different than the rest of our bodies and, to this end, we like to be able to automate processes. We don't want to have to bother the conscious mind with something if it can be delegated to the unconscious. According to Alannah I. Mendelson from the Department of Psychiatry at New York's Columbia University, habits represent "a fundamental paradox in the human experience: despite our sense of control and purpose in our lives, a significant proportion of our daily behavior is actually driven by habit."[18] We're decision-making machines, but a lot of what we do is not consciously evaluated and decided upon. We do it without thinking. This is great in terms of freeing up brainpower for more complicated or important tasks, but bad if we are doing things that we don't want to be doing.

Neurologically speaking, the more a behavior is repeated, the more the associated neural connections are strengthened. Over time, these neural pathways become more efficient and the behavior becomes automatic.[19] That doesn't mean the conscious mind doesn't have to get involved at all, of course—you learned the habit of brushing your teeth before bed when you were a child and it's so ingrained that it's probably rare that you forget to do it. You don't need to make a plan for when to do it or write yourself a reminder on the bathroom mirror. It doesn't feel like too much effort because you're so used to doing it. But there is still an element of conscious control and decision-making happening there. If you're reading this and currently struggling with your mental health to the extent that brushing your teeth actually does feel like an enormous effort, I see you. I've been there too and it absolutely can get better. Hang in there <3.

Habits are fairly reliant on stimuli—something outside your head that activates the process. They are often tied to specific contexts or situations. The unconscious mind learns to associate certain environments, times of day, or emotional states with carrying out a habit. When these stimuli are disrupted, your brain might not then be triggered to prompt you to perform the same automatic behavior. For example, on holiday, when staying in a different place and not following your usual bedtime routine, have you ever found you've forgotten to do something you'd usually do without thinking, like brush your teeth (to return to the previous example) or take out your contact lenses? Or have you walked out without your keys because the front door was open when you left the house and you didn't put your hand on the latch, like you usually would? Something was different and your usual habit was interrupted. (I know that if I don't make myself a cup of tea when I first go into the kitchen in the morning, then I won't remember to take any supplements that day.) Or how about that disorientating feeling when you're in a country where they drive on the other side of the road to what you're used to? When you come to cross the street, you have to make your head turn in the opposite direction to check for traffic than the one that the bit of your brain responsible for the habit wants you to turn it in. Discombobulating.

The bit of the brain that automates habits is called the basal ganglia,[20] part of the limbic system. Evolutionarily speaking, this is the oldest part of the brain—you might have heard it being referred to as the reptilian, primitive, or animal brain. The amygdala and hippocampus live here too. Just as the fight-or-flight mechanism can kick in and react without consulting our prefrontal cortex first, the basal ganglia is often just doing its own thing. Hence we can unconsciously carry out a habit without consciously thinking about it.

In his book *The Power of Habit*, Charles Duhigg calls the thing that stimulates you to carry out a habit a "cue," your habitual reaction to it the "response," and the reason for it—the thing you get out of it—the "reward." When your brain receives some sort of reward in the form of a dopamine hit, it reinforces this whole procedure, firming up those neural pathways and making us even more likely to respond to the cue in the future. It's worth understanding this if we want to break or create certain patterns, as we are very much creatures of habit. In fact, according to one paper based on experience sampling, "Habits—A Repeat Performance," around 45 percent of activities tend to be repeated in the same location most days.[21] So how do we get our prefrontal cortex to pay attention and intervene when our basal ganglia is merrily repeating the same ingrained behaviors that don't help us? Or ask our basal ganglia to please take up a new habit that we do want in our lives?

According to behavioral psychologists, the key is in disrupting this cue–routine–reward loop. If you've got into the habit of pouring yourself a glass of wine or shopping online when you've had a stressful day at work, and you decide you want to cut down on these things, then in an ideal world you would remove the source of stress (the cue). However, quitting your job might result in a different kind of stress altogether ... You could disrupt the routine, initially by not going straight to the fridge/laptop, or by moving the item or even getting rid of the temptation altogether. But that's not going to satisfy the reward centers of your brain, which are now sitting there like a cat next to an empty bowl waiting for the dinner it thinks is due. This is when you try to find another source of dopamine to replace the Sauvignon Blanc/lime-green T-shirt you'll never wear: calling a friend, playing a video game, having a bath, etc.

It's the same principle if you want to create a habit loop that you do aspire to. It's annoying if you feel like the end result should be a good reward in itself but you find yourself struggling to establish the habit anyway. For example, you know you feel good afterward if you get out and go for a walk at lunchtime, and yet it never seems to happen. *Why, brain?!* In this case, what we know about habit loops suggests we need to further load up the reward part of the equation. Let's say you find a really good podcast that you *only* listen to when out on your lunchtime walk. The dopamine flows, those neural pathways are strengthened, you connect "walk" with "feel good," time of day with action, and, after a while, you find yourself getting up and reaching for your jacket at one p.m., barely having to think about it first.

Why we love patterns

Interestingly, some of the other tasks that the basal ganglia gets involved with are forming emotions, the development of memories and pattern recognition.[22] Being able to spot patterns might seem like something that would mostly come up in an IQ test or fun little brain-teaser, but it is actually hugely important.

We love patterns. (And I'm not just talking about my

personal penchant for stripes.) It's important and useful to know how much we love them for a number of reasons. Firstly, and most simply, our brains are naturally attracted to them and they make us feel safe. I mean, of course we prefer it if we feel like we understand something and know what's going to happen next, don't we? We like expressions such as "Red sky at night, shepherd's delight" and procedural detective dramas in which we try to spot clues, reassured all the while that the bad guy will be caught and arrested by the end. In fact, we are so good at spotting patterns that we can even pick out incomplete ones and fill in the rest in our heads.

L tt rs m ss ng fr m a s nt nc d n't g n r lly st p s fr m b ng abl t nd rst nd th t s nt nc .

It might have taken you a few seconds but I think you probably figured that out? And did you notice that all the missing letters are vowels? A gold star for you—you spotted a pattern. A p tt rn. Humans are very good at mentally filling in gaps to create a fuller picture. And we can also disregard information that isn't relevant—or, crucially, that we don't *think* is relevant.

Pattern-spotting is a big part of what sets our cognitive abilities above those of other mammals. Newborn babies are immediately drawn to faces or face-like patterns,[23] and research has even determined that a third-trimester human fetus *still in the womb* is already drawn to face-like patterns, before ever seeing a face,[24] suggesting there's something properly inbuilt about this reaction. Lots of animals learn to recognize elements of their physical environment and each other, using that information to make decisions and predict what's going to happen next, but as our prefrontal cortex evolved, it became one of our most advanced skills. If you think about it, what is science but the search for patterns, which are translated into laws or facts that help us understand what is going on around us?

Back in the day, if we weren't sure, not venturing out of the cave because we'd observed a connection between bear poo and the presence of bears, or not eating the leaf with markings that looked a bit like the one that poisoned Urgg, was the safest option. Spotting patterns made thinking and understanding quicker, helped us to avoid potentially lethal risk and delegated some work to the unconscious part of the brain, using previous experience to assess and guide our behavior. This has been so super-effective for us as a species that, as we evolved, it became a sort of building block in how our brains work. According to one paper in the journal *Frontiers in Neuroscience*, "SPP [superior pattern processing] is sufficient to explain many such higher brain functions including creativity, imagination, language, and magical thinking."[25] When you think about it, almost everything we know how to do comes down to noticing and repeating patterns . . .[26]

However, our brains are not perfect. Of the many thousands of decisions we ask them (consciously or unconsciously) to make every day, they are going to get some wrong. Remember the idea that correlation doesn't mean causality? It's what we were looking at in that "sad vegetarians" study earlier. In other words, there might be a strong relationship between two things, they might often occur at the same time, but that doesn't mean one causes the other. For example, a rise in ice-cream sales may be accompanied by a rise in crime. There is no link there—or not one that anyone's been able to fathom— but both independently increase when the weather is hot. Patternicity, or apophenia (both brilliant words), means seeing patterns that aren't there. If you are living with schizophrenia, you may experience an extreme version of this. But we all do it sometimes—from scientists analyzing results, to conspiracy theorists finding clues where there are none, to a piece of burnt toast that somehow looks just like Kate Winslet.

The bias conundrum

One of the by-products of this hardwired evolutionary ability/need to spot patterns is cognitive bias. The concept was first introduced by Amos Tversky and Daniel Kahneman (who we will meet again later) in 1972. We think we are being very logical and acting on the facts we have before us, without recognizing that our thinking is flawed or undermined in some way. There's a bug in the system but we don't realize it. There are different kinds of cognitive bias.[27] For example:

- **Confirmation bias**. This is maybe one of the best known. We pay attention to the facts that fit the pattern of what we already know or believe and ignore anything that could undermine our existing beliefs.

- **Hindsight bias.** We look back and see something as inevitable and predictable based on how events did unfold, even though we did not have and couldn't have had any clue it would go that way at the time.

- **Sunk cost fallacy.** Gambling addicts will often look at their losses with this bias. We put so much worth on what we have already invested in something that it stops us from assessing the value or benefit of keeping going with the project. You could also apply this one to staying in a bad relationship because of the time you've already invested.

- **The halo effect.** This is when how you feel about someone influences how you perceive their character or morals. For example, when someone seems so nice that you don't want to believe they may have done something unpleasant.

- **The Dunning–Kruger effect.** It's easy to laugh at this one, as it means the overestimation of your skills or ability. But I think we've probably all done it. Apparently, 80 percent of drivers think they are above average.[28]

I think the point to make here is that we all have biases. We can't really avoid it. "Unconscious bias" is a term you hear a lot now, which is good in the sense that it's useful to be aware of this flaw in the system. But I have heard it used as an accusation, as a sort of moral failing, which I don't think is quite right. If our inherent biases lead us to prejudice or to jump to unfair assumptions about someone, then that is not OK and needs addressing, clearly. But our brains are looking for shortcuts, for patterns, and this will result in biases. That doesn't make us bad people—it's what we do to learn more and to recognize and consciously correct for those biases that is important.

Our amazing, sophisticated brains have evolved to allow us to do some seriously impressive things—but their first duty, as per the survival of the species, was to keep us safe. So we will overcorrect for things, see patterns where there are none, seek reassurance from incomplete pictures that don't reflect reality. I don't think we should be beating ourselves up for that. And we could maybe have compassion at times for the other humans around us with their own imperfect brains, who are also muddling through a world that is increasingly filled with stimuli and complications. But when we know a bit about how we are wired and why, I think it gives us the chance to take a moment to question our instinctive responses, course-correct if necessary and consider some neurological context for our "flaws."

Tell me a story

So far we've learned a lot about the unconscious processes bubbling away in our skulls. I hope you don't feel too out of control, with all the things your subconscious is up to without running them by your conscious brain first! In the next chapters, we're going to look at what happens when our brains start interacting with other brains, in relationships, communities, online, and in society in general. Before we do, though, I just want to finish with one more aspect of conscious and unconscious processes that I think is particularly interesting.

Earlier, I mentioned the popularity of police dramas, how our brains are attracted to the familiarity of the way plots unfold within the genre. Or any genre, really; I like the medical ones, myself. In fact, according to Christopher Booker (what a perfect name for a journalist and author), there are only seven basic plots in storytelling, and all novels, movies, TV narratives, etc., are a version or a combination of these. So, for example, "the quest," where the main character has to go on a physical journey, like *The Wizard of Oz* or *Frozen*. Or "the rebirth," where the protagonist learns the error of their ways and reforms, like *A Christmas Carol* or *Groundhog Day*. Imaginative storytelling is one of those key human things that we don't think any other species does. It is integral to the way we understand the world and is basically elaborate pattern-forming and recognition. When we get annoyed because we're watching something and we think, "That person would never do that!," our frustration comes from the character behaving in a way that doesn't fit the pattern we expect.

If you have ever done therapy, or just been interested enough to learn a bit about it, you'll probably know that there is often a focus on unpacking the stories we tell ourselves—consciously or unconsciously. These stories are how we make sense of our lives, our actions, and the things that happen around us. We want to find patterns in what we do and we want there to be an explanation— even if it's not the right one, as, to our brains, having a story is better than none at all. When we throw up our hands and wonder "Why am I like this?," what stories are we telling ourselves about who we are? That we're too lazy? Too stupid? In our own stories, are the people around us somehow so much better?

Renowned psychotherapist Esther Perel talks a lot about the importance of the stories we tell ourselves. She says, "We use our stories as reminders, as protection and prevention."[29] They can reinforce our identity and make us feel capable, but they can also keep us stuck in the past if we keep telling the same story and aren't able to find new, evolving explanations. She has a lovely expression: "Write often and edit well."

This is a huge topic and our stories are of course deeply personal to all of us. We may have moved past Freud's analysis of the ego, superego, and id, but there's no doubt that our unconscious, and all that bias and pattern-spotting, is bubbling away in there. Whether you are in therapy, hoping to do that, or feel it's not something that interests you at the moment, it's worth being aware of the incredible power our unconscious has to put a spin on our stories, without our knowledge.

On social media, we see people blamed for "centering themselves" in situations that are not really about them, and we also see people celebrated for positive "main character energy." The truth is that we are wired to think about and protect ourselves in the first instance. That doesn't make us inherently selfish, per se, it's just that many of the things that make us "good" people—caring for others, seeing their point of view, wanting to do good in the world—are rooted in some tangled social structures and not necessarily embedded in our neurobiology. In other words, we have to learn this stuff, to a large extent, and, like all lessons, it's a process, so there is a chance—sometimes a need, you could say—to make mistakes in order to keep learning.

Let us now venture outside our own heads—our thoughts, our conscious and unconscious, how good we are at imagining an apple—and move on to asking what happens when our brains come into contact with other brains . . .

4

KNOWING ME, KNOWING YOU?

"HELL IS OTHER PEOPLE," WROTE the French philosopher Jean-Paul Sartre.

"No man is an island," wrote English poet John Donne.

"I'm just popping to the loo!" said I, lying, when I
needed to be alone for a minute.

Human beings need other human beings. We are
hardwired to be sociable animals and the relationships
we have with each other have been key to our survival.
That's just basic evolution. Communities = better for
your life expectancy than going it alone. But that doesn't
mean we are always good at getting along with each
other. Putting aside the big picture for the moment—
mankind's long history of picking fights and starting
wars—creating and maintaining relationships with those
immediately around us can be hard enough, before we
even start to think about how communities and wider
groups work—or don't work—with each other.

So how do our brains drive us to make connections

with our fellow humans? We often say things like, "It feels good to feel 'seen' by someone," but what is that feeling and why is it important to us? The world has become seriously complicated since early humans figured out you have to cooperate to accumulate. Are our brains coping with social media and the crazy, constant demands on our attention? What can science tell us that may help us to untangle the problem of how we can understand, but sometimes also so wholly misunderstand, each other?

Dunbar's number

You may well have heard the assertion that humans are only capable of maintaining 150 social connections. That's apparently the maximum size of our mental "community," and after that our internal mailbox is full. If you're wondering where this came from, it was put forward by an anthropologist at Oxford University called Robin Dunbar. In 1993, when Dunbar and his team did research into sizes of groups or networks of people—in Anglo-Saxon villages, modern workplaces, hunter-gatherer societies, military units—they kept coming back to 150 and developed the concept of Dunbar's number: the number of stable relationships people are cognitively able to maintain at any one time.[1] Once a group of people gets larger than this, it seems it will organically split up into smaller groups. As an example of how this number might affect someone socially, those with larger, extended families have been observed to have fewer friends, since much of their "capacity" has been used up in maintaining those familial relationships.[2]

As we keep seeing, our human brains love a neat explanation, a definite figure, so it's not surprising that Dunbar's number has entered popular culture as an easy-to-quote "fact." When you dive deeper into his theory, though, there's actually quite a lot of room for maneuver on the magic number—as well as what is meant by a "meaningful" social connection (Dunbar doesn't actually use this term, but how to define it is a very important question that we'll come back to). According to Dunbar, 150 is an average, with an individual's capacity for social connection likely to range somewhere between 100 and 250. In his 2021 book *Friends: Understanding the Power of Our Most Important Relationships*, he explains that the total should really be broken down into a series of numbers, with concentric circles representing levels of friendship. These extend from "intimates" and "close friends" at the center, out as far as "friends," and then *past* Dunbar's number to "acquaintances" and finally "known names" in the outermost circle, clocking in at an average of 1,500.

I think I would score a relatively low number. Even as someone who loves their friends dearly, I find the maintenance of friendships—in terms of the basic keeping in touch, making sure we've spoken recently—to be quite challenging, depending on how overwhelmed I feel in other areas. I know so many people who seem to be in constant text communication with innumerable friends, always up to date, always on top of what everyone's up to . . . and yet somehow they're not on the phone at every minute of the day, either. It's baffling to me. I think it's partly because I'm not that great at sharing the minutiae of my life as standard. So much of day-to-day communication seems to add up to just letting people know who you've seen or what you've eaten or where you've arranged to go next Wednesday—I think I just assume people won't be interested and so have ended up with a bit of a reputation as someone who doesn't tell anyone anything. I'm always open to these updates from other people, though. But I digress.

It's worth making the point that Robin Dunbar's initial research, which led to this number working its way into the popular consciousness, was first published in the 1990s, when the internet was still in its infancy and way before social media. Since then, there have been lots of continuing studies that have supported, challenged, and furthered this research, asking how it might work in our modern, hyper-connected era. Perhaps surprisingly, in broad terms, it still seems to hold up. Interestingly, Dunbar's number has been used by developers who design platforms and online worlds. Whether this is evidence that it does represent a fundamental principle of how human networks function, no matter where they are formed, or a sort of self-fulfilling prophecy—in the sense that we design new things based on what we already believe to be true and correct, whether they are or not—I don't know. But it does seem to show that Dunbar's number isn't something we can ignore when we're asking questions about our capacity as humans to connect to each other.

Why is connecting so important?

Maybe the next question to ask is why our social network is so important to us. And what does this mean for some of the challenges we come up against in everyday life, as we try to stay in touch with our friends, not fall out with them, and even make new friends?

In terms of basic evolutionary theory, forming social groups was crucial to the success of our species. Most primates live in groups—Zanzibar's red colobus monkey forms communities that range in size from 12 up to 150 (like humans), and there might be 800 in a mandrill "supergroup," while orangutans are described as "solitary but friendly." Humans, however, took this to a whole other level, particularly when you throw the development of advanced communication into the mix. Do you remember in Chapter Two when we talked about the amazing capacity of the human brain to learn new things and how important that was for our evolutionary ability to adapt to different environments all over the planet? Well, every day's a school day, etc., but being able to share what you've learned *and* cooperate to put that knowledge into action is what gets you from a smarty-pants primate to planet-dominating super-species.

Also in Chapter Two, I mentioned how humans' brain size increased as we stopped living in trees and started to figure out things like cooking. But our brains didn't continue to get bigger indefinitely and are actually thought by some to have gotten smaller, perhaps even in the last 3,000 years.[3] Researchers have hypothesized that this brain shrinkage could have resulted from the evolution of social structures that allowed for more collective decision-making and sharing of information. As part of a larger, more cooperative society, we can share and store information between us, taking pressure off the individual. We don't have to know or remember every little thing because we can now rely on others within our social groups for particular expertise or to take on certain roles. Yes, it's the true human manifestation of the hive mind. The internet before the internet. Large brains, as we know, require a lot of energy input to fuel them. So if there is a collective intelligence, we don't need to have so much memory or processing capacity per individual. Or so one theory goes.

Somewhere along the line, though, it went from "more people make 'kill mammoth' easier" to connection with others being a central pillar of both our mental and physical health. I think most people can understand that loneliness and depression often go together, but according to figures cited by the CDC, the United States' public health body, social isolation has been associated with a 29 percent increase in the risk of heart disease and a 32 percent increase in the risk of stroke.[4] Not connecting with other humans is very, very bad for us.

We talk about "chemistry" between people, and there's certainly a whole lot of chemistry going on in the brain to help us feel connection. When you feel love, attraction, comfort, or bonding with someone, there are many neurotransmitters working away at that. For example, you've probably heard of oxytocin—this one's actually a hormone that also acts as a neurotransmitter—which is sometimes called the "cuddle hormone" or the "love hormone" because it helps us to feel trust and intimacy with someone.[5] It's released in different scenarios—including during sex, breastfeeding, and childbirth.[6] That might seem like a wonky mix of situations, but the common denominator here is a feeling of bonding. Another important neurotransmitter you will likely know is dopamine, which is connected to the brain's reward centers and is released in response to situations where you feel pleasure.[7] That feeling of well-being you get when you've had a really good laugh with friends has a lot to do with dopamine.

That's a super-quick overview of some of the reasons science gives us as to why connection is so important. In a way, the complexity seems to reinforce how central it is to us—we've evolved like this for a reason and it's clearly been vital for our species' survival. But though I think it's really useful, as understanding this can remind us not to undervalue or dismiss social relationships, it's obviously not the whole picture. We may share the same neurobiology and common ancestors, but we are all individuals trying to figure out who we are and how to live in society. And that's not a comfortable thing for all of us all the time.

Introverts and extroverts

We might all need some form of social interaction, but how much, how often, and of what kind varies, depending on so many things. I find it interesting to see how common it's become for people to describe themselves casually in conversation as either an introvert or extrovert, and the popularity of online quizzes that apparently tell you which you are.

If I had to choose one or the other, I'd definitely be an introvert. I prefer small groups to big parties, I am overwhelmed and drained by too much socializing, and, as discussed, I'm more of a listener than a sharer in many of my relationships. Though I do sometimes wonder if some of this is a story I am telling myself. Because I have suffered with anxiety, is it sometimes easier for me to look at a situation that seems on the edge of or outside my comfort zone and dismiss it as "not for me" because I've decided I'm an introvert, and it's not something an introvert would like? Rather than something I, Gemma, might potentially enjoy but would have to push myself to give it a go and find out?

The way we talk about introverts and extroverts in popular culture makes it sound like a binary thing—pick a team and that's who you are. But Carl Jung, the Swiss psychiatrist who came up with the theory at the beginning of the twentieth century, believed that we all have an introverted and an extroverted side, that we are not purely one or the other. "Such a person would be in the lunatic asylum," he said. The way psychologists now talk about introversion and extroversion has moved on from Jung's original writing on the subject, though it remains hugely influential and most personality models and tests have the concept somewhere at their core. Most professionals would agree that we tend to exist on a spectrum or continuum, rather then neatly fitting into one of two available boxes. We might be outgoing, but value quiet time at home to recharge. We might not be comfortable in one-on-one interactions all the time, but be brilliant speakers or performers. Lots of stand-up comedians describe themselves as introverted.

So where do these preferences come from? Even though we're not purely one or the other (a mixture of both is called an ambivert, which most of us are, really), what makes someone more intro- or extroverted? I would have assumed these sorts of personality traits were something largely shaped by our experiences— maybe how much we socialized as children, or something. But it turns out that about 50 percent of our introverted tendencies are genetic,[8] and there are some measurable differences in the brain: it's partly to do with our neurotransmitters.

Neurotransmitters are chemical messengers within our nervous system that help to pass signals between our neurons. There are lots of different types but here are just a few you will already have heard of, including some mentioned earlier in this book:

- **Serotonin:** Helps to regulate mood, sleep, appetite, and many other functions.

- **Dopamine:** Part of our reward system, also affecting concentration, memory, and motivation.

- **Endorphins:** Usually mentioned as a good reason to exercise! Also natural pain-relievers.

- **Adrenaline** (or **epinephrine**, if you're that way inclined): Responsible for our fight-or-flight response to fear or stress.[9]

Research has shown that introverted people are more sensitive to dopamine.[10] In practice, this means that whereas an extrovert might be chatting all night, enjoying loud music and new surroundings, leaving the party feeling energized, an introvert might soon be craving the relative peace of their own home. It's not that introverts have less dopamine, but with the way their brains' reward system functions, the same amount of sensory or social input can leave them feeling overstimulated and worn out. As explained by human psychology researcher Peter Hollins, "With a charged social battery, an introvert is indistinguishable from an extrovert—it's what they do afterward, when they are tired, that differentiates them."[11] At the beginning of the night, an introvert might really enjoy all the socializing and liveliness, but because their reward system is more easily triggered, the happy limit is reached earlier and too much extra can leave them feeling drained. Extroverts have more dopamine receptors in their brains,[12] which means they need more dopamine to get the same happy feeling, as they're less sensitive to it—at the end of the night they're begging the DJ for one more song.

Research on the neurochemistry of personality has also suggested that introverts favor a different kind of neurotransmitter: acetylcholine.[13] Just like dopamine, it's linked to pleasure, but acetylcholine makes someone feel good from different types of activity, when they're calm and quiet. It's not better to be more introverted or extroverted—they're just different!

So why have we become such fans of these terms? One simple answer takes us back to what we were talking about before—our brains like patterns and easy explanations. You go in this box, I go in this box. It's also a way of explaining our personality to other people and understanding ourselves. Rather than saying to a person who has kindly extended an invitation to something that I think is probably not for me, "I feel reluctant to take you up on this because I am someone who finds large groups and multiple social interactions draining and I am aware I need some time alone today to recharge," I can simply let it be known that I am an introvert, and everyone knows what that means. In this sense, it's a helpful shorthand.

We learn in therapy that we can tell ourselves negative stories that limit us. But we also tell ourselves stories to justify or explain our feelings or behavior. Because they make us feel better. So, rather than "I am pathetic and needy because I don't like being at home by myself with no one to talk to," we can say, "I am an extrovert! That's why I want to go out tonight—I am someone who is energized by interacting with other people!" And there is nothing wrong with that—at least, not in my book.

Labels

"Introvert" and "extrovert" are words that we use to label each other and ourselves, and the practice of using labels is something I have been thinking about a lot. How they work, how they can be good for us and bad for us. Whether they help us to connect or can drive us further apart.

In one sense, ADHD is a label. When I received my diagnosis, I had something to call the collection of experiences in my head that I'd previously had no name for. It enabled me to discard the unhelpful labels I had given myself—like "disorganized" and "unfocused"—in favor of something more neutral. To my mind, it's not intrinsically a positive or negative thing that I have ADHD, it just *is*. Plus, it's a useful way to indicate to other people how my brain works. Not that everyone understands what it means or how it can manifest in different ways for different people, but almost everyone has at least heard of it. That shorthand again.

Having the vocabulary to name and express something is almost always a good thing—when it's used to further our understanding. We now have many different terms to express sexuality, for example. When I was younger, the labels most folks were familiar with were more limited; most of us wouldn't have been aware of terms beyond, say, gay or lesbian, such as pansexual, asexual, or demisexual. If you're someone trying to work out who you are, then having some words to put to your feelings, a term to walk around in to test whether it feels right for you, is not only reassuring, but also potentially helps you to find people who are like you and identify your community.

But what about the reductive nature of labels, the way they can tempt us to demand a succinct explanation from someone that allows us to box them up and leave it at that? What if someone is still figuring it out or is, for any reason, reluctant to have the rest of the world put a label on them? That's the other side of the coin here, and something that pushes us away from each other rather than connecting us more closely.

I am thinking in part about Kit Connor, who played Nick Nelson in *Heartstopper*. The show is a sweet love story between two boys in high school. The first season aired in 2022 and meant a lot to many people who don't feel like they see themselves reflected often enough in popular media. Unfortunately, however, the show created a certain amount of hysteria, and some fans hounded Kit, who plays a character who realizes he is bi, as they were adamant that he should tell the world whether he too is bi. I understand that many people feel strongly that queer parts in TV and film should go to queer actors. But to harass someone on social media like that, especially someone who is only eighteen years old—and who described to UK *Vogue* the sudden and extreme level of fame the show brought them as "scary" and "overwhelming"—seemed cruel and sad, not to say very much against the spirit and message of the show. When someone uses a label for themselves it can be empowering, but nobody "owes" us a label. They should be offered, not demanded.

Identity and belonging

This all brings us to the important but sticky subject of identity. Evolution has hardwired us to exist in groups and our neurobiology reinforces this in our brains—but there's a lot more to it than that, isn't there? When you think about it, we need other people around us to help us make sense of who we are. The relationships we have and the way we are treated by others goes a long way to shaping our beliefs, our personalities, the way we see the world, and how we see ourselves.

That Sartre line I opened the chapter with—"Hell is other people"—is often quoted as a sort of joke: "God, aren't people an absolute nightmare!" But in the context of the play it is from (*No Exit*), it is usually interpreted to reflect the subjectivity of our brains and how complex relationships can be. In other words, we can only see the world through our own eyes, while we still have to deal with the views and judgments we receive (or think we are receiving) from others, and it's unavoidable that this shapes our self-identity.

Let's not get sucked into an existential wormhole here and maybe back away from French philosophy— because I don't know much more about French philosophy. I only mention it because the challenges of relationships with other people, whose brains we can't see into, and whose motivation can never be totally plain and certain to us, have clearly been occupying the thoughts of brilliant humans since . . . well, since we had the cognitive capacity to wonder about such things, most likely.

The Enlightenment (otherwise known as the Age of Reason) was a period roughly spanning the 1700s that, in Europe and the US in particular, saw a rapid, simultaneous advance in the rate of scientific discoveries and number of challenges to the status quo. (It was also a time of colonialism, when a white, Eurocentric view of the world was cemented, and the foundations were laid for many of the problems we are still dealing with today.) There hadn't been so much of a sense of the individual as a concept before this point; broadly speaking, people knew their role in the world and it was assumed you'd just follow the path you were set on. During the Enlightenment, in art and politics and science, people started to talk more about the individual as a unique, single unit, and our rights and responsibility to society.

But it can feel these days like we can be almost *too* taken with our sense of individuality. As if there is a continual need to define our own identity, what sets us apart from others as an individual, perhaps at the expense of recognizing what is *not* different about us or the value of being just one equal member of a community. Social media obviously has a big part to play in this and we will of course be unpacking it further. But it's an odd one, because we come back to the same paradox we often do when we start talking about social media—that it is an amazing tool with which to create connection and community, but also a medium that encourages us to focus on ourselves, to keep our settings on "transmit" rather than "receive."

As I mentioned earlier, since around the 2010s, a phrase we've come to hear more and more is "I feel seen." It was often originally used by people from marginalized or underrepresented groups to express how they felt when they saw their experiences reflected in the mainstream media or discourse, and (whether you think this is a good thing or not) has come to be used in many situations in which people feel someone or something (like a film, for example) validates or recognizes an aspect of themselves. So you might say you feel "seen" by another person because they show empathy and understanding of your situation, or something about you as a person. Someone sends you a meme, even, and you feel "seen" because they thought of you, or knew you would like it. It's true that language changes and evolves all the time, but we have to have a need for a word or phrase or we wouldn't use it. How mainstream and well used this expression has become seems to show that it's a sensation we all recognize—perhaps something we all need.

I wonder if, in a way, it is an extension or even a sort of inversion of the concept of "belongingness." According to psychologists Roy Baumeister and Mark Leary, belongingness—the innate desire for social acceptance—is a fundamental aspect of human nature and one of our biggest motivators.[14] They argue that a lot of the motivators that other psychologists have identified—like a desire for power, intimacy, or approval—actually all come back to an overarching need to feel we comfortably fit in to a group or community. Plus, so hardwired is our evolutionary need to be part of a group that, they say, it fundamentally affects our ability to think well of ourselves.

Before Baumeister and Leary, Abraham Maslow produced his "hierarchy of needs." It's pretty famous, so you may well have heard of it. It works like a pyramid. At the bottom are things we need for basic survival—water, shelter, food, etc. If we don't have these, they're what we're going to focus on at the expense of pretty much everything else. If these needs are satisfied, we can move up to the next level—safety, which is also pretty essential. Maslow included emotional safety and financial security here too. If you're worried about money, for example, this makes sense—it's hard to think about anything else when you don't know how you will pay the bills, buy food, etc. But at the very next level, Maslow placed love and belonging. Maslow argued that it's only when we have a feeling of belonging, in terms of secure family and social connection, that we are going to be able to start fulfilling our "higher needs"—things like self-esteem, self-respect, and self-actualization, which mean pursuing your talents, interests, and goals. I think it's a really emotive thing to look at it like this: the idea that feeling like you belong is the bridge between the basic "you may well die if you don't have this stuff" and the more complex "you probably won't be truly happy if you don't have *this* stuff."

How this plays out in terms of our brain chemistry is, unsurprisingly, pretty complicated, and scientists are still figuring it out (read: arguing about it). But one thing I think is definitely worth knowing is that feelings of (or fear of) social exclusion or rejection activate the amygdala—you remember, that hyperaware, slightly jittery guy who is constantly on the lookout for threat. This suggests that we experience a bad social interaction in a similar way to how we experience actual physical danger: it makes us feel unsafe and uneasy. We'll come back to how feeling like we're under threat when we aren't can make us overreact and behave, shall we say, not as we would like, in a later chapter.

So when we say, "I feel seen," are we saying, "I feel a sense of being accepted by a person/group which is reassuring to my nervous system"? Perhaps, more specifically, our age of individuality has put a slight spin on this idea of belongingness—rather than recognizing something that feels safe and familiar and sensing that we are a part of it, are we saying that we feel somebody has recognized and included us as an individual? I mean, I don't know, and I'm not sure anyone does for sure. Maybe I'm splitting hairs. But as we throw around phrases like "I feel seen" that have emotional ramifications, I do think it's good to ask ourselves what they really mean to us. Even if we can't truly answer the question, if nothing else it might contribute to the net good, right? If we want to help other people feel seen and want to nurture a sense of safety in ourselves, thinking about how that might work and why it's important could only make us more empathetic.

Relationships

With the connectedness of the modern world and our increased access to more people in it, questions seem to crop up now and again about our capacity to care. When there are so many people in our lives, so many people's experiences we can see played out in real time, how can we keep up and maintain the same level of emotional response for everyone? The ability that technology has given us to contact, discover, and stay in touch with people who are both "known" (in the sense that we have met them in person) and "unknown" to us is mind-bogglingly advanced compared to a couple of decades ago. Surely there's some limit to how many people we can care about at once before our brains short out and break entirely?

I can know how many people there are in the world and have an abstract, innate sense of caring for them, and yet it's overwhelming to try to imagine those people in all their complexity. Zero in on the idea of one person and you can imagine a whole life for them, sure, but try to fathom just how intricate the life of each individual is in a pool of *billions* and, if you're anything like me, your brain turns to soup. It feels a little like trying to picture how many stars there are in the sky. I can be told this number, be interested in it intellectually, try to imagine it, but at some point, my brain seems to reach its limit of cognition and I physically cannot imagine that many things. I'm not the only one. Our brains are optimized to deal with small quantities. We generally find it quite hard to visualize vast numbers, be that thousands or billions, quite possibly because for most of our species' history, we simply didn't have the need to.[15] We didn't encounter thousands of people or spend trillions of dollars. Going back to Dunbar's number and similar studies into our capacity to connect and maintain connections, I find it oddly validating to learn that there are real, proper limits on this sort of processing, and it's not just me who's a bit boggled by some of the big-number thinking.

When I was writing that sentence above, about people who are known and not known to us personally, I struggled to choose words to express what I wanted to say. To start with, I wrote "people we know in real life." But what do we even mean now when we say "real life"? Is that to say social media isn't "real"? That doesn't feel quite right when we look at relationships. These platforms are such an ingrained part of our lives now. We are still the same people when we're DMing someone as when we stop to speak to them in the street. Social media doesn't exist in some sort of inconsequential parallel universe.

I meant people who we feel we know at some sort of personal level and have at least a loose sort of friendship with, as opposed to, say, a celebrity whose films we have seen and whom we may have read or seen interviews with. But there's a wide spectrum between those things. We can exclusively or mostly know someone online but still feel connected to them. So how do we define the online connections we have with people—whether we interact with them or simply feel we know something of their lives? I wonder just what Dunbar's idea of a "stable relationship" entails when you look at it in the context of social media?

At the time of writing, I am following 2,141 accounts on Instagram. And, all right, we can discount a good portion of those as not actually being people (instead dedicated to extreme carpet-cleaning or eldest-daughter memes, for example), but even then, there are certainly a lot more than 150 people I follow on that platform alone. So, what about all those people you're "online friends" with? You follow each other and exchange the occasional DM, story reply, or otherwise friendly comment. It is two-sided—maybe it's gone on for a while—but you've never actually met in real life and you don't know anything about each other beyond what you choose to share on whichever platform you've connected via. Does that count? And does a relationship actually even have to be two-sided?

Parasocial relationships

The first social media platforms were built to connect us to people we already knew and allow us to stay in touch. Maybe the developers were thinking ahead to the world we live in now, where you can meet and feel connected to someone just in an online space, but I don't think that's how most people then imagined the future. If you were a teenager before social media, then it's easier to appreciate the impact it had during those early days—Facebook, the classic example and first really mainstream platform, was based around networking with people you were at university or school or worked with. You specifically added "friends." Another big game-changer if you were a bit older was Friends Reunited. This allowed you to look up people you had known in the past and reconnect. When the more common interactivity between users on platforms moved from "friending" to "following" (particularly with Twitter, which had become fairly mainstream by 2010), the dynamics certainly shifted in who we chose to interact with and how connected or removed we felt from them.

Parasocial relationships are something I hadn't heard of until relatively recently. According to the National Register of Health Service Psychologists, a parasocial relationship is a one-sided relationship in which one party extends energy, time, and interest and the other person doesn't know they exist.[16] I'm not sure I love the tone of this definition, but I think that's because I'm coming at it from my own experience and when I think in terms of, say, people who follow *me* on Instagram, "doesn't know they exist" feels a bit cold. I know you exist! But I see that, factually, it's true in the sense that when we build a picture of someone we follow, taking in information they choose to share, it doesn't require any involvement from them beyond their posts, and by and large the interaction we have with them is surface-level—likes, comments, etc. I think this can be true even in online relationships where two parties follow each other and interact in this way relatively often, to be honest. When I try to think of examples where a person and I have mutually followed each other and interacted for years, it's weird to think that those "relationships" could feel different to me than they do to the other person. If we met in real life, would they want to chat? Do I feel more warmly toward them than they do me?

I think we can agree that there's a definite line between a casual online friendship and someone you actually know. Where does occasionally commenting on each other's posts cross over to become a legitimate friend-ship? That's not a criticism or intended to undermine the value that these interactions can bring. For example, for me, following other neurodivergent people online has often made me feel reassured and supported. It's that sense of belonging or being "seen," I guess, even when these people can't literally see me . . . I get messages all the time from people to let me know that something I've shared has been helpful for them. And my life has been greatly influenced in so many positive ways by the people who follow me. So, in that way, I don't feel that it is completely one-sided, certainly not in terms of impact—but when you look into the term "parasocial relationship," followers would surely fall under that umbrella.

You'll have your own view on this, which will depend on lots of things, but particularly how much time and emotional energy you invest in social media. For some of us, nothing will compare to meeting up with people in person and social media will just be an extra tool to keep up to date with the lives of people we care about. Closer to the other end of the spectrum, if you are someone who is restricted by how much you can go and physically be in the world—say, you have a limiting disability or suffer from acute social anxiety, or you live in a small, isolated community where there are few spaces in which you can meet people to connect with—social media, and the internet more widely, is a clear lifeline. But we all live in an increasingly online world, and so to dismiss these so-called parasocial relationships as automatically less than others, or unimportant, feels reductive to me, like we're missing the bigger picture.

If someone we have followed for a while suddenly does or says something that we feel goes against their usual behavior, or we've held assumptions and find out they aren't actually fact, we can feel just as let down as if a friend had done something we find hurtful; the pattern we expected to see continue is disrupted and it can feel very jarring, making us angry. But equally, if they share something painful that is happening in their own life, we can share their pain, despite never having met them. In an essay for internet culture–focused newsletter *Embedded*, entitled "The hard part of being a follower,"[17] Kate Lindsay examines her own emotional reaction to learning of author and online personality Hank Green's cancer diagnosis:

> When I saw the video title—"So, I've got cancer"—my breath caught in my chest like I had received a text from a friend sharing their diagnosis . . . The practice of "following" someone simply hasn't been around long enough for us to grapple with the unpleasant parts of life that are expected, like the realities of getting older . . . It's weird to realize that I've invited more relationships into my life to worry about, to one day grieve, and it is frustrating that there's no real model for how to do so. There's a natural caretaker instinct that, as a follower, I have no outlet for.

I found this a touching reflection on a kind of relationship that we often hear referred to in a largely negative or even derisive tone. There's a sneery perspective that investing time and emotion into these parasocial dynamics is a waste, and that the resulting relationships are of no consequence, but, as Kate discusses, there are genuine bonds that are formed and genuine care along with them. While they do seem to hold the potential for disappointment (like all relationships, right?), there are entire communities that spring up around parasocial objects of attention and, on the whole, do bring an overwhelmingly positive social element into people's lives.

Friendship

We know that the relationships we experience in our early years—when our brains are still developing and we are soaking up information about the world and how we can expect it to treat us—have a big impact on who we become as adults. Without diving back into the whole "tell me about your childhood" therapy pool, I think there is enough general understanding of psychology now that we know it's important for children to be loved and treated well by the people around them—family and friends. Once in adulthood, the way we think about relationships often changes and the majority of our focus seems to fall on romantic love. Hear the word "relationship" and you might automatically think of a romantic partner, I'm guessing? I could launch off into a whole other chapter of wonderings about why this might be (representations in the media, the novelty of new feelings as we grow up, wanting to be wanted and seen as wanted) but, one way or another, there can be a lot of pressure to "pair off" and find a partner. The bulk of our time and energy can be absorbed by maintaining those intimate bonds, and what can sometimes get left behind, or perhaps taken for granted, is the huge influence that our platonic friendships can have on us.

We need people in our lives, but forming strong, emotional connections with really good people makes everything so much more vivid and fulfilling. Whether it's a childhood best friend, a new friend, or an online friend, finding someone who has similar interests, the same sense of humor, or a shared passion can bring a welcome sparkle into our day with the feeling that they just *get* us.

I'm intrigued by this idea of "clicking with" someone.[18] Have you ever had the experience when you meet someone for the first or second time and feel like you know each other already? Or like you sort of *recognize* something about them? And the other side of this is, of course, when you just can't seem to connect with someone. When you misunderstand each other's meaning, jokes don't land, and it feels like you're casting around for anything to say to keep the conversation going. Why *is* this?

It obviously helps if you have things in common, shared ground on which to build some initial conversations, but it can't just be about that, as you can click with people who are very different to you. A more scientific term for when you find yourself getting along with someone in a comfortable way is "interpersonal synchronization."[19,20] It means that individuals who are socializing with each other begin to unconsciously share body language, ways of communicating, and even things like speech patterns over time. This makes us feel safe and bonded. One type of interpersonal synchronization that you will probably be aware of is mirroring—when we unconsciously reflect the body language of the person we are speaking to. You know: they lean in, you lean in. They frown as they begin telling a story, so you do too. (Mirroring can also be a conscious or learned behavior; autistic or otherwise neurodivergent people often mirror the behavior or body language of people around them as a form of "masking," helping them to blend in with neurotypical peers. This can be very mentally taxing for the neuro-divergent person.)

I think we sometimes blame ourselves if we struggle to connect with someone in a social setting. For example, if a friend introduces you to someone they think you'll really get on with and you just . . . don't. But part of the reason for this could lie with our brains. You know when we say someone "wasn't on our wavelength"? This may literally be true. In a 2018 study titled "Similar neural responses predict friendship,"[21] the authors describe using fMRI to monitor the neural responses of groups of people who knew each other as they watched films. They found that those who were the closest friends also had the most similar brain activity in response to what they were seeing. Next were friends of friends, and so on, with the neural response becoming more different as the social connection became more tenuous.

In the past, psychologists and scientists have looked to environmental factors that make it more likely we will

get along with someone—like similar educational background, family set-up, job, ethnicity, etc. But this suggests
there's more to it than circumstances and outlook. Thalia
Wheatley, one of the psychologists who ran the study,
said it suggests that "We are exceptionally similar to our
friends in how we perceive and respond to the world
around us . . . which fits with our intuition that we reso-
nate with some people more than others. There seem to
be neurobiological reasons for that."[22]

I like this because you could argue that it supports the
idea that we don't have to stay in our predetermined
social groups. Yes, it's much easier to get to know someone when you work or study at the same place, but if
brain activity also plays a part in that feeling of being
simpatico with someone, it means that sharing lots of
demographic factors is not a prerequisite. Though what
the study didn't do—which I would find fascinating—is
measure the neural responses of strangers to video clips
and then use them to predict whether they will become
friends or not.

Let's borrow an illustration from Maslow and imagine a friendship pyramid, with the pool of your wider
acquaintances forming the base and your handful of
closest friends right at the top. Maybe midway down
your pyramid you have people who might not be your
absolute besties but who make you feel safe and known.
I think here I'd put people like an old friend who you're
not super close to but it's always lovely to see them. Or a
work friend who you have no other friends in common

with, but you meet up and talk about work stuff that no one outside your industry would get. A feeling of "warmth" comes up a lot in descriptions of these sorts of relationships. As you'll have noticed by now, I love it when there is a scientific theory or fact to back up some term we just casually throw around. And, joy of joys, this is yet another example.

In a 2013 study run at the University of California, psychologists Tristen Inagaki and Naomi Eisenberger asked participants to hold either an unheated ball or a heat pack.[23] They monitored brain activity and, as you would expect, the parts of the brain that register temperature lit up in those holding the heat pack. They then gave the subjects some messages from their family and friends. When these were neutral statements of fact about the person, nothing much happened, but when they were kind and loving messages, the same areas of the brain lit up as when the participant held the heat pack. So when we say, "That makes me feel warm inside," it literally does!

This has some interesting implications for forming new friendships as well. Results from other psychological studies have demonstrated that this warmth–warmth connection works the other way round, with participants who were given a feeling of physical warmth (holding a hot coffee versus an iced coffee, as in the experiment) more likely to judge a target person to have a "warmer" personality.[24] If you're in the habit of ordering iced coffees and feel like you aren't meeting a lot of friendly people lately . . . maybe try warming up your hands! This feels like a legitimate life hack to me. Even further, maybe it could also partly explain why we feel so buzzy about socializing in the summer time. We might literally like people more when it's hot. Mind-blowing.

I find reading about studies like this, which try to unpack the science behind our complex social interactions and need to exist in groups, absolutely fascinating. I enjoy the challenge of trying to apply how a finding or theory might relate to my own experience of interacting with other people. I don't imagine that science will ever be able to explain all of it, though. And you could argue that we don't really need it to. We are most of us so highly attuned to things like group dynamics and body language that science can often just present us with terms for things we instinctively understand. It might be interesting to know that studies have found that it takes on average around fifty hours with someone to move from acquaintances to friends, for example, and a solid 200 hours for them to become what you'd consider a "close" friend—but examining the time it takes doesn't speak much to how it feels.[25] Or why in certain circumstances we can spend half an hour with someone and feel an immediate bond.

So, now take the top tier of your imaginary friendship pyramid. When you think about your absolute best friends who you would trust with anything, it probably doesn't feel like you can unpack exactly why those relationships are the ones that became so important to you.

(Though I do think it's a lovely and important thing to reflect on sometimes, so we don't take them for granted.) While we are all unique entities who can only ever experience life living in our own heads, the people around us also reflect who we are, shoring up and allowing us to express our own identities, as well as supporting us when we are struggling, of course. I mentioned in Chapter Two that when I was struggling at the very lowest point with my mental health, I was lucky enough to have the right people around me at the right time. Some of those people I hadn't even known for long at all but had that "click" with—now I kind of want to put us in an fMRI scanner and see if our "wavelengths" are the same.

There's an episode of Elizabeth Day's *How to Fail* podcast that I've gone back and re-listened to several times, where she interviews author and modern philosopher Alain de Botton (I highly recommend it: Season Six, Episode Two). They talk about lots of our human failures, but one part that has particularly stuck with me is the idea that we're never going to get all our needs met by one person. Your partner might not be the best at understanding your professional dilemmas. Your best friend can't—well, might not like to join in with your hobbies. Your work friend might not be who you want to meet at the weekend. It's not fair to expect someone to be everything you need them to be all the time; even if it's our dearest friend, our wants, needs, and the demands on us are just too confounding for anyone to be 100 percent, perfectly responsive all the time. As well as tempering any unfair expectations we might have of the closest people in our lives, this realization may also offer up some freedom for those who feel that they themselves aren't able to be the Swiss Army knife of a friend that someone is asking them to be.

5

WHY DO WE GET STUCK IN
THE COMPARISON TRAP?

THERE'S A LINE IN THE poem *Desiderata* by Max Ehrmann: "If you compare yourself with others, you may become vain or bitter, for always there will be greater and lesser persons than yourself."[1] Honestly, the breadth of things you learn about when researching a book. That's great advice, isn't it? You're always going to be good at some stuff and bad at other stuff. If you feel smug every time you realize you're better at something than someone else and resentful when someone can do something you can't—well, that's not going to be a very healthy way to live. Got it, thanks. But can it really be avoided?

I certainly have a habit of comparing myself to others in lots of different areas. I know that in the past I have looked to someone who is doing really well in a similar job to mine and their success has made me feel like I am failing in some way. And there have been times when

I've been struggling with my mental health and seeing other people effortlessly manage some pretty basic life stuff that I was finding challenging made me feel like a slightly shit human. I'm not ashamed of that (in hindsight, anyway). I think it happens to all of us. And with the second example in particular, I can look back and feel compassion for who I was then and what I was going through. I wish that I could have avoided the sting of comparison at that point—it's not like I thought it was particularly helpful—but I have to acknowledge that it's the way I felt. I wonder how you feel about comparison and whether you worry about the same things I do? If I interrogate how I tend to compare myself to others, I can see that it's mostly contained to people I know, to some degree, even if that's friends of friends or people I follow online. I think I am much less likely to compare myself to complete strangers or people I don't even have a para-social relationship with. I find it easier to apply logic and think, "Well, I don't know anything about their life and what they have doesn't affect me at all.' When I know more about someone as a person, it's more likely I'll compare myself to those details.

To go back to my original question, social comparison theory says that no, we can't avoid comparing ourselves to others. This theory was first put forward by a social psychologist, Leon Festinger, in the 1950s,[2] and revolves around the idea that people innately want to compare themselves to others to help them evaluate their own abilities and opinions, to establish where they fit into a perceived "hierarchy." We crave the context of other humans to understand ourselves, essentially.

As we saw in the previous chapter, we humans are hyper-social animals and forming groups was key to our species' development and survival. Social comparison is thought by evolutionary psychologists to have been useful for lots of reasons when we lived in tribes. For example, knowing where you stood in the pecking order, whose superior abilities in one area might be beneficial for you, where you were likely to succeed or fail based on what you had just seen someone else do was all very handy input—and a primal version of reading the room, I guess.

What all this points to is that our brains seem to be hardwired for comparison. As with everything, some of us are going to be more prone to certain types than others. But as studies have suggested that up to 12 percent of all our thoughts are based on some form of comparison,[3] if someone says, "I never compare myself with others," then it could be that they don't realize they're doing it. Personally, I find it reassuring to know that comparison is something our brains are just set up to do. I can accept that comparing myself to others is inevitable—what's within my control is how I go about it and understand and process any negative emotions that it throws up. Because in asking, "Why am I like this?," we are often really asking ourselves, "Why am I not like them?" And when we fall too hard into comparison, it can have a big impact on our self-esteem.

The comparison carrot

Comparison isn't always a bad thing, of course. For example, it can help you to appreciate people in your life who have different skills to you. One of my best friends is so good at staying in touch with people. She seems to effortlessly exchange just the right amount of communication and is always on top of everyone's news in a way that I am not. I can't help but be a little bit envious—even though I know that we both love our friends; it's just not "me" to be in daily message contact with lots of people—but mostly I am glad that she thrives in this way and appreciate that it's part of what keeps our friendship ticking. I don't think she'd even see it as a skill deserving of admiration, as to her it's just normal. But I notice and admire her for it precisely because, in comparison, I know it's not something I am able to do.

In social comparison theory, comparing yourself to someone you perceive as "above" you in the area you're considering is called "upward comparison," and comparing yourself to someone you perceive as worse in that area is "downward comparison." Both can be problematic, of course, but, sticking with the positives for a moment, upward comparison can be a very useful source of motivation. For example, imagine you are used to being on a similar level to your friend in a particular subject at school, and then one day you notice that they seem to know a lot more than you do. You realize it's because they have been working harder in preparation for the upcoming exam. If this makes you see that you have been coasting and ignoring the looming tests, and it prompts you to pull your finger out and do well, that was some pretty useful comparison you just did there, wasn't it?

I had comparison coach Lucy Sheridan on my podcast, and before the interview I asked the podcast community if they had any questions they'd like me to ask her. I received a lot of emotional responses, which made me reflect on just how much anxiety can be caused by comparison—not only the conclusions we draw, but the act itself. The many online rallying calls of "You do you!," "Own it!," and "Do your thing!" are well meaning, but I sometimes wonder if they can make it worse. We have spent thousands of years of evolution comparing ourselves to others and caring what they think of us. To expect ourselves to be able to turn that off with no trouble ironically feels like extra pressure, another potential spiral to get sucked into: *Am I comparing myself to other people more than other people compare themselves to other people? What's the right amount to compare yourself to other people?!*

Lucy and I discussed what it's like to be stuck in the "comparison trap," when you feel almost pinned to the floor by what you perceive as the weight of other people's success and achievements. This is a horrible place to be in because it's hard to move forward from—you you might go searching for more and more detail to add fuel to the comparison fire burning in your brain, or feel like someone who has achieved something you wanted has "taken" it from you or made it less likely you will get it too.

Piled on top of this can be a sense of shame that you are begrudging someone else's success, that you're a terrible person for having these ugly thoughts. Because yes, that's right, along with draining your confidence, another less-than-comfortable outcome of comparison is jealousy. Although, this can almost be a taboo subject. In particular, we are not supposed to feel jealous of our friends if they do well. We're supposed to be cheering our friends on, holding them up, celebrating their milestones. And we do—but what if, in all honesty, we feel resentful or a bit sad that we are missing out? When it comes to strangers or those who we know less well, we are intelligent enough to know that what people put on social media often doesn't reflect the full picture of their lives. Yes, someone can post a picture of themselves looking bloody gorgeous on a night out to celebrate their latest promotion, but we don't know what else is going on for them. We're aware of all this, but still we find ourselves becoming tangled in the swamp of comparison once again . . .

During our discussion, Lucy talked about her journey toward focusing on comparison as an issue, having struggled massively with this tendency herself, and explained how she got out of it, as well as describing more recent points in her life when, despite being a comparison coach, she has felt the familiar pull of comparing herself negatively to others. She spoke about what she now knows can bring this on, how she can observe it starting to happen, and what she does about it. Something that really stuck with me is that if you can get yourself in a good place mentally, it's much easier to remind yourself that other people's achievements are primarily evidence that something is possible. And, if you're lucky, that may present a useful opportunity to learn more about how to make it happen.

Say, you want to be a writer. If you don't personally know anyone who is a writer, it might feel harder to figure out how you even go about doing that. However, if someone in your extended circle has some success early in their own writing career—and particularly if you can find out more about how they did it—it shows you that it's doable and may present you with some helpful information. That could be techniques for structuring, advice on how to write a proposal, or even just some words of encouragement from someone who's been in the same boat. Lucy has a useful mantra to remind yourself of this in any similar situation: "Good for you, and the same for me." Someone else achieving or getting closer to their goal rarely takes anything away from you—it simply shows you that it can be done. Think about it in the right way and you can see that it's good for you too.

I know this isn't always easy to do. We are all more prone to the negative effects of comparison when we are already feeling low—specifically when we are feeling a bit stuck. If we are unsure of our own direction of travel, it can feel like people are enjoying their happy, charmed lives and leaving us behind. Whereas if we have a plan and we know what we want, we are more likely to access the "comparison carrot" mindset and feel inspired and motivated by other people's success. Lucy suggested that, at the very least, if you feel the familiar tug of comparison, you can ask what this feeling is telling you. If you get a jolt of envy when someone posts amazing photos of their trip to Mexico City, is it a signal that you would really love to travel more? And, in that case, is that something you can focus on to enable you to do so in the future? If seeing photos on social media of someone else's fun night out makes you feel sad, is this telling you that you are lonely and need to reach out to your friends and get something in the diary? Or maybe even meet some new people?

Comparison is inevitable—but it's up to us whether we use it as a stick to beat ourselves over the head with, damaging our self-esteem, or as a way to motivate ourselves to identify what we might like in our lives. You don't have to get it right all the time, though. As we'll see later when we look at online culture, our poor brains have a lot to deal with. Try to see the humblebrags for what they are, remind yourself that people are allowed to celebrate their successes, and if someone's feed is just plain getting you down, it's fine to take a break from that.

Before we move on to some of the different (and sometimes sneaky) forms that comparing ourselves to other humans can take, I think it's worth considering *who* we choose to compare ourselves to. The first and possibly most obvious question is whether that person is presenting an authentic version of themselves and their situation. For example, some influencers have a brand to protect and will want to show a specific view of themselves. They might post pictures of their immaculate, beautiful living room, if that's what they are known for, but not their chaotic cupboards where they've stashed all the non-pristine junk they don't want in the photo (and that, friends, very much works as a metaphor for what we all sometimes do in life!).

The other thing I think it is useful to be aware of, when trying to understand how our brains are making comparisons, is that research has shown that we tend to compare ourselves to the most visible members of our groups in certain areas, and they are often the best or highest-performing in that area.[4] So, if I'm thinking that I really haven't been getting enough exercise, my brain will likely automatically go to someone I associate with exercise. I'll probably think of a friend who really loves running and gets out for a run at least three times a week, or someone I follow who's training for a marathon. I might then fall into the trap of beating myself up for being lazy because I don't do anywhere near as much exercise as her. I need to stop and consider that she is an extreme example—running is part of her identity and one of her favorite hobbies. But it's not mine. If I compare myself to the people in my wider friendship group, I see that I am more keen on walks in the countryside than some and less motivated than others—I'm actually pretty average. That makes me feel more secure and puts me in a place from where I am able to make positive decisions about how to get myself moving more often, because it's enjoyable and not because I "should." Perhaps unsurprisingly, the authors of this study concluded that if we are less focused on the above-average in our comparisons, it has a far less detrimental effect on our view of ourselves and our abilities.

The spotlight effect

In her book *Everything I Know About Love*, Dolly Alderton describes talking to a therapist about her "worst nightmare"—a bunch of people sitting around in a conference room gossiping about her. After a pause, the therapist simply asks, "Do you really think you're that important?" I love this. It so neatly encapsulates how we all kind of think we're more important than we are.

In our day-to-day lives, consciously and without being aware of it, we are constantly trying to figure out what people think of us. That's our highly social brain at work again. To do this, we compare our thought processes and experiences to other people's behavior—we can only live in our own heads, after all, so it's not like we have many other options. However, inevitably, the conclusions that we draw are pretty much always going to be skewed by something called "egocentric bias." Do you remember the examples of cognitive bias from Chapter Three? Those bugs in our thought processes that we don't know we have and which can lead us to draw somewhat wonky conclusions? Well, this is another one.

Egocentric bias describes our tendency to center ourselves and our failure to recognize that our understanding of the world or people around us is always going to be channeled through our own limited viewpoint. It might manifest as someone who's an expert in their field not understanding that other folks don't have any knowledge of it, remembering yourself as having had a bigger role in a situation than you did, or the way couples and housemates sometimes argue about who does most housework—you obviously do, because you see all the chores you do, right?! You are not witness to all your partner's contributions, and vice versa.

There are many ways in which egocentric bias can have an impact and it's definitely a good one to be aware of, as it can be countered. By seeking out different perspectives and actively exploring different viewpoints, we can get closer to the objective truth in a situation. We'll come back to this when we talk about a concept called intellectual humility in a later chapter, but let's focus here specifically on something called "the spotlight effect."[5]

If you're not sure what this is, I'm willing to bet that you'll recognize it . . . You know the feeling that everyone is looking at you, that you've said or done or even worn the wrong thing and *everyone* has noticed and now probably thinks you're an idiot? That. Say, you're walking down the street and you trip up a little over an uneven paving slab. Your face feels hot as you imagine all the people walking behind you who are now sniggering to themselves and thinking how embarrassing your stumble is. You try to somehow walk with increased assuredness, or figure out what body language can make your shoulders communicate the message "I wasn't bothered by that in the slightest." From behind.

I'll share a real one of mine in the name of solidarity. As I've already explained, my autobiographical memory is terrible, so excuse the fuzzy details, but, in my first year at uni, there was some departmental social event, a getting-to-know-each-other sort of deal. A quiz was involved and I got roped into reading out some questions, including one about *Les Miserables*, which I'd never read, or seen. Still haven't, actually. Anyway, I read out this question and wrongly hedged my bets on the pronunciation, so rather than reading out "Jean Valjean" the French way, as it should be, I said "*Jean* Valjean" . . . like a pair of denim jeans. There was a smattering of laughter around the room from some people who knew it was wrong . . . and the moment was over. On with the rest of the quiz! You might be wondering why I've bothered to tell you such an inconsequential story. But this happened well over *ten years ago* and the memory of it still makes me die a little inside. It genuinely pops into my head about once a month. Maybe that's why I've still never seen *Les Mis*, as I can't deal with my silly little embarrassment. It's a perfect example of the spotlight effect as, being logical about it, I'm quite sure nobody else there ever thought about it again—probably not even ten minutes later, let alone a decade. Let's hope getting that out in writing is therapeutic and I can finally be rid of my shame at being uncultured.

That trip down memory lane aside, it's worth noting that the spotlight effect is not an inherently negative thing—it could equally apply in a positive situation, where perhaps someone has completed a task perfectly and overestimates the amount of attention other people are paying to it, assuming that everyone is super-impressed. Although, I have to admit I find this example far less relatable.

For better or worse, most of us believe we are being noticed more than we are. This is interesting, because we may simultaneously be aware that we are not that observant. We can even reflect on our egocentric bias and know that we spend a lot of time focused on ourselves—so most likely everyone else is doing the exact same thing and giving much more thought to themselves than anyone else. And yet, this idea that we're being scrutinized and everyone is ready to judge what we say or look like is hard to shake completely.

If you suffer (or have ever suffered) from anxiety, particularly social anxiety, you'll know how powerful the spotlight effect can be—when you do really feel that there is a spotlight on you, you are hyper-visible, and everyone is looking and judging. It's not like being aware of the spotlight effect and egocentric bias is going to solve that but, personally, I find that knowing it has a name and an explanation is comforting; that means other people are experiencing it too. It serves as a reminder to try to rationalize this negative thought pattern, when I can, remembering that other people are likely so blinded by the light of their own spotlight that there's really no room left to worry about me mispronouncing a character's name. As Dolly Alderton's therapist would no doubt remind me: I'm really not that important.

Comfortingly, the science confirms that people are definitely paying less attention than we think. In a 2000 study that is quoted a lot,[6] an undergraduate student was asked to go to class wearing a Barry Manilow T-shirt— seen as an embarrassing thing to do (sorry, Barry)—and and predict how many people would notice. When his classmates were surveyed afterward, far fewer than he had been expecting had clocked his T-shirt. While this demonstrates that the year 2000 was longer ago than I would like, as I'm sure many uni students now wouldn't have a clue who Barry Manilow is (come on, "Copacabana"!), it also illustrates something that plenty of similar experiments have shown too: people aren't noticing most of what you do. In fact, on average, people have been shown to overestimate the level that others notice them by a whole 50 percent

In CBT (cognitive behavioral therapy), which can be used to treat social anxiety, one technique is to deliberately introduce "balancing thoughts."[7] For example, if you say something stupid and find yourself believing that everyone's estimation of you has gone down, you might deliberately consider how, actually, you corrected yourself afterward, and the people present have heard you say enough intelligent, sensible things in the past that they are unlikely to alter their opinion based on one time you misspoke. If that doesn't work for you, you could always try adopting "Hardly anyone notices Barry Manilow!" as a mantra. I mean, it *might* work. Let me know!

Self-conscious emotions

The reason, of course, why the spotlight effect is so powerful is because we are all, to varying degrees, afraid of being embarrassed—which is more likely and felt more acutely if more eyes are on us. Anecdotally, I can attest to this. The more the follower number on my Instagram has crept up over the years, the more I have been plagued with self-doubt about making a mistake; not because I think I'm a horrible person and people are going to find out, but because any spelling error, unforeseen ignorance, or photo where my dress is tucked into my pants in a badly placed mirror is more likely to be noticed by someone.

Embarrassment belongs to a group of emotions that psychologists call the "self-conscious emotions." Also into this box go shame, guilt, jealousy, empathy, and pride.[8] Very small children don't have these particular feelings; they generally start developing between fifteen and twenty-four months. First of all, you have to have a concept of self—as in, "This is me and all these other things in the world are not me"—and then you have to have some sense of a standard to compare yourself against, whether that's what other people have (a toy you want), or expect of you (to be able to climb stairs), or your behavior (to eat your broccoli). In other words, when you have figured out some of the rules of the society or group you're operating within, and what other people do or don't do, you can start to figure out how you measure up.

When reading through the list of self-conscious emotions, I have an almost physical reaction to the words. "Shame." *Shudder.* The actual feelings are hard to define and feel like they have layers to them, but are generally unpleasant to experience. Think about what it's like to experience a twinge of jealousy, for example. Just typing "twinge" then felt like a bit of a clichéd description, but it's perhaps overused because it feels so accurate. Though it's hard to put "jealousy" into words, that "twinge" would strike a chord with most people, I think. And yet, apart from empathy, and maybe pride, they seem to me to be quite lonely emotions. As humans, we don't want to feel like we are being negatively evaluated by others in our social group. If we do, or we feel we would be if they knew something about us that we have decided is shameful, it makes us feel cut off from people, even though we know rationally that we all experience these emotions at times.

These things are, of course, hard for scientists and researchers to study. Take embarrassment, for example. What embarrasses one person wouldn't necessarily bother someone else. It varies from culture to culture as well as individual to individual. For example, for some people, if they were in a group conversation and someone referred to them as "very talented," that would be a lovely compliment. Other people would feel uncomfortable and embarrassed, even though we'd all agree that to be thought of as talented is a positive thing. One area of the brain that is thought to be heavily involved in the self-conscious emotions is the frontal insula. Using fMRI scanners, neuroscientists have seen that it "lights up" in subjects' brains when they see someone cheat, register disgust on someone else's face, and empathize with others, among other things, such as listening to music or hearing a joke.[9] According to neuroscientist Arthur D. Craig,[10] this part of the brain receives sensations (like all mammals do) and changes them into emotions (which is thought to be unique to humans and, to a limited extent, great apes). So we register that someone is laughing at us and feel embarrassed. Or we notice that someone is wearing the dress we wanted but couldn't afford and feel envious.

I think this feeling is a cornerstone of the overall "Why am I like this?" mood. Whether we're wishing that we were more confident and able to shake off the worry about outside opinions, or we're annoyed at ourselves for feeling jealous over some petty little thing, these are emotions we usually don't want. From a social point of view, there are lots of reasons why things like guilt and shame might be useful things for humans as a species. I'm sure you could guess at many of them—for example, feeling guilt when we hurt someone lets us know that we have done something wrong. When the ties that bind communities have been so vital for our survival, it makes sense that we have developed neural and social mechanisms to reinforce them and dissuade us from doing things that threaten them. Even blushing—which many people who are prone to it really don't enjoy—seems to have a social use, as studies have shown that people who blush easily when embarrassed are seen as more trustworthy,[11] and are thought of more highly when they have made some sort of social faux pas. When someone does something "wrong," we appreciate it if they know it.

If we know more about which brain regions are active when we experience self-conscious emotions, it may improve how we help people who live with various differences, from autism to social anxiety, who might experience social interactions differently. In the meantime, it might be helpful for all of us to remind ourselves that *everyone* experiences shame, guilt, and embarrassment sometimes, even though the spotlight effect is making us feel like we are the worst person/biggest imbecile on the planet and *everyone* knows about it. These painful emotions are the price of entry to being human, in a way—without them you don't have community, trust, loyalty, and many of the other profound and fulfilling things that are the high points of being a person. So, thank you, frontal insula. I don't like feeling some of the things you make me feel, but I know you have my back really.

Imposter syndrome

One phenomenon in which I think the spotlight effect, egocentric bias and the urge to negatively compare and undervalue ourselves come together is imposter syndrome. This feels like a much more frequently admitted issue in recent years, with many famous, high-achieving and hugely respected women talking publicly about how they experience sometimes crippling self-doubt, no matter how much success they enjoy—and, in fact, that this increases the *more* success they have. I find it reassuring on the one hand that successful people are willing to talk about this, but also somewhat alarming that it's so universal and seems to affect people more when they have proved themselves again and again.

The term originally came from a paper written in 1978 by psychologists Pauline Clance and Suzanne Imes, though they termed it "impostor phenomenon."[12] They described it like so: "Despite outstanding academic and professional accomplishments, women who experience the impostor phenomenon persist in believing that they are really not bright and have fooled anyone who thinks otherwise. Numerous achievements, which one might expect to provide ample objective evidence of superior intellectual functioning, do not appear to affect the impostor belief."

As we've seen, when a term gains traction and is used a lot, it's usually because it encapsulates something that resonates with a lot of people, describing a common experience or feeling that we didn't have quite the right phrase for before. I think many of us have felt like we are not qualified or knowledgeable enough to be doing the thing we are doing. It's usually associated with work and careers but pops up in other situations too—for example, if you are accepted to a course of study but then feel like you're not clever enough to be there. You may feel like you are somehow a fraud and the spotlight is about to swing round on you and draw everyone's attention to the fact that you are way out of your depth. It's something often associated with women, though it can be experienced by other genders too, and, for reasons we will get on to, it can be acute for people from ethnic minorities. Even Michelle Obama, on tour to promote her best-selling book, *Becoming*, has spoken publicly about *still* feeling imposter syndrome.[13] If she is personally familiar with it, then it's hard to argue that it's not a pervasive and far-reaching issue.

In a slightly different context, imposter syndrome is something I've even found has come into play during my experience of being diagnosed with ADHD. Not so much in terms of questioning my abilities, but questioning whether I'd had an extra hurdle to struggle with or (as I'd believed for so long) was on a level playing field with everyone else and just not as good as them. There were steps involved: I filled out questionnaires, my mum submitted paperwork about how I acted when I was a child, I had a lengthy discussion-based assessment with a psychiatrist, et cetera. None of the answers I gave were untrue. But I couldn't help but think that somehow I'd just accidentally been terrible enough at life to be diagnosed this way; I was so lazy and so lacking that I was experiencing the same level of dysfunction as someone with a neurodivergent brain . . . but it was all my fault. (That's not me calling people with ADHD lazy or lacking, just to make that clear. It's all about me being mean to myself.) I actually said this to the psychiatrist in a subsequent appointment, a few months after I first got the diagnosis—that I was still kind of worried that I'd unwittingly tricked him into diagnosing me. He asked me whether, even if I couldn't trust myself after a lifetime of masking, I could at least trust that he was qualified. Touché.

I think most people would be happy to acknowledge imposter syndrome/phenomenon as a feeling some of us struggle with, but not everyone loves the terminology and many have questioned the way in which it is discussed. It's worth saying at this point that it's more of a self-identified, pop psychology term, rather than something that can be clinically diagnosed by a professional according to a set of established criteria, like most psychological conditions. In 2019, one paper reviewed sixty-two previous studies of imposter syndrome to try to get some answers, and found that the prevalence reported by individual studies varied hugely, from 9 to 82 percent. This is perhaps to be expected, given that the criteria defining what imposter syndrome actually is (and therefore the questions you ask people to figure out if they experience it) are kind of wishy-washy.[14]

This paper also noted that outside the academic world, we all refer to it as "imposter syndrome," whereas psychology professionals and academics still tend to call it "imposter phenomenon." This might seem like massively splitting hairs, but to some people it is important. Medically speaking, the definition of a syndrome is "a combination of medical problems that shows the existence of a particular disease or mental condition."[15] But is it really a disease or a mental condition? Or is this a subtle way of implying that there is something "wrong" with the people who experience it rather than, say, the environments in which they are trying to operate?[16] In a survey of 2,500 UK workers, it was noted that women and those in the millennial age bracket were particularly affected by feeling like a fraud, while trans respondents were by far the most highly impacted, with 64 percent regularly feeling like a failure at work.[17]

According to the *Harvard Business Review*, even though men and women are similar in the way that they browse and look for jobs, women are 16 percent less likely to apply for a job they've viewed, and apply for 20 percent fewer jobs overall. The reason behind this is down to an oft-cited stat you might have come across before: that women will hold back on applying unless they meet 100 percent of the criteria, whereas men will apply if they meet around 60 percent.[18]

Although we know that all genders do report experiencing imposter syndrome, the incidence of self-doubt reported among high-achieving women, people of color, and those of marginalized genders suggests to some that it is society that has the problem. While white men have had most of the power in the West since time immemorial, which means they see people like themselves at the top all the time, others may have internalized a belief that they are not supposed to have a seat at the table. You might get there, look around, realize that no one looks like you and—no matter your achievements to date—the prejudices you grew up hearing make you doubt your ability. You also might feel like you are in the spotlight because not that many people at your level look like you and so, in a sense, you are more visible. There's an additional (unfair) pressure to somehow represent your whole demographic in your job performance. In an article for *Forbes*,[19] creator of the Race Equ(al)ity Index Mandy Bynum Mc Laughlin explained:

> For Black women, there is a felt responsibility to be the voice for everyone, because they are a minority representation, which, when added to the emotions felt from simply being in a majority male and/or white room and holding our own, is a lot to take on . . . The pressure internally and externally to be high performing while navigating microaggressions, the perceptions of Black women's ability to lead constantly being in question, along with the inability to emote anything—let alone anger or frustration—without being labeled aggressive or threatening, are huge

factors in what any Black woman might be facing in a leadership role.

Some people feel that, in such cases, to medicalize imposter "syndrome" as something an individual "has" is to undermine them and insidiously imply that they are not suited to success.

If you are someone who has felt that anxiety, worried that your experience suddenly counts for nothing and you are about to be exposed as a fraud, then you might find this take on it helpful to consider—you don't have a "syndrome" at all; anyone would feel that way. On the other hand, if you've been struggling with feelings of inadequacy that have been really affecting your life, then having a name for it might be a comfort to you—so you'll happily keep your self-diagnosis of imposter syndrome, thanks very much.

However you feel about the term itself, what we do know for sure is that imposter syndrome/phenomenon can cause burnout, stress, and depression;[20, 21] these psychological conditions are recognized clinically and can have very serious consequences in people's lives. Either way, it's an issue that needs addressing.

If you find yourself suffering from self-doubt in any context, work or otherwise, I think the first thing to remember is that doubting yourself is not the same as "being shit." You're a person worthy of care and all the good things in life anyway, even if you're not at the top of your field or the most talented person in the room! We all have moments when we panic that we are going to fail spectacularly, or that those around us are much better qualified or more knowledgeable. Imagine if you never questioned your abilities at all—surely not normal. Plus, if you never feel challenged, then you are probably never stretching yourself. It's natural to feel nervous ahead of a new challenge, and self-doubt may prompt you to develop your knowledge and skills further so you can feel more confident.

But if you are feeling a crippling anxiety that you don't deserve to be where you are, and no amount of rationally considering all the impressive things you have success-fully tackled in the past helps, then know that many, many very clever, competent people have been there and you don't have to suffer in silence. In the UK survey I referenced earlier, 94 percent of the people who said they've suffered from imposter syndrome had never dis-cussed it at work.[22] Studies have shown that people suffering from imposter syndrome can feel like they are the only person struggling and the fault is solely theirs,[23] which we know not to be the case. Imposter syndrome or not, through no fault or anything other than "the nature of being human," our brain's wiring will from time to time lead us to compare our panicked insides to people's calm exteriors and jump to the conclusion that everyone else has got this, and we, exclusively, have not.

Main-character energy

As I've been writing this chapter I have found myself reflecting a bit that ... it's quite hard being a person. Both comparison itself and egocentric bias are sort of inevitabilities—as I've said before, we only have the ability to process our experience of the world through our own eyes, as hard as we try, and yet we crave a sense of understanding who we are in relation to other people around us. We're caught between advice to "stay in our own lane" and the fact that we aren't running the race with blinkers on. Many of us have this low (or loud) hum in our heads of "Am I doing this right?" and "Does everyone feel like this, or is it just me?" So we look to other people for some indication, but, in doing so, risk falling into a downward spiral of comparison, focusing on someone else at the expense of ourselves and what we want.

Aside from comparing ourselves to those around us, we also have to contend with people's expectations of us—how we measure up against cultural or social "norms," which for some people can be a cause of unease or insecurity. From body-image standards to relation-ship statuses, hitting certain "milestones" to how focused we are supposed to be on work, what family might expect from us, what our friends are doing, and what wider society seems to find acceptable can be the source of a lot of pressure. Other people's expectations can be par-ticularly confusing when there are multiple camps all placing ideas on you: one minute you're being told exactly what to eat, how to move, or what to wear in order to fit a certain aesthetic, and fifteen seconds later you're told that the only way to be "cool" is to ignore all that and be completely individual, not like anyone else at all. (One difference I have noticed since I was a teenager is the shift from "I'm not like the other girls" energy to "Hell yes, I'm like other girls; girls are fantastic." Huge improvement. Bravo, Gen Z.) In addition to this, some of us will compare ourselves to those around us, particularly growing up, and come to the realization that we are different in some way and will need to go elsewhere to find our people, which can be a difficult experience. If you often find yourself wondering, "Why am I like this?" because you feel so different from everyone around you, that may not always be the case. Your time will come!

Thanks to the way our brains have evolved, and our social structures alongside them, comparison takes many different forms. I find it really helpful as I try to understand my thought processes to be aware of things like the spotlight effect and egocentric bias. Of course, we are all the main characters in our lives; the inner monologue we hear in day-to-day life, everything we go through, is filtered through our own lens of experience. So it's important to remember that it isn't selfish or self-centered to examine things first from your own perspective, but it's something that we can be conscious of as we navigate our relationships with other people, reactions to events happening around us, and even how we feel about other people's accomplishments. Hopefully, through being kind to ourselves and curious about what our brains are up to, we can extend that to others too.

The way our species has evolved has landed us, as humans, in this brilliant but complicated space where we need each other in so many ways. Where we can work together to achieve amazing things but also misunderstand and work against each other. The state of the planet right now means we have a lot of problems that we and future generations are going to have to address. And for that we are going to need to draw on our incredible ability to connect and cooperate. The rise of the internet has had such an impact on us already in just the twenty to thirty years since it became a fixture of our daily lives. So, let's move on to look at what that means for our brains, how we view the world, and our ability (or not) to connect with one another.

6

IS SOCIAL MEDIA CHANGING
OUR BRAINS?

WHEN I WAS LITTLE (at the end of the previous century *elderly laugh*), "following" someone most likely meant you were a spy, a stalker, or behind them in a conga line. The technology that the mainstream media was most panicked about was video games, specifically the ones that involved shooting and fighting. As they became more realistic (although we're talking in relative terms here—they seem pretty crude by today's standards), there were concerns that they were encouraging and normalizing violence, which was having a detrimental effect on children and young people. There were many think pieces written and concerned groups of parents asking for more regulation. If you go back to the 1960s, it was TV that was being blamed by older generations for "corrupting the youth." This probably all seems pretty familiar—though of course now it's social media that is attracting concerned headlines for its power and influence over young people.

It seems that every generation grapples with new technology and the effects it's having on young people and society at large—whether those effects are real or grossly exaggerated to fit the prevailing narrative. This does make sense on a primal level: as a species, new things can make us feel intimidated or like we are losing control. Our hyper-connected world seems like it's moving at a faster pace than ever before, and we know that our brains like patterns and routine; when change occurs, the amygdala interprets it as a threat and reacts accordingly. Change? No, thank you—it's fight-or-flight time. It feels right to question how we use new technologies and how much they are benefitting us. But while it's easy to look back with the benefit of hindsight on how things like TV or cinema or even the internet have changed us, it's much more difficult when we're still in the thick of these new developments.

Neuroscientists and psychologists are doing research into how social media might be affecting our internal wiring and how we think and feel, and sociologists are examining what effect it is having on our communities and societies. But in the meantime, it's down to us to figure out how we want to use social media on a day-to-day basis, and to decide what we are OK and not OK with. When is social media a force for good, and is there anything we can do to address its darker side? Is social media making us more open-minded or more insular?

How worried should we be about things like screen time and mindless scrolling? And is social media changing our brains?

No one has definitively answered those questions yet, and I'm not going to tell you what's right and wrong either, but there is plenty of research already out there that could offer an interesting perspective. Even if we don't know precisely what the science-backed "best practice" for social media use will turn out to be, it's safe to say we'd be unlikely to follow the advice anyway, right? I've heard a thousand times that it's better to stay away from screens before bed, and it's just not going to happen. We can set usage limits for certain apps, but we can also ignore those reminders—and, more to the point, we're the ones guessing what the right limits are, anyway. What works for one person, or the averaged-out "ideal," often doesn't suit us—because we're all different. I think, at this point, the best thing we can do is think critically and try to remain self-aware. With the information we do have available, can we figure out a way to make sure social media is contributing positively to our lives?

Being your authentic self

As I've mentioned before, I'm not someone who shares every detail of my life with people, including my close friends, even though I'm very happy to hear about everyone else's news and what's been going on in their day. I'm not deliberately holding back or being secretive; it's just not something that comes naturally to me. The same goes for my online life. It's not that I don't want to talk about anything personal. I have found it so reassuring and helpful to be open about my own issues around mental health, for example, and I am so grateful for the conversations I've had with others in this area that have come about because I've shared something or they have. But what we decide to put out into the world—big, important things as well as the details of day-to-day life—is a personal decision for everyone to make. Though, how we go about presenting ourselves as people in the online space is an interesting and nuanced question.

Something that makes me happy is when I meet someone in real life who follows me or with whom I have previously only interacted via social media, and they say something like, "You're just how I imagined!" I think I like this because while I am far from an oversharer, I do want to make sure that what I put online is real, that it is me, and that I am being (buzzword incoming) authentic. And when I get that kind of feedback out there in the world, it feels like confirmation that I am managing to get it right.

Going back to the difference between on- and offline relationships that we looked at in Chapter Four, I suppose the big, obvious distinction is that when you have a parasocial relationship with someone you know only through social media, you are interacting with a curated version of them. However open and real they are being in a video or post, they have chosen to share that. You haven't just run into them unexpectedly at your big Sainsbury's. You don't know if they're rude to waiters, if they get grouchy when they're tired or how they interact with their friends—which are things that you might notice if you knew them outside of social media, and which could give you a more three-dimensional and spontaneous view of who they are as a person. I wonder if our awareness of this discrepancy is connected to our increased focus on (and demand for) authenticity online.

In the early days of social media, before reels and stories, when you could only post pictures (I know, I'm basically imagining it in black and white as I type), it felt like people asked less of each other. You could post what you wanted and it felt . . . lighter, less significant. "Look at this handful of M&M's." "This stain on my tea towel looks like John Lennon." Et cetera. My first Instagram post was a very blurry photo of a screen seen through a window; even I wouldn't have known what it was without the caption. But as social media grew to be a medium which we could use to do more, to *connect* more, we started to want to know that what we were seeing online was a genuine representation of the people we were following and developing these parasocial relationships with.

This was, of course, no bad thing. A lot of good came from it—particularly in the sense that spaces were opened up for important conversations to be had and communities to be formed. At the same time, "authenticity" was becoming a catchphrase in the worlds of business and marketing. Which wasn't a bad thing either, per se, but we also know what can happen when businesses see an opportunity to jump on something that was, ironically, authentic and inclusive before they got there and use it to promote themselves. As a quick example, I'm thinking of brands adding rainbow flags to products around Pride month, despite having done nothing for the LGBTQ+ community.

I don't think being authentic means sharing everything. I actually think it is more authentic in a way to have boundaries around what you share—although these will, of course, vary from person to person and even at different points in our lives. We all have boundaries for what we're willing to talk about with different people—you'd probably tell your best friend things you certainly wouldn't tell a coworker—and yet keeping things to yourself when you're in the habit of posting online is sometimes discussed as if it makes a person disingenuous or vain. It's definitely a subject that comes up a lot on my podcast, as for many of the people I speak to, social media is a big part of their job or their campaigning, and the podcast community seems to have a lot of questions about this too.

One of the trickiest parts, I think, is that vulnerability on social media is complex in the way that it impacts the person speaking out. On the one hand, you can often be rewarded for sharing the most intimate parts of yourself—we're all a bit nosy and like getting glimpses of other people's dirty laundry. People engage well with that content, the algorithm is fed and the poster gets that rush of dopamine, the reward for laying their soul bare for all to see, and so is encouraged to keep doing it. Do they actually want to, deep down? I don't know. The other side of this is that you're never going to please everyone you encounter online and there will always be someone who reacts harshly to something sensitive you have chosen to share. When we're dealing with public profiles, how do you square wanting to be real with your own community with the fact that you're opening yourself up to all manner of commentary from the darker sides of the comment section?

We all find it difficult to imagine what goes through someone else's head when they don't act the way that we would. (Stay tuned for more on that later.) I personally would find it really uncomfortable or even inappropriate to discuss some of the topics that I've seen people share online—from the finer details of an argument with their partner to moments of an emotional crisis experienced by their young child—but I also know that doesn't make me right and them wrong. I'm sure there will have been loads of people who appreciated them disclosing that information because they're going through the same thing, and I genuinely think that's wonderful, even if I wouldn't do it myself. I have more boundaries around my relationships, but then I'm happy to talk about my mental health, which I'm sure to some people actually feels more personal and exposing than anything else. All this is to say, our relationship with social media and how we present ourselves isn't one size fits all, either on- or offline.

Authenticity is a good thing. But it doesn't mean we owe everyone everything.

Humans versus "the algorithm"

I sometimes struggle with the algorithm-heavy nature of social media, which wants you to find your niche and stick within it. It seems to encourage a tendency to package people up into neat little boxes for our consumption, which doesn't often marry with, well, being a person. Because people are more than a handful of hobbies, interests or "content pillars"—and certainly more than their mental health or illness.

We've already looked at the usefulness (or otherwise) of labels. When it comes to social media, these come in the form of hashtags and keywords, which the algorithm uses to direct our attention and push us further into "more of the same." This affects people differently depending on how they use social media but, I think, a lot boils down to the same issue. People who create content prolifically or for a living are perhaps more likely to be strategic in the way they present themselves and, at the end of the day, might depend on their engagement levels to maintain a livelihood. On the other end of the content scale are people who use social media apps but are more focused on absorbing content—maybe they don't post at all and only log in to see what other people are doing. Algorithms affect their experience in a broader sense, perhaps not encouraging them to pigeonhole themselves,

but presenting them with these one-dimensional representations of real people: the woman who bathes kittens,
the person who makes rugs, the guy who takes ice baths.

Aside from what we're doing, the way we look has also
become increasingly homogenized, in a phenomenon
widely known as "Instagram face." Barreling into popular discourse in 2019,[1] the term refers to the trendification
of facial aesthetics; at the time it was largely lip fillers and
skin smoothing. This is all tangled up with the algorithm, with the theory being that having one particular
"look" is rewarded with higher engagement, which
enhances its algorithmic standing in the app so it is seen
by more people, judged as aspirational, and replicated.
Repeat. Since then, we've moved through all sorts of different trends (and platforms, actually—"TikTok face,"
anyone?) to the land of filters that claim to determine
whether you're cat, bunny, fox, or deer "pretty,"[2] each
spawning its own new branch of algorithmic confor-
mity. Can that be a good thing?

It's funny how we've started speaking about "the algorithm" as a singular, mysterious entity, as I have been.
Like, "Look what the algorithm served me up today." "My
algorithm is all hedgehogs right now." Each platform
uses its own software, of course, so there are actually
many algorithms determining in a large part what we
see and what the internet can do for us. If you weren't
aware and are wondering, the pre-internet meaning of
the word "algorithm" is a procedure to solve a mathemati-
cal problem, often involving repeating the same processes

over again. In computing, it similarly describes a sequence of tasks that has to be completed to solve a problem or achieve a goal—like "find cat videos."

I think we feel as though algorithms are mysterious entities because, well, they are. Search engines and social media platforms have built algorithms that they are *very* reticent about sharing the details of. Researchers looking into how our online world is affecting our brains would love to know more, but then so would rival companies, no doubt. So they remain shrouded in secrecy. There are many issues thrown up by how we are presented with information and posts online. Not least that the technology has often been shown to replicate biases and prejudice present in society. And just because you have looked at something, you don't necessarily want more of the same—particularly when that is going to be bad for you. For example, the many cases of young people who have found themselves looking at more and more content related to eating disorders and self-harm.

Social psychologists researching this area have said that social media disrupts our natural way of learning from others, which is one of the reasons it is both powerful and we can struggle to cope with its influence. A review paper published in 2023 explains that, historically, we have been wired to learn from "prestigious" individuals in our groups.[3] This term used by sociologists just means people we look up to, whose skills or knowledge, for example, command the respect of the rest of the group. We compare upward, instinctively decide that someone is a good person to imitate or be allied with, and follow their lead. This is called a "social learning bias," but it's often been a good thing as it encouraged cooperation and building communities. The problem, some social scientists think, comes when people or things appear on our feeds with lots of likes or retweets and our brains assume they are more "prestigious" than they are, so we pay more attention than we might otherwise. Someone shouting conspiracy theories to no one, standing on a box in your local town center, is one thing; someone stating nonsense as fact when they already have millions of followers is another.

According to social psychologist William Brady, a researcher working in this area, "It's not that the algorithm is designed to disrupt cooperation. It's just that its goals are different."[4] Our brains want us to find people to learn from (it's probably worth mentioning here that we get a dopamine hit from that too) but the social media platforms want us to stay on them for as long as possible and will draw our eye to things that already have received lots of attention. It's up to us to decide whether that thing has anything to teach us, but thanks to the way we are wired—and the way people who develop the codes know we are wired—this is not always easy in practice.

The other way that the algorithms work with our brain systems—with results that are not conducive to being a happy, well-balanced human—is in the way they send us into opinion culs-de-sac or echo chambers. Of course, we have to take some responsibility for this ourselves, and I'm going to be talking more about echo chambers in the next chapter, but if we are constantly being fed with stuff that our previous activity makes it seem we would favor, it can be so hard to get a sense that there are other opinions or ways of looking at an issue out there. It's not like we have the option of going to stand in an Ancient Greek agora these days, hearing all sorts of people debating their opinions and sharing information.

As a fellow user of social media, I think the simplest means at our disposal to maintain our humanness (despite the rather different goals of some very clever computer code) is to try to look at as much different content as possible and avoid mindlessly scrolling through everything we are served up. If you find something interesting that you feel you wouldn't usually see, then like it. If you're seeing a lot of videos on the same unwelcome topic, there are often options marked "see less of this," "hide," or "not interested." Make the algorithms work for you as much as you can. If you actively diversify who you follow and the content you seek out, then the algorithms will follow your path, rather than the other way round. Know that we have this social bias and try to check yourself before you assume something is correct just because it's been widely shared.

Are we spending too much time online?

This is a puzzling question to start to unpack as, like many things, it's all relative. (Unintentional *Friends* reference.)

One person might spend a number of hours on social media, watching YouTube videos and reading the news, and suffer no ill effects. Someone else might spend comparatively less time online, but they are doom-scrolling to the point where it makes them feel anxious and they can't sleep. If you're spending hours on social media apps but mainly using them to DM your friends, is that the same as watching videos from strangers? Would sending those same messages via WhatsApp or iMessage be better somehow?

In a 2022 survey of American teenagers by the Pew Research Center, around half said they would find it hard to give up social media and 36 percent said they thought they spent too much time on it.[5] According to the results of a survey of 550 children and young people around the world, conducted by Amnesty International and published in 2023, 74 percent check social media more than they would like. Half had had bad experiences, including racism, bullying, and unwanted sexual advances, and many were concerned about privacy and the "addictive" nature of personalized content and notifications. It's worth noting, though, that according to the same report, many praised "the diversity of ideas, users' creativity, and opportunities for activism" that social media provided them.[6]

This makes me think that there are a few different elements to consider here, particularly when we are thinking about social media. Firstly, there is the question of how much we check our phones and whether it feels like this is within our control or not. Do we feel compelled to be on social media all the time and, if so, for what reasons? FOMO? Because our friendships mainly take place online? Or because we can't seem to stop ourselves picking up our phones and tapping that icon ... If you want to check in on yourself about how automatic your use of social media has become, a simple but effective method I'd recommend is to shift around the layout of your apps. When you absentmindedly open your calculator app twenty times in one afternoon, without even being consciously aware that you were about to open Instagram ... it's sobering.

Then there's the question of what happens to us when we are using social media. This is a different question to "Do we spend too long online?" but the two are often lumped together as one thing, which is to miss some important elements of the conversation. In the Amnesty study I mentioned previously, the young people surveyed said they were worried about the addictive nature of social media, but they also talked about negative or frightening things that they had experienced online. When people make statements like "social media is bad for our mental health," the implication is that just using the platforms is inherently damaging; it doesn't consider the idea that things like trolling, online bullying, and the spreading of misinformation could be addressed by the social media companies themselves. It almost seems to be saying that anything that is negative about social media right now is part and parcel of it and couldn't be changed, which I don't think is right.

Conceivably, there's a version of the future where we can "fix" social media; take the things we know are good for us, the community and access to information, and get rid of the parts that haven't worked for us. Crucially, that means we have to know what those harmful bits are . . . and it seems this information may not always be willingly shared. Something of a watershed moment for the way we look at social media came with the testimony of Facebook whistleblower Frances Haugen in 2021. Product manager Haugen left Facebook (this was before it had rebranded as Meta) and took tens of thousands of its internal documents with her,[7] including proof that the company knew its products were damaging teenagers' mental health but did not act.[8] Having some concrete evidence that platforms were complicit in harming young people fueled a lot of debate around the way that we all use them, which continues today. (The aforementioned branding change also occurred hot on the heels of these revelations, as Facebook's name became more and more synonymous with insidious fake news, political warfare, and, now, poor mental health—with critics arguing that the timing was no coincidence.[9]) The data about young women was particularly worrying, with the *Wall Street Journal* reporting that the internal evidence showed how 32 percent of teen girls said that when they felt bad about their bodies, Instagram made them feel worse.[10]

A lot of it comes down to what was discussed in the previous chapter: comparison. Social media is almost the perfect breeding ground for it. Emma Thomas, former chief executive of charity Young Minds, says that social media *can* be beneficial, but also highlights the feelings of pressure that comparison can cause: "Being surrounded by constant images of the 'perfect' life and seemingly perfect bodies can also have a big impact on how you feel about your own life and appearance, and it can be really hard not to compare yourself to others."[11] Exactly. And this effect surely can't be exclusive to young people. But if they're making us feel bad, why do we keep using these platforms?

Why is social media so addictive?

A few years ago I joined in with "Digital Detox Day." I did pretty well all day—although I was aware that my hand kept automatically reaching for my phone—until midafternoon, when I absentmindedly clicked on the Instagram icon and proceeded to like a friend's post. I immediately unliked it and closed the app, almost like I was silently tiptoeing back out of a room I'd suddenly realized I wasn't supposed to be in, before anyone noticed.

I told this story to Zoe Sugg when she came on my podcast to talk about life online, as she was one of the people involved in promoting the day to encourage people to step away from their phones. Zoe had had a similar experience and we talked about how alarming it was that something we'd thought was going to be fairly easy (it was only one day without social media!) was actually much harder than we'd expected. It wasn't that I was craving an Instagram hit—or not consciously, anyway—it was more that my brain is so used to checking social media that it overrode my conscious decision not to look at it.

So what is going on here, with the subconscious app taps? We recognize that social media is not always good for us—we can be aware of this even as we continue scrolling through content that isn't making us feel good—and yet we still go back to it again and again, so often finding ourselves checking it without actively having decided to. What is happening in our brains that makes us do this?

The first suspect we need to haul in for questioning is dopamine. Offering far more than just the joy you might get from an outlandishly bright jumper, dopamine is alluring and very persuasive—underestimate its power over you at your peril. Dopamine has its finger in a lot of pies, brain-wise, but one of its key domains is the reward centers of our brains. This hedonistic hormone/neurotransmitter zips around giving us that pleasurable little buzz that encourages us to seek out more of what makes us feel good.[12]

Evolutionarily speaking, reward systems were very important. They helped us to survive—and still do, to an extent—by giving us a little gold star when we did things that helped us and encouraged the success of the species, like eating, for example, or sex, or exercise. This made us feel good and taught us that something was a good idea and we should go looking for more of the same. It is known as "seeking" behavior and is a strong motivating factor for how we act, whether we like it or not.[13] Since dopamine is a neurotransmitter and incapable of judgment, it doesn't differentiate between what is actually good for us in the long run and what makes us feel good right now. So, while originally, for our ancestors, rewarding consumption of a high-calorie snack with a hit of dopamine was useful because food was hard to come by, in a world of fast food and Mars bars in every corner shop, that happy buzz from high-sugar, high-fat foods does not serve our needs in the same way. (Enjoyable though it is.) This is also true of lots of things that were scarcer in our distant past but not so much in the modern world that is more set up for our convenience.

As we know, we are hardwired both for comparison and for approval from our group. Again, this was essential when our tribe was key to our survival, but is somewhat riddled with potential problems in our hyper-connected digital world. When we get a like, a follow, or a retweet, the reward centers in our brain light up. *Approval!* Not because we are shallow or desperate—but because dopamine is bowling around our system and, like a true hedonist, it just wants more and more. And it's not necessarily even the reward itself that keeps the dopamine loop going, it's *anticipating* it—meaning it's very difficult to be satisfied.

Have you ever heard the terms "Pavlovian response" or "Pavlov's dog"? These refer to the work of Ivan Pavlov,[14] a Russian scientist who, in the late nineteenth and early twentieth centuries, experimented on dogs by ringing a bell every time he fed them. Eventually, the dogs so associated the ringing of the bell with food that they began to salivate when they heard it, even when there was no food present. Now, a particular noise triggering an anticipatory response ... why does that sound familiar? We spend so much time interacting with our phones and are so primed for those notifications to ping that most of us have experienced "phantom phone sensations"—you know, when you think you felt your phone buzzing in your pocket but you just imagined it. One study found that 83.5 percent of people reported experiencing this,[15] which makes me wonder if 16.5 percent haven't put their phones down long enough to miss them.

Facebook, Instagram, TikTok, all your social media platforms—they know all about dopamine, reward centers, and conditioned responses. They know because their businesses depend on it. Their revenue comes from data and advertising, not from consumers selecting and paying for their products.[16] Apps are designed to hook us in and encourage us to spend as much time on them as possible, because the more time we spend using them, the more money they're able to make from their user base. Being pragmatic about it, I don't think that's *totally* evil. We're using those apps—and, overall, finding them entertaining—for free. This is the world we live in and, personally, I'm under no illusion that TikTok was created out of the kindness of someone's heart to give us the warm-and-fuzzies of connection.

The apps' owners need us, the consumers, to use their platforms as often and for as long as possible; it's in their interest—or actually, vital for their survival and growth—to make us addicted. It's not just social media, either. You know the "next episode" button on Netflix and how it slowly fills across before an auto-play? Dripping with dopamine and partly why that next episode can feel so irresistible (even when you should be hitting the hay). Tristan Harris, a former product manager for Google, compares a smartphone to putting money in a slot machine. That urge to pick up your phone to check for messages, likes, mentions—to get a reward, essentially—is like feeding coins into a slot machine and pulling a lever.[17] The addictive responses can also be very similar . . .

I think most of us are aware that social media companies are constantly competing for as much of our attention as they can get. I don't think anyone is reading this thinking, "But, Gemma, what is this conspiracy theory you're spouting?!" But it is important to consciously consider this sometimes, to bring awareness to what the apps are prompting us to do, how we respond and how that makes us feel. If we're asking, "Why am I like this?" because we feel as though we're not as good as other people, we don't have the friends, the outfits, the authority, the motivation . . . it's not unlikely that social media is part of the answer. If you feel bad because you can't stop checking your phone or enviously scrolling through photos of people on amazing exotic holidays, it's not because you're a terrible person. Though they might be reluctant to discuss the fact that they're doing it, and they certainly don't want to share how, the Silicon Valley companies are using all the scientific knowledge they can get hold of about how our brains work in order to hook us.

If social media is largely a happy and positive space for you then that's great. A lot of the time that's my experience too. But if it's not, then the first thing to do is recognize this, observe what you are doing or feeling without judgment, and then start to think about what changes might help. And talk to people. Because almost certainly some of the people you know will be experiencing similar feelings or will have experienced in them in the past.

Social media and mental health

In the first chapter, I talked about how statistics show that incidences of mental illness are on the rise—we also noted that young people's mental health specifically seems to be declining at a pretty alarming rate. In most places around the world, when studies have plotted their results on a graph of age against happiness, the line has usually come out as a U-shape: the happiest people are the youngest and the oldest, with the least happy period being middle age.[18] But it seems that suddenly this may no longer be the case.

In social psychologist Jonathan Haidt's *After Babel* Substack, he argues that the timing of this change coincides with the advent of smartphones:

> Why would this be? What changed in the early 2010s that could have rapidly reduced the mental health of teens around the world? . . . We have argued that the sudden switch of teen social life from flip phones (which are designed for communication) to smartphones (which enabled continuous access to social media and much higher levels of phone addiction), is the major cause, though not the only one. There are unique factors at work in each country, but we know of no alternative that can explain the *synchronized, gendered, and global decline* in teen mental health.[19]

Research suggests that the earlier we begin to have access to social media, the worse it might be for our mental health. In May 2023, Sapien Labs released a report highlighting the link between the age at which someone first owns a smartphone with their mental health in later life. Their data has consistently shown that the current state of overall mental health is progressively worse for each of the youngest generations, and demonstrates that not only is smartphone usage having an impact on young people, but there also seems to be a direct correlation between getting a smartphone at a young age and poor mental well-being.[20] Basically, the older you are when you first have access to your own smartphone, and all the things that come along with that, the better you're likely to score on well-being overall. So how much of a problem is this? Just how young are the latest wave of smartphone users?

Even saying the term "smartphone" makes me feel ancient. The thing is, we now live in a world that seems to be smartphone or go home. They're all pretty clever these days! So when we get to an age at which we need to up our communication with friends—or, more likely, with our parental figures, who feel reassured if our increasing independence comes with a way for them to contact us at any time—we're opened up to far more than making phone calls.

In "Children and parents: media use and attitudes report 2022," British communications regulator Ofcom released survey data indicating that the majority of UK children get their first phone between the ages of nine and eleven, with phone ownership rising from 44 percent to 91 percent during this period.[21] Admittedly, I've never parented a child that age, but initially that struck me as *young*—is that just me? The report showed that 17 percent of children in the *three to four* age bracket have their own phone. I can't imagine they're using them in the same way a teenager would but, still, I was surprised. In fairness, I think I did get my first phone when I was about eleven or twelve, when I'd started high school—but

I'm a relative dinosaur and the Nokia 3210 was decidedly not a smartphone.

If we are going to have an intelligent conversation about social media use, then perhaps one of the first things to note is that the older generations who lived through adolescence and into their adult years without social media—and I include myself on the fringes of that bracket!—are going to struggle to understand a young person whose social life does take place largely through or assisted by social media. And I do wonder whether many of these Xers and Boomers have taken the time to try to comprehend what this is like. I don't want to be too finger-pointy about this, but to pin the increasing mental health issues of young people squarely and simply on social media, which is ruining the minds, morals, and prospects of every single one of our chronically anxious, attention-deficient young people, is a bit of an easy out. Yes, some of the problems do seem to be tied strongly to technology and social media, but what is the suggestion here—to get rid of it? Delete the lot? Be realistic. I'm certainly not arguing that everything that takes place on the apps is fine and there's nothing to critique here, but are we in danger of writing off young people as a generation of social media addicts at the expense of questioning what could and should be done to make online spaces safer and less detrimental to our mental health?

People who are truly invested in social media users' well-being usually do caveat their negative comments with an acknowledgment of the upsides, the positive elements that young people are getting online, and the potential for encouraging influence. In the Ofcom report, for example, eight in ten children in the 13–17 age bracket "used online services to find support for their well-being," and they were also more likely to feel positive than negative about their online life, with 53 percent saying that being online was good for their mental health.

It's true that social media can be detrimental to our mental health and we should be aware of this, for ourselves and others. I'm going to explore how it might be having an effect on our brains in the next section. But before I do, can we just take a moment to observe that the online and offline worlds are not, in fact, different worlds. We don't enter a parallel dimension when we look at a screen. They are connected and inform each other. Social media can be a shouty and confusing place—and that is also how society feels sometimes now. Depression, anxiety, low self-esteem, issues with body image—all of these existed before the internet. It's just that while social media connects us to things that help and inspire us, it also gives us unlimited access to things that are not going to make us feel great.

Are we chronically online?

What are the consequences of all this instant connection and scrolling and brain hacking on the part of the social media companies? Aside from the effects on mental well-being, could there be long-term implications for the way we are wired and how we think? It's a big question that you can come at from different angles. I'll be talking more about how the pace of our online world and things like rolling news have affected the way we interact with each other in the next chapter. But for now, let's stick to brains.

There are new studies being done all the time, trying to find out what the impact of social media and smartphone technology might be, but realistically it's very early days. As odd as it seems, life before social media wasn't all that long ago. When I started high school, none of these platforms existed. It's less than twenty years since Facebook opened to the public. There is more funding available for scientists who are producing research that can help social media companies "improve user experience," as they call it, than there is for scientists who want to investigate the possible detrimental effects.

One question that comes up a lot is whether smartphones and the myriad apps that live in them are negatively affecting our ability to concentrate. As someone with ADHD, I find this particularly relevant. A lot of studies have observed how distraction has become a normal state—our focus is drawn away from the thing we are supposed to be doing and on to our phone, perhaps by a message from a friend, and once the phone is in our hand, we are then distracted from replying to the message by a social media notification or a sudden need to google something our friend mentioned, which leads us into a YouTube wormhole . . . and then it's forty-five minutes later and we're in a scroll hole, not writing that email for work, and it's not entirely clear what just happened. It's unusual for us to sit and concentrate even on a TV show without also scrolling at the same time. This, at some point, makes us feel tired, unproductive, and, eventually, overwhelmed. As one review paper phrases it: "One of the most significant challenges the digital world poses for attention is attentional overload. Attentional overload occurs when the demands of the environment exceed the capacity of an individual's attentional resources."[22]

The term "continuous partial attention" was first used by a tech writer called Linda Stone in 1998.[23] We might think we are multi-tasking when really we are getting distracted from the "primary task" by something else that seems more important. We feel like we are getting things done, but we are in fact dividing our focus and flitting between tasks. Neuroscientists generally agree that our brains can't actually do two conscious things at once. For example, if you are talking on the phone while you chop veg for dinner, you are multi-tasking in that you can do both at once. Your attention is switching between both things to an extent, but you can do them simultaneously because your brain has automated at least some of the physical process of the chopping. If you are talking to your friend and responding to a DM, then you are doing two things that need cognition and you are not focused on either. According to Linda Stone, this is fine in small doses. We are historically good at scanning the horizon for predators while getting on with our daily tasks. But too much of it causes an "artificial sense of crisis," which activates our fight-or-flight mechanism as we continually scan the periphery and our attention constantly shifts focus.

This all feels fairly familiar to me. That wound-up, anxious feeling when I have spent too long scrolling and/or flitting between the apps does seem like it would have something to do with my amygdala and the fight-or-flight mechanism. We often talk about the need to feel "present" in a situation and we are aware that phones are often a major hindrance to that. But I think it's interesting to know that it could be this constant "scanning" mode that is partly responsible. If you have ever deliberately put your phone out of reach but still found yourself struggling to focus on what is in front of you, you probably recognize this as a mode that it can be hard to snap out of. It's also worth noting that the average person checks their phone eighty-five times a day.[24] And if you're thinking, "To be honest, I probably check it more than that," then I'm afraid I have to tell you that the same report concluded that . . . we're pretty much all *under-estimating* how often we do it.

On an only slightly more positive note, while we might not love that it's our devices taking up so much of our available attention, it turns out that distractibility might be more built into our nature than previously thought. Studies have shown that "stimulus-independent thought," aka thinking about something other than what we're doing at the time, could well be the brain's default mode.[25] In a 2010 study, Harvard psychologists Matthew Killingsworth and Daniel Gilbert found that up to 47 percent of our every waking hour is spent "mind wandering."[26] That does sort of make me feel better. Perhaps our heads aren't necessarily being rotted away by phones and screens; they were already distractible and this is just our current preoccupation.

Unfortunately, though, it being hardwired doesn't seem to make it any better for our mood. Though we might think that doing fun stuff is the key to making us chirpy, the study found that activities account for only 4.6 percent of our happiness, while being fully engaged in what we're doing accounts for about 10.8 percent—so, living in the moment contributes more than twice as much toward our happiness as what we're actually doing in that moment. As Killingsworth and Gilbert's paper concludes: "A human mind is a wandering mind, and a wandering mind is an unhappy mind. The ability to think about what is not happening is a cognitive achievement that comes at an emotional cost." Fascinating. With all this talk about mindfulness and living in the moment, it's nice to see some cold hard data to back it up: if you feel like you're suffering negatively from all this partial attention, try to be more consciously present (even if it's only putting your phone down while you're watching TV) and see if it makes a difference to your mood.

Though there are lots of studies being carried out on attention, it's hard for them to reach specific conclusions—as with all research, it depends on the framework and the questions the researchers are asking. There is also the issue of research being interpreted to fit a certain agenda. Take "digital amnesia," or "digital dementia," as it is rather more alarmingly referred to. This is the idea that we are outsourcing so much knowledge and memory to digital devices that we ask our brains to remember much less than we used to, with potentially damaging implications. There is also the "Google effect" whereby we don't commit things to memory because we know that we can just look them up again easily anytime we like.[27] It's not to say there isn't some truth in this, but it can also be used as the basis for alarmist reports that extrapolate the findings of a few limited surveys to conclude that there is an epidemic of memory loss and technology is making us stupid.

As someone who is fascinated by the human brain, I like learning about the latest research into how we are interacting with and being influenced by the technology that we ourselves are creating. It seems to be a hulking great piece of the "Why am I like this?" puzzle. Like all species, throughout our early history, we evolved based on the laws of natural selection. But we have reached the point where we have the ability to profoundly change our environment (sorry, planet Earth) and so survival of the fittest as Darwin described it doesn't really apply to us in the same way. Instead, it seems that the next stage of our development, if we do "evolve" further in any sense of the word, could depend on our own inventions.[28]

All this is interesting, if potentially scary, in a big-picture way. But as it all unfolds, we as individual humans still need to figure out how we are to live in the world day to day in a manner that feels the most comfortable and true to who we are. That means establishing how we want to "live" on social media too. And how to do it in a way that makes us happier.

As I have mentioned, our online lives aren't in some alternative dimension. Maybe social media is changing our brains a bit, but even with iPhone in hand, we are still humans with our messy human tendencies and impressive human skills—cooperation, communication, empathy . . . If only we give ourselves the chance to use them in the right way. In the next chapter, we're going to look at some of the things that divide us. But then we'll talk about some of the opportunities the modern world presents us with to do good and to participate positively in our communities, however we define them. It's not all doom and gloom, I promise.

7

WHY CAN'T WE GET ALONG?

I'VE NEVER BEEN SOMEONE WHO is comfortable with confrontation. In the past (and probably still occasionally now), I could agonize over a mild disagreement or slightly opposed views. I don't like being angry—even if a situation means that I have every right, I still don't like that feeling. I think it might come from a fear that expressing that anger, however justified, will lead to confrontation and other people being angry with me. When I was younger, I would avoid even minor personal confrontation at all costs. As I have gotten older, though, I have come to realize that, in life, sometimes you have to have difficult conversations or things can fester and feel much worse in the long run—but it's been a process. Oddly, I now find this easier with the people I'm closest to than I do with strangers, even though logically I should feel less worried about annoying or being misunderstood by them. I do care what other people think and

I am unlikely ever to be the sort of person who will tell everyone my feelings without fear of the consequences, or loudly proclaim my opinions as facts. I never want to say I'm 100 percent right about something and I sometimes wish I had more confidence to back myself.

Of course, having a difficult conversation with a friend or a family member about something they have done that has upset you is a different proposition from feeling angry about something that is happening in the world or someone's views on social media. But I find it interesting that in all these situations, our reactions, the emotions that come up, and how we feel physically are similar. So what happens to us when we feel threatened in some way? How good are our brains (and bodies) at understanding the actual level of threat? In other words, are the systems in our brains able to tell the difference between a pack of wolves circling our family and a pack of X (which was called Twitter when I started writing this book—help) vigilantes circling today's hot topic? How can we try to understand what is dividing us? Are we living in a world that is angrier than before, or are we just more aware of conflict and disagreement thanks to things like social media and rolling news?

What is anger?

This might sound like a stupid question, as even the most laid-back person gets angry occasionally and we all know what it feels like. But it's not the easiest to describe. Not least because what will make one person furious will be easily shrugged off by someone else.

If we were to ask this question of a psychologist, they might tell us that anger is generally considered one of the "basic" or "universal" emotions. How many of these we experience, and where the boundary is between one emotion and another, is more debatable. Most researchers and practitioners agree we have at least five, while American psychologist Paul Ekman, who has been working in this area since the 1950s, says that humans have seven universal emotions: sadness, anger, contempt, disgust, enjoyment, fear, and surprise.[1] The evidence for this is partly how most of us are able to recognize those emotions in someone else just by their facial expressions, even when we are from a different culture and speak a different language. (Further evidence is the Pixar film *Inside Out*, which I mentioned briefly in Chapter Two and is a completely charming exploration of basic emotions battling it out inside the head of a child. If you think I am being unscientific calling it "evidence" . . . you're right. But, in my defense, Paul Ekman includes an explainer of this film on his website.)

Ekman explains that these main families of emotions contain different degrees. For example, he says the anger family ranges from annoyance to rage. It also includes different forms of anger, such as "resentment, which is the kind of anger in which there is a sense of grievance;

indignation and outrage, which are anger about the mistreatment of someone; vengeance, the anger which retaliates against a misdeed by another; berserk, anger which appears to others to be an uncontrolled response, inappropriate to any provocation, and so on."[2]

So, there are different types of anger on a sort of scale. I think we can all agree with that. Further to this, some psychologists make the distinction between primary and secondary emotions,[3] and some think that anger can be both. A primary emotion is a "raw" emotion, so your first, instinctive response—like a wave of sadness when you accidentally break something that is precious to you. This might be followed by shame or embarrassment because it was a present from someone, or anger with yourself for being clumsy. Secondary emotions are usually more complicated, may last longer and can deflect or mask, or protect us from the first thing we felt.

I think this is an appealing distinction and worth bearing in mind—particularly the part about secondary emotions being used to protect ourselves—as when we, or someone else, is showing anger, that may not be the whole story. For some of us, if we feel shame or embarrassment, which are not nice things to feel, it might prompt an angry response. Or have you ever felt angry with someone because they have "made you" feel guilty? Sometimes it's easier to be angry and direct that outward than it is to try to deal with more awkward or confusing feelings.

Hello again, amygdala

Let's think specifically about the relationship between fear and anger for a minute. I think it's instinctive to acknowledge that they're linked and that this is likely to have an impact if the level of disagreement and disconnect in our world is increasing. Viewed simply, both anger and fear are reactions to something that makes us feel threatened in some way. They both focus our attention, sometimes too narrowly, and cause us to react. Fear often prompts us to run away; anger makes it more likely we will confront or try to counter the "threat."

As we know, the amygdala is the quick-fire-response part of the brain that is responsible for our initial emotional reaction. It has to run this by the prefrontal cortex eventually, but it can activate various physical responses without asking first. For example, it can cause the release of stress hormones (also called neurotransmitters), such as adrenaline, noradrenaline, and cortisol. Whether or not this is what is needed at that moment, adrenaline speeds up our heart rate, and increases the blood flow to our muscles and how much energy is available to power them. Great if you're surprised by a saber-toothed tiger outside your cave; less helpful if you are reading a particularly stressful comment thread before bed. Unfortunately, our amygdala and its stress hormone messengers are not easily able to tell the difference and have something of a one-size-fits-all reaction.

I am, of course, talking here about the famous fight-or-flight response. Although, there are other options in how we respond to stress triggers—to this we can add "freeze," when we feel momentarily almost paralyzed, glued to the spot as we hyper-focus on the "threat" to the exclusion of all else. A lesser-known part of fight-or-flight is the "fawn" response, in which, if the other possible reactions aren't working, or we think they won't, we can be overly accommodating or flattering to try to neutralize the threat.[4] This is something experienced by people who have had traumatic experiences at the hands of someone they haven't been able to get away from, such as an abusive partner or parent. Masking, when a neuro-divergent person mimics neurotypical behavior patterns in order to be accepted in social situations, can also be a form of "fawning," as they respond to the stress that situation is causing them.[5]

But to go back to fear and anger, and primary and secondary emotions, it's useful to be aware of these things because it helps us understand our own emotions and reactions, and potentially to understand the behavior of others. Emotions are such an important part of what makes us human and they are also influenced by our evolutionary past—they kept us safe from danger and encouraged us toward positive things that helped with our survival, like forming bonds with each other. Anger and fear are not inherently "bad" things, and we can't avoid them. Though, how we process them will depend so much on our experiences to date. These affect how we arrive at our secondary emotions, which is when our prefrontal cortex, as well as other bits of our brain, gets involved. This is something that we do have more control over than our immediate responses to things that happen to us, but, as touched upon earlier, secondary emotions can be much more complicated and feel confusing.

Echo chambers

What is the difference between a strong online community of like-minded folk and an echo chamber? I wish I knew the punchline to this. The reality is that platforms, which can be so powerful in building positive spaces, can also keep us insulated within them. Perhaps this makes it ultimately harder for us to deal with differences in opinion. The culture on social media, backed up strongly by those algorithms that are designed to show us more things that we probably already like, means we are far more likely to hear opinions we agree with and less likely to hear anything to the contrary. When we do hear opinions online that are different to ours, because of how little room for nuance there is in a tweet or a post, and because the algorithm favors sweeping or controversial statements that attract a lot of attention, we can get the impression that everyone who doesn't agree with us holds some extreme and intolerant opinion. But is this really the case, and what effect is it having on how we see the world and treat other people?

I don't think this is being exacerbated because we are necessarily *choosing* to spend more time online, but I think recent changes in society have taken away places where we might previously have encountered people we wouldn't usually. An obvious one is working from home; where many of us would have been commuting and spending five days a week in offices, we may now only go in a couple of days a week or not at all. And while this kind of flexibility is great in many ways, there is nothing like a packed London Underground train to resign you to dealing with humanity in all its forms . . . ! Couple this with the fact that we tend to have most things delivered to us rather than go shopping on the high street, along with the rising price of pretty much everything, which means many of us are staying in more to save money. Travel has always been a great way to break out of your own "normal," as well as a way to learn that wherever you go in the world, people are fundamentally the same—but while it's always been a privilege, it's now unaffordable for so many. Not that we can easily change any of this; I just mention these things because I think it's good to be aware of how echo chambers and their effects on us can be amplified by offline factors too, and also because I find it frustrating when commentators in the traditional media make out that younger people only *want* to interact via social media, when it sometimes feels like other options are limited. Guys, you spent all the money; we're just doing our best here.

So how do we counter this tendency to stick to our own when a lot of what's inherently in us and baked into our most common communication systems encourages us to stay the same? A simplified answer is to increase the diversity of opinion that we're exposed to. But trying to actually do that, for example by following an account or individual with differing views, can be frowned upon by those within your existing peer group, as it may be taken as a token of endorsement or support.

I had a thought-provoking conversation about this with anti-racism advocate Marie Beecham for an episode of my podcast. (Marie's own podcast is called *Know Better, Do Better* and covers social issues, race, and equity. Hard recommend, not least because she is a delightful person.) We discussed how to break out of our comfortable echo chambers in practical ways, and how this can actually help us to be better at communicating our own point of view. One example she gave was about reading books by authors you expect to disagree with; this has the potential to be a bit upsetting and, yes, you might be tempted to hide the cover if you're reading it on the bus, but as we discussed: how can we expect to effectively debate with someone if we don't know how they've arrived at their opinion?

The empathy gap

Cast your mind back to Chapter Three, where I talked about cognitive bias and some of the different forms that can take. Another type, one that we run into very commonly and which can cause division and a lack of understanding, is known as the "empathy gap."[6] This is closely related to egocentric bias, where we can become trapped in our own perspective of the world. It causes people to struggle to imagine or relate to people whose mental state is different to their own at present. This might mean that you look at someone's reaction in a particular situation and fail to understand their way of thinking, or don't take into account that their emotions or perspective have impacted their actions.

This is particularly noticeable in online comment sections. If you enjoy such an exercise, next time you run into a post that some folks are reacting to negatively, see if you can identify the responses potentially being fueled by an empathy gap, where someone is only examining an action through their own current feelings and not even trying to imagine how someone else's emotions or experiences might have led them there. I do this quite often and, while it doesn't make the realm of nit-picking comments automatically less frustrating, I do find it a very engaging way to process other people's commentary. As much as learning about our brains and our biases can be helpful or comforting in understanding how we ourselves feel about the world, there's also a massive potential benefit in applying those lessons to other people and adding a layer of perspective to our inevitable judgments of others. Often, it's far easier to look on people kindly, even when we don't like what they're saying, when we can do what they're *not* doing and try to unpack why they might feel that way. We don't need to have empathy for hateful people, but, at the same time, having an awareness that their hateful behavior may come from a place of isolation, loneliness, pain, or trauma can be helpful. It doesn't excuse them and I don't believe you are conceding anything to anyone by having those thoughts. But it may just help our own sanity as well as exercise our empathetic muscles.

Thinking back to self-conscious emotions, a lot of what those feelings boil down to is that we really just want other people to like us. Good on an evolutionary basis, as we've discussed, but there's a difference between wanting to be liked and *needing* to be liked—and that's where some of us fall down. When we ponder the emotions that come up when we frustratedly ask ourselves "Why am I like this?!," are you instantly thinking how you feel about yourself . . . or how you're being perceived by other people?

The empathy gap can even be used to explain how you look back on your own actions and beat yourself up about them. If you remember ways you've behaved in the past and think, "I can't believe I did that," "Why did I find that so difficult?," or "How did I ever think that was OK?" then you might be experiencing bias toward your present mental state and struggling to find empathy with who you were at the time.[7] Big, big "Why am I like this?" energy. I'd say this is pretty common among people who've experienced mental illness—when you've moved out of a particularly bad time or seen significant improvements in your mental health, it can be hard to look back and recognize the person you were or the ways you acted during that period. In a similar response to that of people who've never experienced mental illness at all, it's tricky to look back and understand yourself at a stage when taking a shower felt like a monumental task, even if you know that was true in the moment. It might not feel great to remember the difficult times, but, equally, it's part of who you are and is useful when you need to have compassion and understanding for others who may be struggling.

A particularly emotional and perhaps extreme example of this gap in empathy can be found in our discussion around suicide. Certainly, for as long as I can remember, a common word that came up when people talked about suicide was "selfish." Now, in recent years, you find more people calling out that narrative and explaining that taking one's life is *not* a selfish act. It's so, so much more complex than that. But, still, this persisted for a long time and I think the empathy gap goes a long way to explaining why. For people who've never experienced suicidal ideation, or maybe even for people who have but have recovered from those feelings—because you absolutely can move forward and out of that state of thinking—it can be supremely difficult to empathize with the emotional state of a suicidal individual, to imagine what severe depression or other forms of mental illness can make you believe. As someone who has experienced suicidal thinking, I find it easier to overcome part of that empathy gap and fathom how it's possible to feel that way. But even though I have felt it myself in the past, I *still* find it hard to comprehend completely—so I understand why it's so hard for others to grapple with, at the same time as believing that it is hugely important that we try.

Empathy for our fellow human beings is such a vital thing to bind us together and help us navigate through conflict. But it's a knotty and sort of elusive subject, and there are lots of reasons why we might struggle to feel it, even when we might want to. One paper, called "The Science of Empathy,"[8] defines it like this: "Empathy is a complex capability enabling individuals to understand and feel the emotional states of others, resulting in compassionate behavior. Empathy requires cognitive, emotional, behavioral, and moral capacities to understand and respond to the suffering of others." The paper notes that it depends on neural pathways in the emotional, motor, and sensory areas of the brain—which is why we might physically flinch when we see someone get hurt, as if it is happening to us, while also feeling bad for their pain. And yet, "when emotionally overloaded, overwhelmed, exploited, or burned out, the capacity for empathy declines," because we can't keep up the level of emotional labor needed to continue feeling and processing this complicated emotion.

You've probably heard the term "compassion fatigue" or "emotional burnout." Compassion is similar to but not quite the same as empathy; where empathy refers to our *ability* to understand or share the feelings of someone else, compassion is characterized by feelings of caring that are motivated by a desire to alleviate suffering. Compassion fatigue is a term that is used to refer to the negative effects of repeatedly suffering secondary trauma—that means dealing with terrible things that are happening to other people. Emergency service workers, nurses, therapists, and social workers are all people whose jobs mean they are often assisting people in their worst moments, day in, day out. (I know there will be lots of other examples too.) Without proper support, they can suffer symptoms like feeling numb or disassociated, a lack of motivation, and hypervigilance.[9] It's like their capacity for empathy has been exhausted, which can even make someone feel ashamed if, say, they are a compassionate person who has chosen a job in a caring profession.

It's easy to see how frontline workers like these would be affected by what they see and hear first-hand. But studies suggest that compassion fatigue is affecting many more of us; back in 1996, a research paper titled "Compassion Fatigue: Communication and Burnout Toward Social Problems" established that being over-exposed to crises via the media contributed to emotional fatigue among the adult population.[10] Now think about how the media landscape has changed since 1996. We are faced with rolling news and social media that delivers us updates on the terrible things happening around the world at a rate which we have never had to deal with before—and frankly aren't equipped for.

If your reaction to a terrible story in the news has ever been to feel numb, while your friends all seem angry or sad or motivated to join a campaign, there could be a reason behind it. Have you been dealing with other stressful events in your life lately? Have you been watching the news for six hours straight? Is your emotional cup running empty? That doesn't mean there is something wrong with you, or you're a bad person. Quite likely, your brain is just struggling to keep up with the work it needs to do to allow you to feel empathetic. As a side note—but a related point, I think—psychologists have noted that you don't have to be able to feel empathy to have a clear sense of right and wrong. Some people with autism, for example, find it hard to recognize the feelings of others. But they may still have a strong moral code and acute recognition of injustice. They just come to it in a different way—such as by reasoning and logic. So it's not as though you can't be a good person without empathizing widely with the people around you. Research suggests that people who develop compassion fatigue via the modern avenue of social media may experience symptoms similar to those of PTSD, including changes in personality or mood, trouble sleeping, and emotional numbness—causing desensitization to the experiences of others.[11]

The difficult thing about acknowledging this is that there isn't a simple answer. We can't just . . . not listen to anything about what's happening in the world, can we? Uncomfortably, being in a position to feel emotionally drained by watching news coverage about suffering happening far away is one of enormous privilege. The people being directly affected by something that we're only hearing stories about, or seeing relayed on social media, don't have the option to switch it off, and so bearing witness to their pain feels like something of a moral obligation.

This is a particularly emotive topic since it sounds really horrible to say that we're worn out by something as innate as caring. I think the term "compassion fatigue" has a tendency to be taken literally—as in, tired of being compassionate, not willing to do it anymore— but I don't believe that's usually the form it takes. It's not that we stop caring, but that the amount we have been caring, and still do care, makes us less able to carry on. So how can we avoid compassion fatigue and not be sidelined by the guilt that can accompany acknowledging our privilege?

A 2021 paper in the journal *Journalism and Media* examined how the representation of individuals in media coverage can be used to foster "social empathy" and how that could be used to counter compassion fatigue.[12] Citing examples from the Instagram account "Humans of New York,"[13] the study noted that by informing readers about "neighbors or groups they may not know or understand" through the lens of humanizing concerns such as careers or romantic relationships, commenters felt more socially orientated and positive. However, in a study analyzing *New York Times* columnist Nicholas Kristof's people-focused reporting style (through which he actively attempts to overcome compassion fatigue), the results unexpectedly showed that the topics and geographic proximity of the stories were more likely to influence reader engagement than story-telling style.[14] It seems this is not a problem that's easy to fix with some tweaks to journalistic approach. If we can't avoid this emotional exhaustion altogether, can we at least find ways to remedy it?

Research in this specific area is fairly new, but a 2022 study focused on counselors in the Covid-19 era explored "compassion practice" as an antidote to compassion fatigue.[15] By focusing on mindfulness, self-compassion and holding reasonable expectations for what individuals could achieve under difficult circumstances, subjects were better able to maintain compassionate responses to others. Practical advice for individuals like you or me who might find themselves feeling overwhelmed includes setting boundaries to limit news consumption, or setting specific times for it, rather than doom-scrolling, as well as practicing self-care and reinforcing a sense of shared humanity by connecting with our communities on issues we care about.[16]

I think it essentially comes back round to the empathy gap. When we feel we can relate to someone, we're better able to feel compassionate toward them—and that includes giving ourselves a break when we find things tough. Later, we'll look at the "oxygen mask theory" of making sure we're well first in order to help others. We are cognitively biased to make this difficult, but trying to consciously bolster ourselves against emotional fatigue can help us to maintain levels of compassion for other people, making us more effective, socially active global citizens.

Polarization

The "intergroup contact hypothesis" was first proposed by an American psychologist called Gordon Allport in the 1950s. It suggests that contact between groups of people who would not usually cross paths increases understanding and reduces prejudice. That makes sense, doesn't it? If people can come together and see that those whom they perceive as different and "other" to them are reasonable humans with whom they can share common ground, even if they are never going to agree on everything, it seems like a Very Good Thing. However, Allport outlined four key conditions that have to be in place for this to work: the group has to come together on the basis of equal status of all members; they need to have common goals; they also need a reason and motivation to cooperate; and there needs to be some sort of support from an outside authority.[17] Since the 1950s, this theory has been developed and used in lots of different ways, but I think we can all see how finding spaces with these optimal conditions can be difficult in our online, often polarized world.

I'm not going to launch back into algorithms and the morals of tech companies, but whatever their intentions might be, the vast amount of information and opinions we're exposed to on social media is in itself encouraging us to be more divided. Research published in 2021 found that when the number of posts we're exposed to increases and we aren't sure how accurate they are, our rate of learning slows (!) and polarization increases. Polarization, particularly when we talk about politics, means that people shift away from moderate attitudes toward one of two opposing ideological extremes. When faced with an overwhelming amount of information, people gravitate toward and choose to read posts that are closest to their existing beliefs, in order to reduce their feelings of uncertainty about the state of the world.[18] Remember when I mentioned confirmation bias earlier? I present to you . . . the consequences.

It won't shock you to read that social media contributes toward an "us versus them" mentality, but it can be jarring to step back and realize how it might apply to you. Let's assume, for discussion's sake, that you're "left wing" to some extent, i.e., you favor socially liberal ideas. When you hear about polarization, it's easy to look outward, and across; you might immediately think about extremely right-wing views and roll your eyes in exasperation. It's important to remember that we are none of us immune: someone with the opposite viewpoint is probably thinking the same about you.

A systematic review found that while research into social media's role in encouraging polarization has increased in the last decade, there's a strong focus on both X (formerly known as Twitter) and US samplings, at the expense of research into other locations and platforms, as well as a distinct lack of research into whether or how social media can *de*polarize.[19] Essentially, the field has really latched on to this idea, but might need to broaden its view a bit.

I'm really interested in where the line falls between learning about opinions that are different to yours and forcing yourself to listen to people who you find truly unpleasant. Of course, this will be different for everyone. I don't think any of us should feel we have to be engaged with society's ills all the time. If cat videos and memes are what you mainly want from Instagram, then more power to you. It doesn't have to be where you get your news. Many of us crave a nice, friendly space in which to connect with people with whom we have things in common. That is perfectly fine—and, based on what we looked at in Chapter Five, in keeping with our knowledge of our basic evolutionary wiring: we feel safer in a group of like-minded souls. In a similar vein to compassion fatigue, we can't contribute to the net good if our own mental health is suffering because we are over-exposing ourselves to prejudice and narrow-minded views.

There is a similar issue here, though, in that "opting out" is a position of enormous privilege and not really compatible with our humanity. I think some of us can feel guilty when we know how many opportunities exist at our fingertips to learn about other people's experiences far outside our own. If you, like me, are aware you are living a life of huge privilege when compared to lots of others around the world, it sometimes feels like the

WHY AM I LIKE THIS?

least you can do is educate yourself about those experiences. But where to start, and how to begin to take on board all there is know?

We may become so overwhelmed by current events and the debates raging around them that we shut down. We might need to take a break from the news for a while, which is absolutely fine. However, this shutting down can take the form of refusing to listen to anyone who doesn't agree with us, or instantly branding people as "toxic" because their views are different to ours. It's not that some people's views aren't terrible, of course, but when we start labeling people—"snowflake," "woke," "antiwoke"—are we getting our point across or effectively closing off any conversation? Sometimes, we just don't have the conversation in us. How resilient we are and how we develop that resilience is a personal matter for each of us. However, I do think it's a question that's worth actively engaging with.

Toxic, triggering, or just "I don't like this"?

Speaking of "toxic," that's just one example of the therapy-speak we've picked up and now use in daily conversations. We talk about "boundaries" and "coping mechanisms"; we see videos about spotting "narcissists" and "gaslighters." Common examples like "inner child" lead all the way back to Freud. In recent years, it seems that the word "triggering" has become ubiquitous to the point where it actually seems to trigger those on the right, ironically

making them furious at the idea that you "can't say anything these days" as some "snowflake" will get upset. Yes,
we are all veterans of the culture wars now!

In psychology, a "trauma trigger" is considered to be a
stimulus that brings up a memory of a traumatic experience in a visceral and upsetting way. It's particularly
associated with PTSD. So, if you were once in a car accident on a rainy day, bad weather while traveling in a car
might cause this kind of memory. But so might an otherwise innocuous smell or sensation, like a particular air
freshener that was in the vehicle that day. I can understand how some people feel frustrated that "triggering"
is now sometimes used as a synonym for "upsetting" or
"something I don't want to hear about," as that is very
different to the original meaning. However, I have also
heard people who are living with PTSD say that they
don't really have a problem with this "slide" in meaning,
as they feel that the word being in common usage is
helpful in bringing awareness to how words and images
can impact people in ways that someone casually using
them might not be aware of.

If you've ever wondered about the origins of trigger
warnings, they seem to have originated on feminist web-
sites in the early 2000s, with the intent of flagging
potentially disturbing content related to sexual abuse
and violence that might impact the sites' audiences. They
then started to pop up in academic circles, particularly
in the context of warning undergraduates that some of
their course materials contained potentially distressing

topics, as it was thought by some that this would disrupt students' learning. An article about triggers in the *New Yorker* quotes philosopher Kate Manne, who wrote in 2015 that not telling students in advance about these things was like "occasionally throwing a spider at an arachnophobe."[20] As an arachnophobe myself, I would very much prefer that this doesn't happen, but many people have questioned the analogy—partly because a list of triggers is potentially endless. We have no way of knowing what traumatic experiences an individual may have had and therefore what they might find upsetting— they might not know themselves until it happens. And partly because subsequent research has suggested that trigger warnings don't actually do any good. Some people have argued that putting "WARNING" on something may actually work as a nocebo—which means someone experiences a negative outcome because they have been told to expect it. It's the opposite of a placebo, basically, which is when we experience a positive effect simply because that's what we are told will be the result.

I'm not sure what I think about this. On the one hand, you could say that trigger warnings are a sign that we, as a society, are becoming more aware of individuals' mental health and more willing to accommodate it. Or, on the other hand, much like one view of "imposter syndrome," that it's pushing something back on an individual and making them feel like they have the problem, whereas actually we all, at different times and in different ways, suffer the ramifications of the problems in society. I would certainly prefer it if people weren't allowed to post massive house spiders on their Instagram stories. (I dread September for this reason.) These rules, however, are of course more complicated to establish.

Which side are you on?

In the years I've been on social media, one of the biggest changes I've noticed is the increase in the speed at which people are expected to react to things and how there seems to be so much pressure to have a public opinion on everything. Whenever something makes headlines or some sort of controversy erupts, there seems to be an expectation that we will all state our position, pick a side, use our voice. Immediately.

I know I have my own slant on this because of my experience of social media. I'm acutely aware of the privilege of my platform—it's frankly a lot to have ten million people on the end of a silly little app on your phone—but that means I'm very careful about using it properly and not accidentally adding to the hellfire of online misinformation. When I feel like I know what I'm talking about and, crucially, feel that adding my voice to a conversation is actually useful, I'm in, speaking, on board, and feel better mentally prepared to deal with the consequences (read: angry DMs).

I've actually understood more about my feelings here since I was diagnosed with ADHD. A common symptom (although not experienced by everyone with ADHD, and not exclusive to them either) is rejection sensitive dysphoria, or RSD. This means that someone can experience intense emotional pain in response to failure, rejection, or criticism—and, honestly, when I read about this, some of my online experiences made a lot more sense. I have found it acutely distressing to realize that I have, for example, shared a post that contains inaccurate information on slide five and now someone is angry with me. Maybe it would be easier if it was just one or two people, but when it's a whoooole bunch of messages? Literally full-on meltdown crying and a panicked sense that everyone in the world hates me. That's the trickiest part, really: that RSD causes such a strong and unpleasant emotional response even when a criticism is totally valid.

Because I'm now worried about what you think of me (see above), let me say that I'm not trying to make excuses or garner sympathy. There's no "boo hoo, people are shouting at me." That's one reason why I'm very conscious about what I share, but another reason takes us back to one of the cognitive biases I mentioned earlier—the Dunning–Kruger effect. This inbuilt flaw means that we struggle to evaluate how little we know and therefore have a tendency to be overconfident, which can even dampen our ability to think rationally.[21]

I think, in my case, it's basically an overreaction to knowing about the Dunning–Kruger effect. If that describes overconfidence in one's ability or knowledge, I have ... under-confidence. As Shakespeare himself stated: "The fool doth think he is wise, but the wise man knows himself to be a fool."[22] I'm so paranoid about doing something wrong and contributing negatively that I totally freeze up and don't know what to do at all. Am I weaponizing incompetence? Good God, I *am* chronically online.

Anyway, enough about me and my self-conscious dread. Obviously, I'm not the only person in the world dealing with the pressure to get everything right all the time, or wanting to avoid incurring any wrath. I'm not sure how we got to this point, where if you don't immediately and unreservedly pick a team, or if you try to contribute a more nuanced idea to the conversation, inevitably someone will tell you that you are endorsing the extreme opposite view or you don't care at all.

It's true that we seem to be asked for our opinion more and more these days in general. We are constantly being asked to rate and review things, from the quality of a WhatsApp call to our internet banking app to a sandwich bar we popped into last Tuesday. It's all fuel for our increasingly data-driven world, of course, and the algorithms that power it. (I know I feel kind of blindfolded at the prospect of buying something with no reviews.) Is it good for us to be . . . I'm going to say *coerced* into our hot takes?

As we've touched on before, twenty-four-hour rolling news, and the speed at which stories unfold and are dissected in both social and traditional media, means that the pace of current events feels extremely fast. When I was a kid, adults got their news from the morning newspaper that had gone to press very late the night before, plus some breakfast news on the radio. Throughout the day, there were hourly radio bulletins on commercial radio and the BBC, and the news was broadcast at roughly one p.m., six p.m., and nine p.m., depending on which channel's news you preferred. There were local newspapers and some evening newspapers—oh, and Teletext, which I have vivid memories of watching at my grandparents' house when I was little. (But you'll have to google that if you are under thirty.) That was about it. Sky News, the first rolling news channel in the UK, actually launched in 1989, but most people didn't have Sky television then.

Fast-forward to now: there's a whole host of news channels to choose from and all the newspapers are online too. It's easier than ever to select based on political affiliation, so you can be even more riled up by a host who knows just how to push your buttons with their own take. You might have two or three separate news apps on your phone that will notify you with "breaking" updates throughout the day (the urgency of which is often questionable, in this writer's opinion). Aside from the dedicated apps, you probably also spend a chunk of your time on social media, where news is interspersed, dissonantly, between red-carpet outfit analysis and someone painting their fence.

Part of the problem in terms of news versus our brains is that we feel as though getting answers and knowing more should help us feel in control. But it often doesn't.

Psychologist Markus Brauer, who worked on a study about the emotional effects of "information seeking" and social media during the pandemic, explains that uncertainty is "a difficult psychological state for us."[23] So it's natural to want to find answers, but in that time of huge uncertainty, watching the news on TV and looking at social media had a detrimental effect. Brauer and his colleagues note that these were unprecedented times, but I think if we all consider how we feel when we get sucked into internet quicksand trying to find answers to a situation that is complex and still unfolding, it seems likely that this is not unique to the pandemic.[24]

Educate yourself!

A common response to a quick reshare or someone raising their hands to say, "I don't have the background knowledge to understand this" is: "Well, EDUCATE yourself!" I mean, yes, to a point. No one wants to be called ignorant, particularly when we have more opportunities than ever before to learn and hear directly from people with first-hand experience—global citizens, baby! And it's also frustrating being on the receiving end of someone else's ignorance. But I do think it's good to remember that ignorance is not the same as *willful* ignorance, which is not exactly the same as prejudice. And to resist the knee-jerk reaction of scolding people for these things equally.

I don't know if it stems from my background in teaching, but it's a particularly strong belief of mine that we don't know what we don't learn. We're born lumps of clay, blank slates, and we're taught all sorts of things throughout our lives. The empathy gap and all our jumbled-up biases can make it difficult to stop and remember that other people haven't had the same life experience we have, whether they're less or more experienced in a particular topic, and so we feel disbelief and frustration when we're trying to have a conversation and there's a canyon of misguided or uninformed opinions between us. I'm not saying I'm above this—depending on the discussion at hand, it can be a little bit jarring or absolutely devastating to see people share beliefs that you know in your bones are wrong.

My main bugbear with the "Educate yourself!" thing is that I think it has the opposite effect. It's a phrase meant to chide and punish people rather than *actually* encouraging them to learn. "You'd better educate yourself, because right now you're stupid; you have five minutes to do so and you'd sure as shit better think the same as me at the end." I'd go as far as to say it disincentivizes people from learning—have you ever noticed who gets the most backlash for speaking up about social justice, climate action, or other emotive topics? It's usually the people who are already at least interested and trying to get involved in the conversation. Other folks, who stick to "safe" areas or steer clear of anything even vaguely political, aren't expected to comment and so they don't—it's a cycle that keeps them feeling safe and discourages them from participating. What I think everybody wants—or I hope so, at least—is as many people as possible being encouraged to engage with issues, gaining knowledge, and practicing compassion for other human beings. I don't think we're always doing a great job of that.

We just can't know everything. We can certainly go away and try to learn more, but that can take a while, and, as we have seen, the demand to "state your position" can be insistent and immediate. "Tell me what you think about that so I know if you're good or bad." Giving people a certain amount of grace is beneficial both in not shutting them out of that education and making the interaction feel less confronting to you too. Do you want to immediately shame someone or could you help them actually to learn something? Have you assumed what they mean or think based on your own biases? We'll expand in a minute on primary and secondary reactions—would you rather hear someone's instant, reactive, blurted-out hot take, or hear what they actually think once they know what the hell is going on? The reality is that some of us grow up with first-hand experience or teaching about a topic and others don't, and it can take a while to identify your blind spots. For example, if you've grown up in a family or a location where you're constantly being told that climate change is the nonsense ramblings of worrywarts with a political agenda, you're probably not absorbing information from a neutral standpoint. On a more personal level, if you have never suffered with depression and no one close to you has either, you may have picked up on some of the stigma that has floated around in society for years without even realizing. I mean, even if you *have* suffered from a mental illness like this, you may well have internalized some prejudices—such is the pervasive nature of stigma! Anti-racist educators have tried to tell us this for ages. Walking around and saying you're not racist, you "don't have a racist bone in your body," actually isn't as useful as acknowledging the fact that we've all grown up absorbing the racism and bias in society around us, then working to actively combat it.

So, yes, educate yourself. I mean, that's what we're all trying to do, isn't it? There may be a lot going on in the world that is anxiety-inducing, to say the least, but there is still so much that is enchanting. Our brains do want answers but they also don't want to be overloaded or threatened, and most of us need time to process and to think. It's not always immediately obvious what it is you're missing and, let's face it, every day is a school day. We cannot expect ourselves, or others, to be experts on anything in a matter of minutes, and although the planet and news cycle are whirring 24/7—you cannot.

Why are you really angry?

To bring us back round to the "why" of it all: while I'm working to extend compassion to people, that includes compassion for those making these heated demands for a statement. Where does their anger come from? I think I do understand to an extent. There is so much we can't control and a lot of frightening things going on, to which we have instant access via our phones, so it's natural that we sometimes feel powerless. And when we feel powerless, we can feel scared. In a time when many have lost faith in politicians and it feels like the world is getting steadily worse, social media can be an outlet for frustration, pain, and fear.

The Nobel prize–winning behavioral economist Daniel Kahneman wrote a very famous book called *Thinking, Fast and Slow*.[25] In it, he described how our brains operate in two different modes; I like to think of these as our primary and secondary reactions. System 1 thinking is quick and feels instinctive. We rely on this for immediate decisions and responses. However, it's riddled with biases and prone to relying heavily on an emotional response. System 2 thinking is slower and requires conscious effort, but it enables us to analyze, solve problems, and approach questions logically. When stressed, we are far more likely to revert to System 1 thinking, as we feel pressure to respond with answers immediately. This can block System 2 thinking and mean that we never get to the stage of approaching a question more rationally.

It's not bad to be angry—in the past, people's anger has been used as fuel to challenge injustice and bring about change many times over. It's natural to be afraid and it's hard not to feel overwhelmed, particularly when that dopamine loop harnessed by social media algorithms is drawing us back to our screens again and again. But we need to recognize that the way we are wired means that when we feel fear and anxiety, it prompts emotional and impulsive reactions, meaning we can lash out or retreat and stop engaging. Fight-or-flight, in other words, floods our system with cortisol and adrenaline. Our emotional reactions trigger more emotional reactions in other people, who feel attacked and/or not listened to. And then you get X. (Kidding. Mostly.)

While there's nothing wrong with anger—we can honor it; we can make room for all our feelings—I don't think it's where we want to end the story. We can try to look for what underlies the anger—are we scared, confused, sad, threatened, desperately seeking some sort of release? What do we want to do with that? If we never use this introspection to fuel action or make us more compassionate, how can we ever expect to get along?

8

HOW CAN I MAKE A DIFFERENCE?

MOST OF US FEEL LIKE we want to contribute to the net good. To help others and make the world a better place in whatever ways we might be able to. Don't we? But when we are constantly plugged in to all that is still wrong and unfair and sometimes scary, how do we stop ourselves from becoming overwhelmed? There's sometimes the sense that the choice is between being "selfish" (massive air quotes) and tuning out from the big issues, even to protect our own mental health, and being someone who engages totally with a multitude of causes. But, like so many binary choices, I think that's a false dilemma. You don't have to choose one or the other. But it's very difficult to do good things and gainfully take part in important conversations if you are struggling with your own mental health—or feeling paralyzed by the weight of a general sense of sadness at all that's wrong in the world.

"Making a difference" is kind of a nebulous phrase. In some situations, it can sound bland, or like an empty platitude. It will also mean different things to different people, but what I mean by it here is quite simple—just how can we remain engaged with and attuned to what's happening around us and take opportunities to help, influence and support? We can't avoid encountering negativity in the world on a daily basis, so how do we protect ourselves against becoming passive and defeatist? What is actually happening in our brains at these times and can knowing more about this help?

Sometimes we will make a contribution and do something positive by being part of something bigger, like joining a campaign, raising money for a cause, adding our voices to others to bring about a change. But I think it's important not to overlook the more everyday ways in which we can offer help, like supporting people around us or being a part of a positive community. There will be times when showing up for a friend, for example, might feel like a small gesture or no big deal, but it makes a big difference to the person who really needed some care and attention at that moment.

Before we go further, I want to make sure it's said: you are worthy already. If you don't run campaigns or create seismic change, if you're not an activist, if you don't have a laundry list of "impressive" things you've done to reel off . . . If you're not the friend everyone goes to for help, if you're forgetful or overwhelmed, if you wish you did more but you're so, so tired—you are a whole person who is deserving of grace and respect. If we talk about making change and you feel like you're already struggling with all the things you have to manage, know that taking care of yourself in the first instance is at times the best way for you to contribute to improving our society. With all these stats we've examined about how our mental health is declining, looking after yours can, sometimes, be the most radical action the world needs from you.

The oxygen mask theory

Have you ever heard someone refer to the "oxygen mask rule" in relation to self-care? It uses the metaphor of the safety briefing on airplanes in which you are told that, in the event of an emergency, you should put on your own oxygen mask first before you help anyone else—the rationale being that you obviously can't do much good if you are short on air yourself! When applied to mental health, it means that if you're struggling and don't take care of your own needs first, it's going to be much harder to support those around you or contribute positively to your community.

This is, of course, sensible and logical advice. It can be a good reminder to stop and focus on your own well-being if you feel like you are not being a good friend or participating in the way you would like to. Rather than beating yourself up because you feel like you should be doing more, do you actually need to take some time for yourself and try to get your own mental health in a better place first? However, I do think it is important to acknowledge that this isn't always going to be straight-forward for everyone. If you are a parent looking after young children, have other nonnegotiable responsibilities, or work in a caring profession and are feeling burned out—or even if you are just in a super-busy period at work—the standard self-care advice to focus on yourself, maybe have a soothing bath or do some meditation, might feel laughably impractical. You might be thinking, "I don't even have my own 'oxygen mask' right now!" If this is you, then all I can say is I hope you have people around you who are in a position to offer their support, and I hope you can accept it when they do. (I also covered this on my podcast with trauma specialist psychologist Dr. Sam Akbar, in an episode about stress and resilience, if you feel like you'd benefit from a more in-depth discussion.)

This seems as good a place as any to talk about burn-out. This is a term that seems to have really cemented its place in our well-being vocabulary in recent years, with many people overwhelmed and struggling, but it's not always used in quite the right contexts. I mentioned the alternative phrase "emotional burnout" when I talked about compassion fatigue, because I think a lot of people can relate to that terminology, but "burnout" itself has quite a specific definition and is related to work. According to the World Health Organization:

Burn-out is a syndrome conceptualized as resulting from chronic workplace stress that has not been successfully managed. It is characterized by three dimensions:

- feelings of energy depletion or exhaustion;
- increased mental distance from one's job, or feelings of negativism or cynicism related to one's job; and
- reduced professional efficacy.

Burn-out refers specifically to phenomena in the occupational context and should not be applied to describe experiences in other areas of life.[1]

Whether or not it's used in the most accurate, work-related context, it seems to be a state that many people relate to—which I think is pretty telling about how we're collectively coping with the demands placed upon us. According to research by Future Forum, there are two groups who are more at risk of burning out than any other: women and people under thirty.[2] Something to bear in mind is that burnout shares a lot of its symptoms with depression,[3] so if you're feeling exhausted by life and not just work, it's equally important to seek some support.

With all that being said, the oxygen mask theory seems more relevant than ever. There will be times when you just don't have much emotional capacity available and you need to focus on yourself. But remember too that sometimes looking after ourselves *can* take the form of helping others. Even just witnessing kindness and caring behaviors has been shown to reduce stress,[4] while performing acts of kindness could possibly mediate symptoms of depression and anxiety.[5] If you are feeling powerless, joining a group of people fighting for change can be exhilarating. If you are feeling lost in your own thoughts, then getting out and doing something for someone else can recalibrate them. I'm certainly not suggesting that you should cure burnout by adding something else to your over-stacked plate, but nor am I convinced that focusing on ourselves exclusively is always the right approach when we are feeling disconnected and cynical. Yes, oxygen is essential, but it also helps to recognize that we are not alone on the plane.

Negativity bias and the news

If you do find yourself struggling under the weight of all the bad news, feeling like you're trapped in a deluge holding a failing umbrella, then there are a few things it's worth knowing about. The first is negativity bias. The way we are wired, studies have shown, means we notice and assign much more importance to things we perceive as negative than those we consider positive. It's partly why we remember insults but forget compliments, and why one bad moment can ruin an otherwise delightful day.

In an evolutionary sense, this is understandable. For

our ancient predecessors, it was lovely to spot those deli-
cious berries growing over yonder, but it wasn't a matter
of life or death, like whether you spotted the saber-
toothed tiger tracks. (I'm starting to feel I may have
overused the cave person and tiger analogy in this book.
I'm sure prehistoric people had other problems and apex
predators to contend with, but this example really works
for my imagination.) As with so many things, the evolutionary development that helped to keep us safe back
then lives on in our brains but is not so much the right
tool for the job in the modern world—even though it
still shows up in a variety of human behaviors. For example, the way we are often more motivated by the threat of
losing something we have than the prospect of gaining
something we would like.[6]

This is relevant not only because feeling like we are
constantly faced with negativity—whether in our own
lives or out in the world—makes us less likely to try
to change things, but also because it has an impact on
the news we see and the way it is served to us. A 2023
paper published in the scientific journal *Nature Human
Behaviour* explained how when researchers looked at
click-through rates on news stories on the website
Upworthy from 2012 to 2015, they found that "negative
words in news headlines increased consumption rates
(and positive words decreased consumption rates) of
articles."[7] So we're wired to engage with the negative
stuff, and it sounds like the more negative, the better:
"For a headline of average length, each additional

negative word increased the click-through rate by 2.3 percent." It's also significant that the site *Upworthy* was founded to deliberately focus on good news stories. In other words, users were going on a positive news site and *still* clicking more on headlines that contained negative words.

Based on what we know about negativity bias, this does make some sense, but the bigger problem comes thanks to that somewhat mystical beast we talked about in Chapter Six—the algorithm. As the algorithms used by different platforms want us to keep clicking, and we are more likely to click on a headline containing negative words, and the more we click, the more we get more of the same . . . well, you can see what's happening here. Doom-scrolling. Everyone up in arms. Sighs of resignation.

Hot takes and knee-jerk responses

Just before we move on to looking at *how* we make a difference, I want to consider one more thing that might skew our desire (or ability) to do so. When I spoke to Lucy Blakiston, cofounder of the popular news account "Shit You Should Care About" for my podcast, one of the things we talked about is how much pressure there is to instantly form an opinion. I discussed this a bit in the last chapter, but it's important to remember that outlets are under this pressure too, and the immediate responses that you read to breaking news aren't always going to be the most thoroughly informed. (Though at least journalists are usually trained to provide a balanced view of things, even if the publication they are working for has its own political angle.) Social media can give us access to first-hand accounts and citizen journalism, which can be crucial especially where politics do affect reporting, but it's also the absolute Wild West. And yet, in a 2023 review of news consumption,[8] Ofcom found that almost half of adults in the UK are using social media to obtain their news. This figure rises to 71 percent in the young adult (16–24) category, while one in ten teens (age 12–15) said that TikTok is their main source of news. Interestingly, when compared to all adults aged sixteen and over, young adults' *motivation* for consuming news is different. Compared to other groups, they are less likely to be partaking out of habit or a desire to know what's happening in their local area, and more likely to be motivated by boredom or wanting to be knowledgeable for their work or studies.

I have to say, I find this particularly thought-provoking since it does seem to tie in to a lot of what we looked at previously: collectively, we feel like all eyes are on us and there's a pressure to know right away exactly what's going on in breaking stories. The fact that so many young adults say they're motivated by wanting to seem knowledgeable and that it's a different category of motivation to *actually wanting to know* . . . that's an important distinction for me.

Going back to thinking about the providers of social

news, I find "Shit You Should Care About" refreshing, particularly because of the way that the team doesn't claim to be experts or an authority, but is willing to engage, curious and open-minded in their approach to understanding current affairs. Leaning in to the fact that there are people behind the platform acknowledges a crucial difference between this era of social-media news brands and traditional, national news outlets. Lucy admits that some of the stories she has written about for the "Shit You Should Care About" newsletter and podcast have reduced her to tears, but she manages to remain so enthusiastic about her work and positive about its importance.

We also spoke about how she researches stories that go viral—sometimes to the point where they are being shared by politicians—and has found that not all of them seem to have any basis in verifiable fact. This is another reason why hot takes and instant responses can shut down meaningful conversation. It's not always that people are deliberately making things up and promoting "fake news," more that it can take time to get to the bottom of a story and figure out what might actually be going on.

I do think there's beginning to be a bit more acknowledgment of this as a problem, and social news platforms seem to be addressing it, if only (says my cynical side) to cover their own backs. I've suddenly started to notice infographics posted with caveats like "emerging story" or a note that the platform hasn't been able to verify sources yet, which I certainly wasn't seeing a couple of years ago, even. One criticism often leveled at traditional news media is that it's too slow or too biased, but the logical part of us surely knows that there's a reason why news outlets have to verify a story before publishing. That hasn't always been the case with social news, but with enough examples of stories being backpedaled, a shift is on the horizon.

All of which is to say that I think it's fine, even preferable, not to have an instant opinion sometimes. Particularly when something has literally just happened. Your offhand comments really can affect the perception of a shared story. And even when you have got to the point where you've learned some more, it's still fine to say, "I'm not sure yet." As we have seen, feeling sad and powerless in the face of scary events happening around the world is natural, but even when this inspires us to attempt to do something to help, it is still a good idea to take a moment to be curious and try to learn more about the nuances of the issue before diving in.

"Virtue signaling" and "slacktivism"

Indulge me in a dictionary quotation here. According to the *Oxford English Dictionary*, "slacktivism" refers to "actions performed via the internet in support of a political or social cause (e.g., signing an online petition), characterized as requiring little time, effort, or commitment, or as providing more personal satisfaction than public impact."[9]

Some claim that slacktivism—a contraction of "slacker" and "activism"—was originally a positive term that simply meant small acts which an individual could perform on a personal level. Like planting a tree or picking up some litter, say.[10] Contributions to the net good, if minor ones. Not something you would expect praise for, but satisfying in their own way. Now the term is, evidently, used more judgmentally to denote a very small action—like sharing a post—that takes almost no effort on the part of the person doing it but makes them feel disproportionately like they have contributed, far beyond what they actually did.

There are a few things to take into consideration here. Firstly, some people don't have the means—in terms of money, or time—to contribute even to causes they care passionately about. For others, liking a post might be the first step on a journey that leads to them joining a campaign off- as well as online. Personally, I am thankful to many people who have shared posts that have allowed me to find out about things that weren't even on my radar before. So I don't think there is any justification for writing off all social media activity as lazy "slacktivism." But there does need to be more to it than just liking a post you have only half read . . .

One example of harmful slacktivism came in the summer of 2020. The murder of George Floyd triggered a necessary refocus on racial justice around the world and awareness around the Black Lives Matter movement quickly swelled. On a day that became known as

Blackout Tuesday, millions of people posted black squares on Instagram; this had snowballed from a day of reflection set up within the music industry by executives Brianna Agyemang and Jamila Thomas.[11] However you feel about that particular wave of slacktivism in theory, it caused problems in practice: hashtags like #BLM had been used by campaigners and organizers to share protest details, donation points, and safety advice, but that information was swiftly drowned out by the tags' use in a tidal wave of black-square posts. There were accusations of "performative allyship," which "refers to someone from a non-marginalized group professing support and solidarity with a marginalized group, but in a way that is not helpful."[12] It's certain that there are many lessons here about the power, limitations and pitfalls of social media when it comes to raising awareness and making change. There was a huge sense of frustration from some that large numbers of people apparently thought they could post a black square and—tick!—that was all their anti-racist work done.

The term "virtue signaling" has been around since at least 2004 but became more popular from 2015 onward; it fully hit mainstream discourse in 2020, largely in relation to the issues I just touched on. When a word is quickly taken up and seems like it is being used everywhere, in traditional media as well as online, it's often because it fulfils a communal need to be able to name something new that has popped up in the cultural conversation. I'd say this was very much the case here, particularly as perceived by people who have experience of offline campaigning, working hard to get an issue into the public eye and then to bring about whatever changes—legal, social, legislative—are needed. I think it's understandable if they find it a bit galling to see someone claim credit for "raising awareness" when they have done little more than a few posts or tweets.

If you google "virtue signaling," at the top of the results you get an Oxford Languages definition (sorry, just one more)—"the public expression of opinions or sentiments intended to demonstrate one's good character"—and the term is flagged as "derogatory." We know that it isn't a term we use to show appreciation or acknowledge moral actions; it's levied as an insult or to criticize someone's behavior.

I can't help but think that this is slightly at odds with some of our most basic desires as human beings. We want other people to like us and think we're good, because it's crucial for our survival that we succeed in communities, but doing something to try to make people like us and think we're good . . . makes them not like us. Navigating human relationships is a lot sometimes.

Confusion aside, I think we can all agree that, yes, it is a Bad Thing for people only to speak about an issue because they think it'll make them look good. Not cool. But can we also try to square that with the fact that we're learning how to do something we used to do differently?

Firstly, we can't know anyone else's true feelings or

intentions—only our own (and sometimes we struggle to untangle even those, let's be honest). Also, in a situation where someone is trying to get the word out about a cause they care a lot about, they may well want people to share posts to raise awareness. If someone asks me to share something and I think it's an important message to get out there, for a cause I'm interested in, should I refuse to share the post in case some people *think* I am only doing it to "look good" or because I want to be associated with a "fashionable cause"? Or, to flip it around, say that was true—I literally couldn't care less about the issue and my only motivation was because I thought it would reflect well on me—still the outcome of me sharing is often going to be the same: the message is amplified and the person who asked me to help them amplify it has achieved what they wanted. In the real world, of course, there are situations where people with public profiles and/or a large number of social media followers can actually prove detrimental to the conversation around an issue; and if you think there is anything on earth for which you will receive universal praise and approval on social media, you will be sadly disappointed.

There are few clear answers here, so let's push the thought experiment a little further to see where it takes us. When I was younger (yes, stand by for another scene-from-my-youth history lesson!), lots of people would make a donation and wear a poppy to mark Remembrance Day, as they still do. (Even now, if people catch a

TV presenter who's forgotten to wear their poppy in November, there is national tutting and head-shaking.) Or you might pop your loose change into a charity bucket outside Tesco and get a sticker in return, which you would wear proudly all day. Casting back to a generation before, people would wear "CND" and "Ban the Bomb" badges, maybe because they really cared about nuclear disarmament or maybe a bit because they were countercultural symbols and therefore came with a certain cultural cachet. Would we label any of these things "virtue signaling" in hindsight?

These days, if I donate to charity online, should I use that "share on social media" button? "I just donated." Why does that feel gross? Is that just me? The charity certainly wants me to use it, as they are in favor of spreading the word as much as possible and it could even prompt someone else to donate. If I don't and I later talk about the cause on social media, someone may assume all I have done is put up a post and that's as far as I care. Whereas I know I have (at least) donated but was . . . what? Too embarrassed or self-conscious to publicly say that? It's true that it can feel icky to use that "share" function, but why does it feel so different to wearing a sticker you got from outside a supermarket on your jumper all day? Because social media feels so public? Because the potentially limitless yet unseen audience has the power to make us feel self-conscious in ways we are still getting our heads around? Or because there is so much judgment floating around that our brains are constantly trying to anticipate it? Trying to mold our actions into ones that nobody can ever find a way to criticize is an impossible game with no winners.

Where can I make a difference?

Going back to the sheer amount of information we have at our fingertips, not only about what is wrong in the world but what people are doing to address it, how do we decide where to put our energy and the other resources we have (e.g., time, money, capacity to understand an issue)? I hope that the discussion at the start of this chapter about things like the oxygen mask theory and negative bias was a useful reminder that it's just not possible to spread ourselves across everything, and to expect that of ourselves risks fatigue and overwhelm. So, OK, what *can* we do?

Of course, the answer for you personally will depend on the whole picture of your life—which I don't have!— but let's look at this question from a few different angles. I think an important thing to consider when we do want to get involved is that while the instinct can be "I can't believe this horrible thing is allowed to happen! I must start a campaign/group/hashtag to show people that I know it's wrong," before we leap into action there will often be people out there who are already doing this work. Would it be more useful to find and join up with them, at least to start with? Do we need to take some time to learn more about the issue and what is likely to make the most difference? For example, no doubt some of the people who posted black squares and used the #BLM hashtag on and around June 2, 2020, really wanted to support this movement. But, with the benefit of hindsight, if they had taken more time to learn about what was happening and the fundamentals of the campaign, would that have represented a much more useful contribution and been of more benefit to our own education? In that situation, at least, almost certainly yes.

When we are used to seeing campaigns played out on social media, and accustomed to the message of "raising awareness," it can feel like the first step should be to get online and talk about the thing you want to change. This is perfectly natural if you are on social media a lot, and of course we have seen many, many examples of how social media has been used as a powerful tool in this way. But it's worth considering the alternatives. For example, is there anything you can do in a more practical way in your community, your school, your industry, your town to help bring about change on a more localized level? Raising awareness of an issue might reach a large number of people and affect them in a small way. But as countless projects and organizations have shown, sometimes it's equally or more effective to impact a smaller number of people in a bigger way. And there's no rule to say you can't do both!

For example, say you are worried about loneliness among older people. You can use social media to remind people who follow you to check in with older neighbors and retweet campaigns from charities like Age UK. Of course you can. But are there volunteering opportunities in your local area that would work for the amount of time and energy you would be able to give? Are there grassroots organizations near where you live that would appreciate a direct donation, if that is what you are looking to do? There are so many people doing "unglamorous" work, invisible to most, which is inspiring and hugely valued by those who benefit from it, and that is something I think gets often overlooked on social media.

In fact, some psychologists recommend actively involving yourself in the most practical way you can as an antidote to "media overload."[13] There is evidence to show that constant news-scrolling can result in something called "learned helplessness," which is when repeatedly facing a negative situation they don't feel they can control makes someone give up trying to change anything, even though they are suffering.[14] It's thought that becoming positively proactive in the areas they are worried about, even on a relatively small scale, can counter this. Numerous studies have found that the positive impacts of volunteering on an individual can include lower blood pressure, a higher sense of general satisfaction in their life, and even longer life expectancy.[15, 16] Like I said, this won't be an option for everyone, but it's good to know that the benefits of taking part in something tangible with a community of like-minded folk comes backed by hard scientific evidence.

On a more day-to-day level, I think it can again come back to supporting others rather than feeling you have to immediately go into "transmit" mode in order to make a difference. I'm certainly not saying it's wrong to be angry about an injustice or that you should *always* wait for someone else to take the lead. It's more about having an awareness of the action you want to take and where that is coming from. I'm never going to love this phrase, but accusations of "virtue signaling" carry more weight when they are responding to a sense of ego, of wanting to be the one who is heard more than wanting to contribute to solving the problem.

It can be lonely and hard campaigning and talking about issues you believe in. Not least because of what so often happens when you put your head above the parapet on social media. So if someone you follow really inspires you and/or you have learned a lot from their posts, it might be worth taking the time to send them a DM or write a thoughtful comment to let them know that their work has had an impact on you. You never know, it might be just what they need to hear that day.

I also think it's possible to make a technically small but still important difference just within our families and friendship groups. Say, as a group, your friends are super-supportive of each other and believe in body positivity, but individually you sometimes put yourselves down in relation to your appearance. Is there a way to have a conversation about this and make a pact that you will always try to talk positively about yourselves? That you will catch each other and cheerfully remind your-selves if you hear any patriarchal noise about body image creeping into the chat? You all feel supported and a tiny bit better, and maybe this even trickles down to the younger women or children in your lives.

Living according to your values

You've probably heard this expression. There have been whole books written about identifying your values and living by them, so I'm not going to attempt to do a deep dive on the subject here, but I do think it's pertinent to mention this in the context of how we can make a differ-ence, for ourselves and others.

The concept has been co-opted by both the business community and the wellness industry, which, depend-ing on the sort of person you are, might lead you to write it off either as corporate bullshit or airy-fairy twaddle. And while I am as suspicious as the next person of the commodification of ideas that have been around for most of human history—by which I mean, haven't phil-osophers always debated what is or should be most meaningful and important in our lives?—research has been done to back this up. For example, a study carried out in 2013 at Carnegie Mellon University in the US found that asking students to identify and focus on their values reduced stress levels, making them better at solv-ing problems.[17] A 2019 study in South Korea found that people who could identify strong intrinsic values (things that come from within, like wanting to prioritize family or friends) were measurably happier than those who had extrinsic values (things that rely on something from outside, like making money or career success).[18]

What the internet would call "living your truth," psychologists might term "values-driven actions derived from personal and social goals."[19] Or, put slightly more generally, most people would agree that it's easier to make decisions and choose a direction of travel if you know where it is you want to end up. This makes sense, although with the caveat that it's always going to be an evolving process and we do need to recognize that we and our priorities are going to change as we go through life.

When you are identifying your values, you are essentially trying to distill the elements of what you care about most. What brings you the most happiness and meaning? Perhaps the things that, when the areas of your life they have the biggest impact on are going well, make you feel most content and like yourself. They might be things like family and friendship groups. Or abstract concepts like freedom or fairness—though in this case you'll want to define exactly what they mean to you. Once you have done that, they become like compasses or touchstones that you can come back to when you need to make a decision or judgment call.

Little kids so often have a burning sense of what is fair and what is not. It's such a beautiful thing and we should try to carry it into adulthood. But at the same time, as we grow up and learn how complicated and challenging the world can be, this can be hard. We can end up with that "learned helplessness" in response to what is presented to us through social and traditional media. But by consciously identifying what is most fundamentally important to us, we can feel more positive about our ability to make a difference and empowered to know what we want to change. Whether that's in our immediate space, our wider community, or even out there (*gestures vaguely*) in the world.

Can it be as simple as "don't be a dick"?

I sometimes wonder if it would make a difference if there were a sort of social media code of conduct. If we could get together and say, "This is the etiquette and this is what we should reasonably be able to expect from one another online." I don't know if there would be any penalties for breaking it; I think I like the idea that there could be some simple agreement of what constitutes good manners online and that would be enough. Just like how you wouldn't turn up somewhere in person and walk straight to the front of the queue—or, if you did, most likely all the people in the queue would be so firm in their united understanding that this is not how queues work that you would know you had broken a social code and trot obediently to the back of the line. (*Such* a British example.)

As I am typing this, though, I feel slightly hesitant. Does this get close to the realms of policing people's behavior? On the one hand, I wholeheartedly believe that a basic level of intra-human respect is very important. It's possible to respectfully disagree and still get your point across firmly. Plus, history is filled with examples of people who brought about change and healed deep wounds between groups by finding a way to speak to their opponents with respect, even when no doubt people from their own communities were shouting at them that the other side didn't deserve any consideration whatsoever.

In the context of this book, a place you have chosen to be and hang out, where you have very generously given me your attention and the space to explain my thoughts, does a statement like "let's be respectful to each other online" sound OK to you? But if I said this online, would people feel like I was telling them to be kind to trolls? To be nice to someone who had discriminated or refused to listen? If I phrased it in terms of "I think people should try to have good manners when interacting online, particularly when discussing emotive topics," does that sound like tone policing? Plus, what constitutes "good manners" is kind of subjective. So would people be angry if they felt that, by that statement, I was saying everyone should behave in a way that I personally find acceptable?

Maybe, reading the above, you think I am being massively oversensitive. "Be polite! Fine! What's so controversial?" Or maybe you have had the experience of saying something that to you was positive and uncontroversial, and yet people responded with outrage. I'm bringing up this scenario here because I think that, as previously discussed, social media *is* a space where we can do some of the work of having important conversations and beginning to make change, even though no one can reasonably expect to start a revolution with a few likes. But if we are constantly shouting each other down and assuming the very worst of every statement we read, how is that impacting the opportunity we have to engage? My fear is that it makes it likely that those who don't enjoy online confrontation, who are very worried about saying the wrong thing, who feel they need to protect their mental health, will back away, leaving the floor clear for people with loud, certain views who couldn't care less about what anyone else thinks. I know that I have definitely "left the room," as it were, when a social media debate got shouty, even when I have cared passionately and known something about the topic in hand. And I have avoided making a comment on an issue, even though I received many messages asking me to and felt I otherwise could, because at the time I didn't feel I was up to dealing with the angry responses when it wasn't exactly what some people wanted to hear. I don't like that about myself, but it is the truth.

So what can we do about this? Realistically, there's probably not going to be a social media code of conduct, however informal, that people will get on board with. But maybe that's OK. What if we each had our own? Maybe this is another case of "be the change you want to see." I wonder if potentially it's a very good exercise to actively think about what we feel is the right sort of etiquette and behavior we would ideally like to see in others—and therefore what we should be doing ourselves. We can't control other people's reactions; we can only control our own. Yes, if someone is being a troll, they don't necessarily deserve kindness. But don't we owe it to ourselves to—as discussed previously—live according to our values?

There is an opportunity here for all of us to proactively engage our brains and decide not only what we, as individuals, think it's OK and not OK to do or say online, but what we should do in future when these boundaries are crossed, either to protect our mental health or to prevent us reacting in a way we are not going to be proud of later. It's totally up to you what your own internal "social media code of conduct" would look like. Maybe you don't believe there is any need for one. That's fine. Mine would take the form of a series of questions, rather than instructions, that I'd ask myself while taking a breath and putting the phone down for a moment, to figure out what's going on in my brain and my body, and if I'm OK with that . . .

- Is this conversation getting us anywhere?

- Is anyone learning anything?

- Am I adding something helpful or am I simply trying to point out someone's error or poor choice of words to score points?

- Have I stopped to think that there is a real person on the other end of this conversation, even when I really disagree with them? (Or *especially* when . . .)
- Would I speak like this to someone if they were sitting in front of me?
- Do I have to react now and form an immediate opinion, or is it the speed and pressures of the social media algorithm that's making me feel like this?
- How *do* I feel? Shaky, weirdly focused, increased heart rate? That's likely the effect of cortisol and adrenaline and a sign my fight-or-flight response has been activated. Good decisions are unlikely to be made here.

It's a fine line to tread when you think that people should be able to go about their own lives as they please, do what makes them happy and be free to be their true selves . . . but you really want to include "don't be a dick" in the list of requirements. Does "don't be a dick" count as policing someone else's behavior? Shouldn't there be a teeny exemption for that one?

Intellectual humility

If you're reading this discussion about being empowered to change the things we want to change in the world and thinking, "But I don't even know what's going on in the world! How does everyone else know all this stuff?!," then this might be a good phrase to remember.

Intellectual humility basically means recognizing what you don't know—and it's a good thing. In fact, it's the best way to guard against all those biases we keep running into. As a review article published in *Nature Reviews Psychology* puts it: "Research suggests that intellectual humility can decrease polarization, extremism and susceptibility to conspiracy beliefs, increase learning and discovery, and foster scientific credibility."[20] Which sounds good, no?

Just to recap, we all have biases. Though biases are sometimes spoken about as if they make you a bad person, it's pretty much impossible to avoid them. As we saw before, it's how our brains are wired. They have to be able to take some shortcuts, or thinking would take ages and we'd never get anything done. Intellectual humility is what makes us question them. It's all the more important when we are in danger of holding on to firm convictions even in the face of evidence to the contrary, or just other people's differing views. It's like open-mindedness but more specifically connected to considering the possible limits of what we know or believe.

So, whether we are hoping to make a difference to our own lives or the world around us, we shouldn't let lack of knowledge or uncertainty in our own viewpoint deter us. Rather, it's an opportunity to go and learn more, to ask questions and to develop ourselves. And it's so much better than the opposite, which is to run in without questioning the origins and reliability of your own opinions. It's fine not to know—if you're willing to learn. If you're certain you've already got it covered, it's likely you're missing opportunities to deepen your knowledge.

I realize that in the previous chapter—two chapters, I suppose—I've had to cover some of the more negative and difficult elements of how we interact with each other, as part of trying to answer the question "Why am I like this?" But I hope this chapter has shown that while we all feel uncertain at times, and it's completely understandable if you feel overwhelmed and saddened by the news, we all have the power to create change.

As we have seen, we humans got to where we are because we developed the ability to cooperate and to balance our cognitive abilities and emotional reactions. All around the world people continue to come together to have important conversations, to learn about each other and to make a difference, in all sorts of ways. We just need to remember that it all starts with curiosity, with appreciating what we don't know and with trying to take care of each other. Even—or especially—when it's hard.

9

CAN I CHANGE MY BRAIN?

I HOPE THAT ALL THIS talk about the things our brains get up to has been enlightening and reassuring, rather than, well, alarming. As I said at the beginning, I have found it hugely helpful to learn more about the processes that shape my thinking and my reactions, to get an objective idea of what's going on up there and why. It reminds me that I'm not an irrational idiot (OK, some days I am a little bit; that's fine, we all are)—there are reasons and explanations for what is going on in my head. A lot of the time—like when I overreact to seeing a spider or do something out of habit—that is some hardwired evolutionary development trying to help me or keep me safe. It's true that I have despaired of my moth-in-a-lampshade ADHD brain for not doing what I want it to, but I still want to remember to say thank you to this brilliant, weird, unique organ that makes me *me*. In fact, I should probably stop talking about it like we are two different entities; although it's helped in getting across what I wanted to say in this paragraph, we are of course one and the same. We are me.

So how are you feeling about your brain right now? Has it helped to learn a bit more about what's going on in there? Will you be conscious of your thought processes and reactions—or potentially those of others around you—in a way that you weren't before?

I realize we have covered a lot of ground here. From prefrontal cortexes to parasocial relationships, the spotlight effect to serotonin. And there's so much more we could have looked at. A lot more tangents that my brain could have gone off on (and very nearly did—thank you, word count limit!). There's always more to learn—for us curious cats and for actual scientists working in the field. One of the things that amazed me when I was researching this book is how regularly the best-regarded experts seem to disagree on the details. That makes me feel excited for all the new theories and discoveries that are no doubt on their way to us over the next few years, that will clarify what we know already and teach us more about ourselves.

In the meantime, though, I thought we should finish by looking at a few interesting examples of science showing us, the hapless toddlers in possession of such machines, how we can harness our brains' amazing power to do more of what we want and less of what we don't. In the sense that, yes, it is great to understand our brains better—but what does this mean for us? Can we change our brains?

Your plasticine brain

The scientific word for our brain's capacity to change is "neuroplasticity." This is what gives us the ability to learn and adapt to our environment; it also means that we can alter our brains through our behavior. Of course, our brains are super "plastic"—which just means that a structure can be molded by outside influences—when we are children. It used to be thought that once we reached adulthood our brains were finished, cooked, and wouldn't change any more. But that's not the case. We continue to change, reorganize, and grow our neural networks, even just by learning to do new things. If we suffer an injury to a particular area of the brain, another area may be able to partly take over its function.[1,2]

The actual mechanics of how this works are (obviously) complicated and take a number of forms—for example, making new synapses (the connections between neurons, the nerve cells that send messages) or strengthening the ones we have already. As we've touched on before, neural pathways that we use a lot develop into sort of . . . established footpaths, as I imagine them, like a well-worn shortcut across a field. The synapses we don't use are eventually eliminated by our brains, in a process called "synaptic pruning."

Each neuron (read: brain cell) has anywhere from a handful to hundreds of thousands of synapses, which can be connections to itself, to neighboring neurons, or even to neurons in a different region of the brain.[3] Synaptic pruning is essentially the process of our brains becoming more efficient, by getting rid of connections that we don't need or aren't using. The most rapid pruning (is anyone else picturing gardening gloves and pruning shears right now?) takes place between roughly the ages of two and sixteen; in the earliest stages it's affected largely by genetics, but later it's based on experiences.[4] That's one reason why mental stimulation is so important for children; it uses their developing synaptic connections and causes them to become permanent, rather than underused and snipped off.

Research has suggested that problems with this "pruning" process could contribute to a wide range of mental health issues that arise during adolescence,[5] and other studies have found that the pruning takes place largely during sleep.[6] This could well explain in part why sleep deprivation results in cognitive impairment.[7] (Can I blame my newborn for any errors in this book? Probably not cool.) Science used to believe that the process had stopped by early adulthood at the latest, but more recently it's been demonstrated that it does in fact continue in adult brains.[8]

If you fancy encouraging a clear-out in your cerebellum, a 2022 study found some evidence that motor learning could be beneficial to the process.[9] Otherwise known as building "muscle memory," motor learning is what happens when we pick up new physical skills such as throwing a ball, chopping vegetables, or typing on a keyboard. There's a sales pitch for you: take a pottery class and trim off the split ends of your brain!

It's not all about getting rid of unused connections, of course; sometimes it's about forming new ones. To keep it as simple as we can, there are two main types of neuro-plasticity: functional and structural. Functional plasticity is the ability our brains have to reorganize themselves. For example, if an area of the brain is damaged, its functions can be moved into other, undamaged areas so we can retain them. Structural plasticity is the brain's ability to change its physical structure, its connections, through the process of learning.[10]

The term for deliberately using techniques to direct our focus and what we pay attention to in order to "rewire" our brain is often referred to as "self-directed neuroplasticity." Practicing something over and over is one simple example of this. Think about learning to juggle, as an obvious one. But it can also stretch to thinking positive thoughts. Our brains learn from repetition, so the more we do something—whether that's a card trick or deliberately focusing on good things over bad—the more we strengthen those pathways in our brain and the better we get at it. Maybe neuroscience isn't so complicated after all . . .

But I'd just like to say here that while neuroplasticity is fascinating—in my humble opinion—it's not magic, or a cure for all ills. I mention that because this scientific concept and some of the associated research have been co-opted by various self-help crazes as evidence that if you buy the right book or follow the right pundit, you have the ability to change your thinking, modify your brain, and therefore achieve whatever you want, or conquer whatever issue you are grappling with. While this is convenient for whoever is selling said book or publicizing said pundit, it obviously comes with the troubling flipside that if you therefore *don't* manage to achieve/cure/get over the thing . . . well, the power to do so lies in your brain, so you clearly haven't worked hard enough to harness it. There are two important facts to note here: 1) this is not at all what the science behind theories of neuroplasticity is suggesting, and 2) the self-help industry is growing all the time and, at the time of writing, is estimated to be worth US $14 billion a year by 2025. This is a lucrative industry that relies on telling us there's something subpar about us and that buying a certain product can fix it. See what I'm getting at?

Want to try some fun and games with neuroplasticity for yourself? In the same way as you might lift weights to exercise your actual muscles, some simple actions can effectively exercise your brain, which can improve, for example, your capacity for emotional regulation and memory. The key thing here is novelty. You know that feeling when you do a new action for the first time—say, you row a boat. When you begin, it feels so weird and awkward. But as you get used to it the action comes more naturally and you can predict which way the boat will go when you pull hard on one of the oars.

Challenges, as well as new experiences, can enhance cognitive function.

Don't fancy boating today? OK, fair enough. Why not try using your nondominant hand to brush your teeth, pour a drink, or operate a computer mouse. Again, it feels weird, doesn't it? But this is forcing you to actively think about what you're doing rather than it being an automatic, passive activity, thereby using neural pathways you usually don't,[11] and maybe forging some new ones! Research has also found that using our nondominant hand means that both the left and right hemispheres of the brain are stimulated. A study of musicians who use both hands to play their instruments found a 9 percent increase in the size of the corpus callosum, the part of the brain that connects the two hemispheres.[12] Aside from doing regular activities in a different way, similar benefits can be unlocked by getting novelty from new experiences, which can be as easy to build into your day as taking a slightly different route on your commute or getting your morning caffeine fix from a new coffee shop.

Meditate to regulate

One activity that's been extensively studied for its relationship with neuroplasticity is meditation. If you were studying meditation and wanted to find some of the most dedicated meditators in the world, where would you turn? Tibetan monks—jackpot. Luckily, over a period of several years, plenty of them have been recruited for brain imaging studies in the Waisman Laboratory for Brain Imaging and Behavior at the University of Wisconsin–Madison. The findings from studying this somewhat extreme sampling found that the monks had, over the course of tens of thousands of hours of practice, in fact changed the structure and function of their brains.[13] Using fMRI scans of both novice and expert meditators' brains, researchers were able to detect alterations in the patterns of their brain function. For example, the amygdalas of the experts were less stimulated by hearing what the report describes as "emotional sounds." In other, albeit highly unscientific words, it seems that the veteran monks' brains had been made functionally more chilled out by their long experience of meditation.

Most of the monks who took part in the study practiced a kind of meditation known as Vipassana. This meditation style is essentially about non-reactivity; you use your senses to be aware in the given moment but without reacting to what you sense or feel. In the ancient Indian language Pāli, Vipassana means "introspection, penetrative vision, observation, and understanding of reality as it is." In simpler and more practical terms for the uninitiated, if you've sat cross-legged in meditation for an hour, you might keenly notice that your knees are stiff or your back aches, but your aim would be not to react to those sensations. Practicing this skill over time theoretically trains a person in not reacting so strongly to the ups and downs of life.

Aside from influencing the chemical pathways in your brain, other studies on meditation have found links between long-term practice and positive effects on the gut microbiome (again, using Tibetan Buddhist monks as their subjects—what a group, very generous with their time/brains/bowels).[14] Compared to controls, the monks' samples were particularly high in levels of certain bacteria including *Bacteroidetes*, *Prevotella*, *Megamonas*, and *Faecalibacterium*, which, according to the research team, have been "associated with the alleviation of mental illness, suggesting that meditation can influence certain bacteria that may have a role in mental health." Aside from a focus on practicing thought patterns, this study offers an alternative explanation for the impact of meditation on mental health through mechanisms that are now often referred to as the microbiota–gut–brain axis. I have to say that my brain is itchy with doubt about cause and effect here. As discussed earlier, it can be very difficult to separate all the factors and pin down a correlation to its cause . . . this study did use control subjects, though, and I have to say I hope that this research avenue proves to be as exciting as it currently sounds. So I guess the question here would be: Change your meditation habits to change your guts to change your brain?

I find it riveting that scientists are studying the reasons behind phenomena that humans have understood for millennia. Or at least, some cultures have understood. Tibetan Buddhist meditation derives from Ayurveda, which is an ancient Indian medical system more than three thousand years old. In the West, meditation wasn't taken particularly seriously until scientists got involved in the 1960s and started "proving" the results—despite it being possibly as old as human civilization and cropping up in different forms throughout the centuries in many different places and religions. You could say that science is starting to show what some people have known all along without feeling any need to read a study about it. Meditation can result in long-lasting changes to the brain, including an improvement in cognitive function and a reduction in age-related brain degeneration.[15,16] It could also prove to be a useful tool in the prevention of diseases that are linked to age-related degeneration of the brain, such as dementia and Alzheimer's,[17] though research is ongoing here.

Shinrin-yoku

I feel like I should say at this point that you don't have to be completely woo-woo to think that there are other ways than scientific research to understand the world and assess whether something has value. Of course not. I love science and it's how I tend to best accept explanations, but I'm not so arrogant as to assume that only things I personally grasp are possible. If you find that doing yoga makes your brain feel like a more peaceful place to be, have ever experienced the phenomenon of a "runner's high" (I'm jealous, frankly), or simply have a warm sense of well-being when all your books are grouped by spine color and size, you may have no need for any scientific investigation into those sensations. And that's A-OK.

Sometimes, though, I find that learning about the science behind a phenomenon or an idea tickles my interest and makes me more likely to try it out. I'm all for embracing mindfulness and self-care, of course, but in a world where these concepts have been commodified and seemingly applied to everything, to the point where they are in danger of becoming meaningless, I do feel more engaged when I know a bit about why or how something might work.

While it's unlikely that you need me to tell you that being out in nature = good brain vibes, I am going to tell you about *shinrin-yoku*, a Japanese term that we in the West translate to "forest bathing," as it's another example of modern science investigating ancient wisdom. The practice has ancient roots within Japanese culture and beyond, but the term *shinrin-yoku* was actually coined in the 1980s by the Japanese Ministry of Agriculture, Forestry, and Fisheries as a way of encouraging people to spend time in nature, taking in the atmosphere of the forest, partly as an antidote to stresses caused by the boom in technology happening at the time, and also for environmental reasons, in the hope that it would make people want to protect their forests.[18] It's not like spending time in nature to promote your well-being is some radical new idea. But, possibly because this is an activity that's been given a specific name, in the 1990s scientists began to research the physiological benefits of *shinrin-yoku*, to try to quantify the benefits of which we may have instinctively already known.

In one study, 155 participants had their blood pressure, pulse, and "profile of mood states" measured before and after spending the day forest bathing. The group was divided into "those with depressive tendencies" (ah, my people) and those without. Both groups showed improvements in the areas that were being analyzed, but particularly the group with depressive tendencies, whose markers were much more in line with those of the "without" group at the end of the day.[19] Other studies have also found a measurable positive effect on blood pressure and the immune system, as well as benefits for those who have trouble sleeping.

Two reasons for some of these health benefits seem to be a higher concentration of oxygen in the forest environment and plant chemicals called phytoncides, oils which form part of a plant's natural defense system against pathogens like bacteria and fungi, which appear to benefit humans when we breathe them in. Beyond the forest, the very act of walking can also be beneficial for relaxation: in fact, a whole form of therapy was born from it. EMDR (Eye Movement Desensitization and Reprocessing) therapy is a style of psychotherapy that allows people to process and move past negative experiences.[20] First developed in 1987 by a psychologist called Dr. Francine Shapiro, EMDR uses side-to-side eye movements in combination with recalling difficult memories, which is particularly helpful for patients with PTSD or anxiety disorders. Through utilizing lateral eye movements, or the "optic flow," that happen as we move through space, comprehending the objects that pass us, we can create a sense of relaxation in the brain.[21] Outside of a therapist's office, we can harness the simple origin of this practice, walking (or otherwise moving forward, perhaps in a wheelchair) to induce a sense of calm. Prescribe me a stroll through the woods, stat.

The power of wow

So how does being in nature change our brains? Or at least alter how we feel for a while? Is it possible to quantify or explain that "ahhhh" feeling of relaxation you get during a particularly good walk? We know instinctively that some environments offer up different "energy" or feel more beneficial to maintaining good mental health than others. What's going on here?

One possible explanation is known as "attentional restoration theory," or ART. This was first proposed in the late 1980s and suggests that when we are constantly exposed to urban environments, we have to actively direct our attention far more often to the things we want or need to notice (looking out for the friend we are meeting, a car coming toward us, advertising everywhere, etc.).[22] When we are in nature, however, we can do less conscious filtering, which means we can generally enjoy the scene more. This might give us more space or mental energy for what are known as "self-regulation processes"—basically having active control over our thoughts and emotions rather than constantly being alert for e-scooters hurtling down the pavement or some stranger trying to snatch our phone. If you're someone who feels relaxed when out meandering through the countryside, this probably rings true.

Another theory about how our brains can be affected by the situation we put them in has to do with a thing that you could call the "awe factor." One definition of awe, from a 2015 psychological study, is "an emotional response to vast stimuli that transcend our current frame of reference."[23] I'm talking about that sort of "wow" feeling when you suddenly become aware that something is so much bigger than you are. It's a feeling of respect mixed with wonder, which gives a sense of scale, reminding you that you're a little human on a big, amazing planet. An obvious example would be when someone looks at some enormous natural feature, like the Grand Canyon or Mosi-oa-Tunya (aka Victoria Falls).

In the 2015 study, researchers found that participants who viewed a towering tree for one minute displayed higher "awe" scores than others who viewed a building of a similar height. Trees are coming off super well in this chapter. Although—as we'll get on to—the sensation isn't just provoked by nature. Maybe you've felt awed by being part of a large spectacle, like a stadium crowd (I know I've certainly experienced that one!).

This is relevant because it's been shown that this

emotional response has a positive effect on some of our behavior in the time after we feel it. As demonstrated in the research I mentioned previously, awe is associated with an increase in prosocial behaviors—in other words, things we do because they benefit others and not just ourselves—including generosity and ethical decision-making. So what's the connection?

A number of studies have been carried out that suggest these effects are in part caused by the feeling of a "small self," which may help people to step back and see themselves within broader social contexts, as well as enhance their concern for others. In other words, it seems that when we are made aware of our relative "smallness," we can become less consumed by our own individual concerns and more likely to see ourselves as part of a collective. In a world where the internet *can* in theory connect people all over the globe, but one in which we can feel more and more isolated from each other, there is something really interesting in this, I think. With all our main-character energy and the amount that we need to focus on ourselves in order to get through the day, to work, to take care of ourselves and our immediate contacts, being reminded that we're all teeny-tiny organisms on the face of an enormous planet, coexisting with billions of others ... There's something pretty magical about that, isn't there? It's worthy of some awe.

In his book *Awe: The New Science of Everyday Wonder and How It Can Transform Your Life*,[24] psychology professor Dacher Keltner explores the relatively young study of awe as a quantifiable field of research and examines how it affects us as social creatures. As we saw before, throughout the history of human evolution it has been our capacity for social comparison, collaboration, and connection that has allowed us to adapt and thrive as a species—our brains are wired to want to work with others. Keltner dives into the role that awe has played in those processes and discusses how we might try to harness our new understanding of the feeling of awe to encourage more prosocial behaviors. Speaking on the podcast *On Being with Krista Tippett*,[25] he explained that this sense of awe also arises from places we might not expect:

> It's other people around us—everyday people—who bring us awe, and what we called moral beauty ... Kindness, courage, overcoming obstacles. You know, saving people's lives. Time and time again, the most common source of awe is other people. And you wouldn't think that given what we look at on [X] and Instagram, but it's a deep tendency to choke up and get tears thinking about what people can do.

I think this is truly lovely. Not only is it the kind of insight into how human beings work that I find fascinating, but it also feels like something very tangible and achievable that we can add to our own lives in the pursuit of self-improvement, or simply enjoying our lives more.

As much as we'd all like to make space in our schedules to spend more time staring at big trees or otherwise awe-inspiring natural stuff, it can be hard when most of us have a lot of other things that make demands on our time on a daily basis. And let's not overlook the fact that, according to the World Bank, around 56 percent of the world, some 4.4 billion people, currently live in urban environments, and a great number of those people simply don't have easy or regular access to forests, woodlands, or other more rural locations.[26] According to the United Nations Population Division, by 2050 a whopping 75 percent of us will live in cities.[27] So there we have inconveniently parallel truths: that spending time in nature is good for us, while fewer of us will be living close to those environments. This is far from ideal for a number of reasons, not least in terms of things like air quality and access to enough outdoor space for exercise and sport. But what I do love is the idea that spending time feeling awed and appreciative of the world around us—including fellow humans, and not just Grand Canyons or large trees—has a measurable effect on how we view and interact with it, making us more generous, socially aware people.

If you can, then, absolutely go and lie under a massive oak; it's not for you, it's for all of our benefit. And whether you live somewhere with access to much awe-inspiring nature or not, you can still pay attention to the kindness and resilience displayed by other human beings. This will provide your brain with a valuable emotional experience, and I'd certainly say it is a way to change your brain that I can get on board with.

Please look after this brain

I know that in an ideal world, we would live in a society perfectly set up for taking care of our brains—a society that acknowledged mental health as well as physical health, and allowed us the space and the understanding to thrive. As we've examined in many of these chapters, though, that isn't always the way it's going, and so it's down to us to do the best we can. I know the examples I've included in this chapter may seem small in comparison to some of the systems or norms we're living with that could be making life harder, but I hope they serve as a reminder that you're not totally powerless in this scenario either. Meditation, spending time in nature or paying attention to the good folks around us aren't paradigm-shifting ideas in self-care, but there is science behind them that you may not have known about and which I personally find wonderfully reassuring.

Fingers crossed, the more we know about how our brains work and the ways we can affect them, the more we'll be able to build a little TLC into our day-to-day. It's a tricky balance—I totally understand that if you are currently experiencing a period of mental ill health, then ideas of lying under a tree to make yourself feel better or trying to foster neuroplasticity in your brain might seem about as helpful as a chocolate teapot. If you are struggling, it's not solely on you to forest-bathe yourself magically back into wellness; you are deserving of professional support. I didn't want to focus on therapy or medication in this chapter as they are personal choices and wildly individual—it simply wouldn't be appropriate as a blanket recommendation—but those are two things that have really helped me during dark periods in the past. Self-care and medical care: it needn't be one or the other.

As I think we are all becoming increasingly aware, our mental health is not something we should only pay attention to when it's not so great. A significant part of looking after our well-being is having a conscious awareness of what helps and what hinders us, and proactively using that information. It's not just vaguely knowing that two hours of uninterrupted scrolling will likely drop us into the comparison trap, whereas half an hour walking round the park while on the phone to a friend will almost certainly improve our mood, but actually putting that knowledge into action.

Remember back in Chapter Three when we looked at habits and how we form them? This is all connected to neuroplasticity, as I'm sure you now see, as we can actively use how our brains form and strengthen neural pathways to challenge the automatic or semi-automatic behaviors we don't like and help us to create new ones that will be better for us.

We have all read self-care advice along the lines of "Have a bath!," "Go for a massage!," "Reduce your blue-light exposure before bed!," and I'm not disagreeing that these are all valid ideas. But what I would like to challenge you to do, as we barrel toward the end of our "Why am I like this?" journey, is to observe yourself and your reactions with a little more scientific curiosity. For example, how does being on social media make you feel? What other things affect your mood? What labels do you put on yourself and do they help or hinder you? Where do you get your news from, and do you ever feel overwhelmed?

Science likes to figure things out by asking questions, coming up with theories and then testing them through studies and experiments. You are a human being and not a science project. Obviously. But you are also the owner of an amazing, complex, and still slightly mysterious brain, one that we know has incredible potential for change and growth. Now that we have gone some way (I hope!) to addressing the question of "Why am I like this?," I wonder if it's time to ask, "How would I like to be?" The answer probably won't be simple, and neither will figuring out how to get there. But it's an exciting place for us to part, don't you think?

Conclusion

"Don't forget you are a space baby. A giant to the ants.
An ant to the giants."

KATIE BENN

I SAW THAT QUOTE ON the artist Katie Benn's Instagram and liked it so much I immediately bought it for my wall. What an amazing thing to remember: that although we live our entire lives inside our own heads, our vast experiences are the only ones we can truly know; each of us is one person among billions of people on a planet among billions of planets.

How do you end a book like this? The only thing I keep coming back to is how I hope you might feel now you're done. We've covered a lot of things that may seem pretty negative on the surface, but I feel that by understanding the reality of how things work, the futility of trying to be anything other than human, we have more space to breathe. There's no point in wishing that you never compared yourself to other people—you will. You're going to notice when negative things happen because that's how we as a species have survived. You'll have feelings about people you've only "met" through the screen of your phone (that you can't stop checking) because you're a person and it's unreasonable to expect otherwise. You might also sometimes forget that they are people too.

You're biased by nature. But you're also capable of secondary thinking, of analyzing and applying that knowledge. You experience the spotlight effect, but you also know what's happening and can tell yourself that feeling is exaggerated. Maybe your friends like going out and you know you'd have a better time staying in—doesn't it somehow feel better to have an idea why? Go anyway, enjoy yourself, and feel justified in leaving when you're done.

Going right back to Chapter One, where we took a brief look at the state of our collective mental health, I hope that knowing things *are* tough right now makes you feel vindicated. The world likes to tell us loudly and often that all we have to do is love ourselves—but that tends to discount all the messy feelings we have along the way, and can even make us feel guilty for struggling to get there.

Being a person is hard. But look at you go! Moseying along with all these things ping-ponging around in your body, influencing your thoughts: negativity bias, flaws in empathy, self-conscious emotions, a need for connection, pattern spotting, competing reward systems ... and still, here you are, trying to learn more about yourself. Making an effort. Caring about being kind, to others and to yourself.

Think about the people around you. Look at yourself and the things you battle every day—then look at the people you love or admire and realize that they're dealing with those things too. Isn't that remarkable? In a world where we try every day to honor and celebrate our differences, we still have so much more in common than there is that divides us.

We are bloody miracles.

I know there will still be people who scoff at the idea that consciously looking after our mental health is important. I probably won't ever change their minds, and that's fine. If you've made it to the end of this book and don't feel like any of the things I've explored have ever made you feel sad or worried or weird, then that's cool! Keep on keeping on, my friend . . . and maybe let us know what the secret is.

If you ever feel small, I hope it's not because the world made you feel that way, but because you're looking around you with awe. Stand tall in your tiny spot in the universe, space baby, and know that you are doing just fine.

Glossary

ADHD—attention deficit hyperactivity disorder; a condition that often results in restlessness, difficulty concentrating, and acting on impulse, sometimes leading to additional problems such as sleep and anxiety disorders.

adrenaline—a neurotransmitter, also known as epinephrine, responsible for our fight-or-flight response to fear or stress.

Alzheimer's disease—a progressive condition affecting multiple brain functions and a leading cause of dementia in people aged over sixty-five.

amino acid—organic molecules that form proteins and so are essential to life; the human body requires twenty (nine of which are known as "essential") to provide energy, grow tissue, digest food, and produce hormones, among many other roles.

amygdala—a region of the brain that plays a major role in emotional processes, as well as memory and learning; closely linked to fear, motivation, and the fight-or-flight response.

aphantasia—the inability to conjure mental images; a condition that can be either congenital or acquired.

bipolar disorder—a mental health condition that causes extreme changes in mood; people with bipolar disorder usually swing between "low" periods (depression) and "high" periods (mania) that can be so pronounced they interfere with everyday life.

CBT—cognitive behavioral therapy; a form of talking therapy commonly used to treat anxiety, depression, and other mental and physical health issues, which helps to relieve symptoms by consciously changing patterns of thought and behavior.

cerebellum—one of the three major parts of the brain (along with the cerebrum and brain stem); responsible for movement, balance, and other cognitive functions, including speech, eye movement, and emotional processing.

DM—direct message; a function of Instagram, TikTok, and many other social media apps.

dopamine—a "feel-good" neurotransmitter that works within our brain's reward centers; also affects concentration, memory, and motivation.

endorphins—neurotransmitters that are particularly stimulated by exercise and help to relieve sensations of pain in the body.

fMRI—functional magnetic resonance imaging; a method of scanning the brain to reveal blood flow to different areas, used for measuring brain activity.

neurodivergent—an umbrella term to describe people whose brains process information differently from the "norm." It can include conditions such as autism spectrum disorder (ASD) or other neurological or developmental conditions such as attention deficit hyperactivity disorder (ADHD).

neurotransmitter—a chemical messenger that passes signals between neurons as part of our nervous system.

Parkinson's disease—a progressive condition caused by loss of nerve cells in the brain that leads to a reduction in dopamine; main symptoms include involuntary shaking, muscle stiffness, and loss of movement, as well as memory, sleep, and balance problems.

prefrontal cortex—a region at the front of the brain responsible for a number of cognitive functions, including speech, memory, risk processing, and decision-making.

PTSD—post-traumatic stress disorder; an anxiety disorder caused by frightening, stressful, or traumatic events that may develop immediately or some time afterward, often causing the person to relive these events through flashbacks or nightmares, as well as other symptoms such as difficulty concentrating and sleeping, isolation, and feelings of guilt.

schizophrenia—a long-term mental health condition thought to be caused by both genetic and environmental factors; psychological symptoms can include hallucinations and delusions, confused thoughts, and social withdrawal.

serotonin—a neurotransmitter that helps to regulate mood, sleep, and appetite, among other functions.

SSRI—selective serotonin reuptake inhibitor; a form of antidepressant that works by preventing the reabsorption of serotonin, thus increasing the amount of free serotonin circulating in the body.

synapse—a junction between two neurons (nerve cells), or a neuron and a muscle cell, that allows an electrical or chemical signal to be passed from one to the next.

tic—fast, repetitive muscle movements that are difficult to control, resulting in involuntary movements of the body (motor tics) or sounds (vocal/phonic tics).

Tourette's syndrome—a condition that causes involuntary sounds and movements known as tics; it often begins during childhood and may improve over time.

umbrella review—one of the highest levels of evidence available in medical research, this is a "review of reviews," or collection and assessment of all the systematic reviews and meta-analyses conducted on one particular topic.

Acknowledgments

Thank you to Millie, who changed the game. To Nat and Izzy for getting me here.

To Adam, for flipping the publishing process upside down to let me lead with people.

To everyone at Transworld: Zoe for taking on this anxious first-time author with such enthusiasm, Steph, Eleanor, Rosie, Izzie, and Beci. To Liz for being the most wonderful surrogate editor and enduring my hormonal phone calls.

To the community of women with missed ADHD who have filled my DMs with an understanding I craved my whole life.

To all the friends who have loved me for me, both before and after I learned to love myself.

To my family, always. My favorite team. My mum, for holding me tight along the way. Watching your child struggle with their mental health must be heartbreaking and you never looked away. H for the pep talks and your endless wisdom. Mish for being my partner, picking up the slack and lifting me back up when this felt impossible. To my little mouse for keeping me company through every chapter, even before you were born.

To all the parasocial relationships and distant cheerleaders. Without you I wouldn't have gotten to do this.

And to you, for giving me your time. I hope you find the awe in yourself that I find in all of us.

Notes

1: WHAT'S HAPPENED TO OUR MENTAL HEALTH?

1 NICE. "Recommendations | Attention Deficit
   Hyperactivity Disorder: Diagnosis and Management."
   National Institute for Health and Care Excellence, 14
   March 2018, www.nice.org.uk/guidance/ng87/chapter
   /Recommendations.

2 Mind. "Mental Health Facts and Statistics." Mind, June
   2020, https://mind.org.uk/information-support/types-of
   -mental-health-problems/mental-health-facts-and
   -statistics/. © Mind. This information is published in full
   at mind.org.uk.

3 American Psychological Association. "Survey: Americans
   Becoming More Open about Mental Health." American
   Psychological Association, 1 May 2019, https://apa.org
   /news/press/releases/2019/05/mental-health-survey.

4 Njoku, Ihuoma. "What Is Mental Illness?" American
   Psychiatric Association, 2022, https://psychiatry.org
   /patients-families/what-is-mental-illness.

5 NICE. "Common Mental Health Problems | Information
   for the Public | Common Mental Health Problems:
   Identification and Pathways to Care | Guidance | NICE."

National Institute for Health and Care Excellence, 25 May 2011, https://nice.org.uk/guidance/cg123/ifp/chapter/Common-mental-health-problems.

6   Mind. "Causes." Mind, October 2017, https://mind.org.uk/information-support/types-of-mental-health-problems/mental-health-problems-introduction/causes/.

7   Morales-Brown, Peter. "Situational Depression vs Clinical Depression: Difference and Diagnosis." *Medical News Today*, 27 July 2023, https://medicalnewstoday.com/articles/314698.

8   American Psychiatric Association. *Diagnostic and Statistical Manual of Mental Disorders*. 5th edition, American Psychiatric Publishing, 2013.

9   Patten, Scott B., et al. "Descriptive Epidemiology of Major Depression in Canada." *The Canadian Journal of Psychiatry*, vol. 51, no. 2, February 2006, pp. 84–90, https://doi.org/10.1177/070674370605100204.

10 Pearson, Caryn, et al. "Mental and Substance Use Disorders in Canada." *Statistics Canada*, 2013, www150.statcan.gc.ca/n1/pub/82-624-x/2013001/article/11855-eng.pdf.

11 Bebbington, P., et al. "The Influence of Age and Sex on the Prevalence of Depressive Conditions: Report from the National Survey of Psychiatric Morbidity." *International Review of Psychiatry*, vol. 15, no. 1–2, January 2003, pp. 74–83, https://doi.org/10.1080/0954026021000045976.

12 Peytrignet, Sebastien, et al. "Children and Young People's Mental Health." *The Health Foundation*, 8 February 2022, www.health.org.uk/news-and-comment/charts-and-infographics/children-and-young-people-s-mental-health.

13 World Health Organization. "Mental Health." World
    Health Organization, 2023, https://who.int/health-topics
    /mental-health#tab=tab_1.

14 Reile, Rainer, and Merike Sisask. "Socio-Economic and
    Demographic Patterns of Mental Health Complaints
    among the Employed Adults in Estonia." *PLOS ONE*,
    edited by Md Nazirul Islam Sarker, vol. 16, no. 10, October
    2021, p. e0258827, https://doi.org/10.1371/journal
    .pone.0258827.

15 Kohl, Ingrid S., et al. "Association between Meatless Diet
    and Depressive Episodes: A Cross-Sectional Analysis of
    Baseline Data from the Longitudinal Study of Adult Health
    (ELSA-Brasil)." *Journal of Affective Disorders*, vol. 320,
    January 2023, pp. 48–56, https://doi.org/10.1016/j
    .jad.2022.09.059.

16 Bryant, Chris. "Vegetarians More Likely to Be Depressed
    than Meat-Eaters—Possible Reasons." *The Conversation*,
    5 October 2022, https://theconversation.com/vegetarians
    -more-likely-to-be-depressed-than-meat-eaters-possible
    -reasons-191707.

17 Henry Ford Health. "Why Is TikTok Giving Teen Girls
    Tics?" Henry Ford Health, 21 March 2022, https://
    henryford.com/blog/2022/03/tiktok-giving-teen-girls-tics.

18 NHS. "Overview—Munchausen Syndrome." NHS, 16
    February 2021, https://nhs.uk/mental-health/conditions
    /munchausen-syndrome/overview/.

19 Chakrabarti, Bhismadev. "Diagnostic Labels for Mental
    Health Conditions Are Not Always Useful." *The
    Conversation*, 10 October 2018, https://theconversation.

com/diagnostic-labels-for-mental-health-conditions-are
-not-always-useful-102943.

20 Mental Health Foundation. "Physical Health and Mental
Health." Mental Health Foundation, 18 February 2022,
https://mentalhealth.org.uk/explore-mental-health
/a-z-topics/physical-health-and-mental-health.

21 De Hert, Marc, et al. "The Intriguing Relationship
between Coronary Heart Disease and Mental Disorders."
Dialogues in Clinical Neuroscience, vol. 20, no. 1, March
2018, pp. 31–40, https://doi.org/10.31887/dcns.2018.20.1
/mdehert.

22 Pescosolido, Bernice A., et al. "'A disease like any other'?
A decade of change in public reactions to schizophrenia,
depression, and alcohol dependence." *American Journal of
Psychiatry*, vol. 167, no. 11, 1 November 2010, pp. 1321–1330,
https://doi.org/10.1176/appi.ajp.2010.09121743.

23 Pilkington, Pamela D., et al. "The Australian public's
beliefs about the causes of depression: Associated Factors
and changes over 16 years." *Journal of Affective Disorders*,
vol. 150, no. 2, 5 September 2013, pp. 356–362, https://doi
.org/10.1016/j.jad.2013.04.019.

24 Moncrieff, Joanna, et al. "The serotonin theory of
depression: A Systematic Umbrella Review of the
evidence." *Molecular Psychiatry*, vol. 28, no. 8,
20 July 2022, pp. 3243–3256, https://doi.org/10.1038
/s41380-022-01661-0.

25 Goedeke, Anne. "Justice for Millions of Americans
Prescribed Antidepressants for a Chemical Imbalance of
the Brain That Doesn't Exist?" *EIN News*, 18 August 2022,
https://einnews.com/pr_news/586580219/justice-for

-millions-of-americans-prescribed-antidepressants-for
-a-chemical-imbalance-of-the-brain-that-doesn-t-exist.

26 Jauhar, Sameer, et al. "A Leaky Umbrella Has Little Value:
    Evidence Clearly Indicates the Serotonin System Is
    Implicated in Depression." *Molecular Psychiatry*, vol. 28,
    June 2023, pp. 1–4, https://doi.org/10.1038/s41380-023
    -02095-y.

27 King's College London. "A Response to 'the Serotonin
    Theory of Depression: A Systematic Umbrella Review of
    the Evidence.'" King's College London, 19 June 2023,
    https://kcl.ac.uk/news/a-response-to-the-serotonin-theory
    -of-depression-a-systematic-umbrella-review-of-the
    -evidence.

28 Smith, Dana. "Antidepressants Don't Work the Way Many
    People Think." *New York Times*, 8 November 2022, https://
    nytimes.com/2022/11/08/well/mind/antidepressants
    -effects-alternatives.html.

29 Jauhar, Sameer, et al. "Fifty Years On: Serotonin and
    Depression." *Journal of Psychopharmacology*, vol. 37, no. 3,
    March 2023, p. 026988112311618, https://doi.org/10.1177
    /02698811231161813.

30 Science Media Centre. "Expert Reaction to a Review Paper
    on the 'Serotonin Theory of Depression' | Science Media
    Centre." Science Media Centre, 20 July 2022, https://
    sciencemediacentre.org/expert-reaction-to-a-review
    -paper-on-the-serotonin-theory-of-depression/.

31 Jauhar, Sameer, et al. "Fifty Years On: Serotonin and
    Depression." *Journal of Psychopharmacology*, vol. 37, no. 3,

March 2023, p. 026988112311618, https://doi.org/10.1177
/02698811231161813.

2: WHY ARE WE LIKE THIS?

1   Herculano-Houzel, Suzana. "In the Light of Evolution."
    In the Light of Evolution: Volume VI: Brain and Behavior,
    edited by George Striedter et al., vol. 6, National
    Academies Press, 2013.

2   Kwon, Diana. "What Makes Our Brains Special?" *Scientific
    American*, 24 November 2015, https://scientificamerican.
    com/article/what-makes-our-brains-special/.

3   Johns Hopkins Medicine. "Brain Anatomy and How the
    Brain Works." Johns Hopkins Medicine, 2024, https://
    hopkinsmedicine.org/health/conditions-and-diseases
    /anatomy-of-the-brain.

4   Ibid.

5   Mora-Bermúdez, Felipe, et al. "Differences and Similarities
    between Human and Chimpanzee Neural Progenitors
    during Cerebral Cortex Development." *ELife*, vol. 5,
    September 2016, https://doi.org/10.7554/elife.18683.

6   Shmerling, Robert. "Right Brain/Left Brain, Right?"
    Harvard Health Blog, 28 July 2017, https://health.harvard
    .edu/blog/right-brainleft-brain-right-2017082512222.

7   Knecht, S., et al. "Handedness and hemispheric language
    dominance in healthy humans." *Brain*, vol. 123, no. 12,
    1 December 2000, pp. 2512–2518, https://doi.org/10.1093
    /brain/123.12.2512.

8   National Institute of Neurological Disorders and Stroke.
    "Brain Basics: Know Your Brain | National Institute of

Neurological Disorders and Stroke." National Institute of Neurological Disorders and Stroke, 2022, https://ninds.nih .gov/health-information/public-education/brain-basics /brain-basics-know-your-brain.

9   Goyal, Nishant, et al. "Neuropsychology of Prefrontal Cortex." *Indian Journal of Psychiatry*, vol. 50, no. 3, 2008, p. 202, https://doi.org/10.4103/0019-5545.43634.

10 University of Queensland. "The Limbic System." University of Queensland, 24 January 2019, https://qbi.uq.edu.au /brain/brain-anatomy/limbic-system.

11 Cherry, Kendra. "Why Phrenology Is Now Considered a Pseudoscience." *Verywell Mind*, 2018, https://verywellmind .com/what-is-phrenology-2795251.

12 Harvard University. "Scientific Racism." *Harvard Library*, 2022, https://library.harvard.edu/confronting-anti-black -racism/scientific-racism.

13 Becker, Heike. "Auschwitz to Rwanda: The Link between Science, Colonialism and Genocide." *The Conversation*, 26 January 2017, https://theconversation.com/auschwitz -to-rwanda-the-link-between-science-colonialism-and -genocide-71730.

14 Janik, Erika. "The Shape of Your Head and the Shape of Your Mind." *The Atlantic*, 6 January 2014, https:// theatlantic.com/health/archive/2014/01/the-shape -of-your-head-and-the-shape-of-your-mind/282578/.

15 Kwon, Diana. "What Makes Our Brains Special?" *Scientific American*, 24 November 2015, https://scientificamerican .com/article/ what-makes-our-brains-special/.

16   Bat Conservation Trust. "Types of Bats—about Bats."
     Bat Conservation Trust, https://bats.org.uk/about-bats
     /what-are-bats.

17   Smithsonian National Museum of Natural History.
     "Australopithecus Afarensis." *The Smithsonian Institution's
     Human Origins Program*, Smithsonian National Museum
     of Natural History, 25 January 2010, https://humanorigins
     .si.edu/evidence/human-fossils/species/australopithecus
     -afarensis.

18   Kingston, Clare. "Did the Discovery of Cooking Make
     Us Human?" *BBC News*, 2 March 2010, https://news.bbc
     .co.uk/1/hi/8543906.stm.

19   Rodríguez Arce, José Manuel, and Michael James
     Winkelman. "Psychedelics, Sociality, and Human
     Evolution." *Frontiers in Psychology*, vol. 12, Sept. 2021,
     https://doi.org/10.3389/fpsyg.2021.729425.

20   Scogna, Kathleen. "How Your Baby's Brain Develops |
     BabyCenter." *BabyCenter*, 2022, https://babycenter.com
     /pregnancy/your-baby/fetal-development-your-babys
     -brain_20004924.

21   Glowacka, Halszka. "Babies, Birth, and Brains."
     Ask an Anthropologist, 6 November 2015, https://
     askananthropologist.asu.edu/stories/babies-birth-and
     -brains.

22   Weintraub, Karen. "The Adult Brain Does Grow New
     Neurons after All, Study Says." *Scientific American*, 25
     March 2019, https://scientificamerican.com/article/the
     -adult-brain-does-grow-new-neurons-after-all-study-says/.

23   Dance, Amber. "Making and Breaking Connections in the Brain." *Knowable Magazine*, Annual Reviews, 18 August 2020, https://knowablemagazine.org/content/article /health-disease/2020/what-does-a-synapse-do.

24   Center on the Developing Child. "Five Numbers to Remember about Early Childhood Development." *Center on the Developing Child*, Harvard University, 2009, https:// developingchild.harvard.edu/resources/five-numbers -to-remember-about-early-childhood-development/.

25   Perez, Alejandro. "When Does the Brain Stop Developing?" *Think Twice*, University of Texas at Austin, 21 February 2022, https://sites.utexas.edu/think-twice/2022/02/21 /when-does-the-brain-stop-developing/.

26   GoodTherapy. "Prefrontal Cortex." *GoodTherapy.org Therapy Blog*, 18 August 2015, https://goodtherapy.org /blog/psychpedia/prefrontal-cortex.

27   National Institute of Mental Health. "The Teen Brain: 7 Things to Know." National Institute of Mental Health, 2020, https://nimh.nih.gov/health/publications /the-teen-brain-7-things-to-know.

28   National Institute of Neurological Disorders and Stroke. "Brain Basics: The Life and Death of a Neuron." National Institute of Neurological Disorders and Stroke, https:// ninds.nih.gov/health-information/public-education /brain-basics/brain-basics-life-and-death-neuron.

3: WHAT WAS I THINKING?

1   Kale, Sirin. "The Last Great Mystery of the Mind: Meet the People Who Have Unusual—or Non-Existent—Inner

Voices." *Guardian*, 25 October 2021, https://theguardian
.com/science/2021/oct/25/the-last-great-mystery-of-the
-mind-meet-the-people-who-have-unusual-or-non
-existent-inner-voices.

2 Westfall, Michele, et al. "Does Someone Who Was Born
with a Hearing Loss 'Hear' an Inner Voice?" *Quora*, 2019,
https://quora.com/Deafness-physiological-condition
/Does-someone-who-was-born-with-a-hearing-loss-hear
-an-inner-voice.

3 McGuire, P. K., et al. "Neural Correlates of Thinking in
Sign Language." *NeuroReport*, vol. 8, no. 3, February 1997,
pp. 695–98, https://doi.org/10.1097/00001756-199702100
-00023.

4 Fernyhough, Charles. "Do Deaf People Hear an Inner
Voice? | Psychology Today United Kingdom." *Psychology
Today*, 24 January 2014, https://psychologytoday.com/gb
/blog/the-voices-within/201401/do-deaf-people-hear
-inner-voice.

5 Vinney, Cynthia. "Does Everyone Have an Inner
Monologue?" *Verywell Mind*, 28 November 2022,
https://verywellmind.com/does-everyone-have-an
-inner-monologue-6831748.

6 Hurlburt, Russell T., et al. "Toward a Phenomenology of
Inner Speaking." *Consciousness and Cognition*, vol. 22, no.
4, December 2013, pp. 1477–94, https://doi.org/10.1016/j
.concog.2013.10.003.

7 Cleveland Clinic. "Aphantasia: Thinking That's out of
Sight." Cleveland Clinic, https://my.clevelandclinic.org
/health/symptoms/25222-aphantasia.

8   Yadav, Riya. "Sigmund Freud and Penis Envy—a Failure of Courage?" *BPS*, 8 May 2018, https://bps.org.uk/psychologist /sigmund-freud-and-penis-envy-failure-courage.

9   Cherry, Kendra. "Sigmund Freud's Psychoanalytic Theories in Psychology." *Verywell Mind*, 2022, https://verywellmind .com/freudian-theory-2795845.

10   Mcleod, Saul. "Unconscious Mind | Simply Psychology." *Simply Psychology*, 25 January 2024, https:// simplypsychology.org/unconscious-mind.html.

11   Hanson-Baiden, Joelle. "The Debate on Repressed Memories." *News-Medical.net*, 10 January 2022, https:// news-medical.net/health/The-Debate-on-Repressed -Memories.aspx.

12   Chew, Stephen L. "Myth: We Only Use 10% of Our Brains." *Association for Psychological Science—APS*, 29 August 2018, https://psychologicalscience.org /uncategorized/myth-we-only-use-10-of-our-brains.html.

13   Bargh, John A. *Social Psychology and the Unconscious: The Automaticity of Higher Mental Processes*. Psychology Press, 2007, p. 32.

14   Hemingway, Ernest. *A Moveable Feast*. London, Arrow Books, 2011.

15   Creswell, John David, et al. "Neural Reactivation Links Unconscious Thought to Decision-Making Performance." *Social Cognitive and Affective Neuroscience*, vol. 8, no. 8, May 2013, pp. 863–69, https://doi.org/10.1093/scan/nst004.

16   Pillay, Srini. "Your Brain Can Only Take so Much Focus." *Harvard Business Review*, 20 December 2018, https://hbr .org/2017/05/your-brain-can-only-take-so-much-focus.

17   Siliezar, Juan. "Daniel Lieberman Busts Exercising Myths." *Harvard Gazette*, 9 November 2023, https://news .harvard.edu/gazette/story/2021/01/daniel-lieberman -busts-exercising-myths/.

18   Mendelsohn, Alana I. "Creatures of Habit: The Neuroscience of Habit and Purposeful Behavior." *Biological Psychiatry*, vol. 85, no. 11, June 2019, pp. e49–51, https://doi.org/10.1016/j.biopsych.2019.03.978.

19   Neal, D. T., W. Wood, and J. M. Quinn. "Habits—a repeat performance." *Current Directions in Psychological Science*, vol. 15, no. 4, August 2006, pp. 198–202, https://doi .org/10.1111/j.1467-8721.2006.00435.x.

20   Duhigg, Charles. "Habits: How They Form and How to Break Them." *NPR*, 2019, https://npr.org/2012/03/05 /147192599/habits-how-they-form-and-how-to-break-them.

21   Neal, D. T., W. Wood, and J. M. Quinn. "Habits—a repeat performance." *Current Directions in Psychological Science*, vol. 15, no. 4, August 2006, pp. 198–202, https://doi.org /10.1111/j.1467-8721.2006.00435.x.

22   Barkman, Robert C. "Why the Human Brain Is so Good at Detecting Patterns." *Psychology Today*, 19 May 2021, https:// psychologytoday.com/gb/blog/singular-perspective/202105 /why-the-human-brain-is-so-good-detecting-patterns.

23   Simion, Francesca, and Elisa Di Giorgio. "Face Perception and Processing in Early Infancy: Inborn Predispositions and Developmental Changes." *Frontiers in Psychology*, vol. 6, no. 969, July 2015, https://doi.org/10.3389/fpsyg.2015 .00969.

24 Reid, Vincent M., et al. "The Human Fetus Preferentially
    Engages with Face-like Visual Stimuli." *Current Biology*,
    vol. 27, no. 12, June 2017, pp. 1825–28.e3, https://doi.org
    /10.1016/j.cub.2017.05.044.

25 Mattson, Mark P. "Superior pattern processing is the
    essence of the evolved human brain." *Frontiers in
    Neuroscience*, vol. 8, 22 August 2014, https://doi.org
    /10.3389/fnins.2014.00265.

26 Shukla, Aditya. "Why Did Humans Evolve Pattern
    Recognition Abilities?" *Cognition Today*, 6 October 2019,
    https://cognitiontoday.com/why-did-humans-evolve
    -pattern-recognition-abilities/.

27 Cherry, Kendra. "What Is Cognitive Bias?" *Verywell Mind*,
    7 November 2020, https://verywellmind.com/what-is-a
    -cognitive-bias-2794963.

28 The Open University. "Are You Better than the Average
    Driver?" *Faculty of Arts and Social Sciences*, The Open
    University, 16 November 2020, https://fass.open.ac.uk
    /school-psychology-counselling/news/are-you-better
    -average-driver.

29 Perel, Esther. "From Esther Perel's Blog—Letters from
    Esther #23: Stories." *Estherperel.com*, https://estherperel
    .com/blog/letters-from-esther-23-stories.

4: KNOWING ME, KNOWING YOU?

1   Neuroscience News. "Dunbar's Number: Why the Theory
    That Humans Can Only Maintain 150 Friendships Has
    Withstood 30 Years of Scrutiny." *Neuroscience News*, 28

August 2021, https://neurosciencenews.com/dunbars -number-social-brain-19210/.

2   Han, Sheon. "You Can Only Maintain so Many Close Friendships." *The Atlantic*, 20 May 2021, https:// theatlantic.com/family/archive/2021/05/robin-dunbar -explains-circles-friendship-dunbars-number/618931/.

3   DeSilva, Jeremy M., et al. "When and Why Did Human Brains Decrease in Size? A New Change-Point Analysis and Insights from Brain Evolution in Ants." *Frontiers in Ecology and Evolution*, vol. 9, October 2021, https://doi .org/10.3389/fevo.2021.742639.

4   Centers for Disease Control and Prevention. "Loneliness and Social Isolation Linked to Serious Health Conditions." CDC, 29 April 2021, https://cdc.gov/aging/publications /features/lonely-older-adults.html.

5   Psych Central. "About Oxytocin." *Psych Central*, 17 May 2016, https://psychcentral.com/lib/about-oxytocin#1.

6   Wu, Katherine. "Love, Actually: The Science behind Lust, Attraction, and Companionship." *Science in the News*, Harvard University, 14 February 2017, https://sitn.hms .harvard.edu/flash/2017/love-actually-science-behind -lust-attraction-companionship/.

7   Cleveland Clinic. "Dopamine." Cleveland Clinic, 23 March 2022, https://my.clevelandclinic.org/health/articles /22581-dopamine.

8   Hobgood, Donna K. "ABO B Gene Is Associated with Introversion Personality Tendancies through Linkage with Dopamine Beta Hydroxylase Gene." *Medical Hypotheses*,

vol. 148, March 2021, https://doi.org/10.1016/j.mehy
.2021.110513.

9   Cleveland Clinic. "Neurotransmitters: What They Are,
Functions & Types." Cleveland Clinic, 14 March 2022,
https://my.clevelandclinic.org/health/articles
/22513-neurotransmitters.

10 Rammsayer, Thomas H. "Extraversion and Dopamine."
European Psychologist, vol. 3, no. 1, March 1998, pp. 37–50,
https://doi.org/10.1027/1016-9040.3.1.37.

11 Hollins, Peter. *The Science of Introverts*. PublishDrive, 2019.

12 Golimbet, V. E., et al. "Relationship between Dopamine
System Genes and Extraversion and Novelty Seeking."
Neuroscience and Behavioral Physiology, vol. 37, no. 6, July
2007, pp. 601–6, https://doi.org/10.1007/s11055-007-0058-8.

13 Xu, Shiyong, et al. "Personality and Neurochemicals in the
Human Brain: A Preliminary Study Using ^{1}H MRS."
Chinese Science Bulletin, vol. 50, no. 20, October 2005, pp.
2318–22, https://doi.org/10.1007/bf03183742.

14 Baumeister, Roy F., and Mark R. Leary. "The Need to Belong:
Desire for Interpersonal Attachments as a Fundamental
Human Motivation." *Psychological Bulletin*, vol. 117, no. 3,
1995, pp. 497–529, https://researchgate.net/profile/Mark
-Leary-2/publication/15420847_The_Need_to_Belong
_Desire_for_Interpersonal_Attachments_as_a
_Fundamental_Human_Motivation/links
/5b647053aca272e3b6af9211/The-Need-to-Belong-Desire
-for-Interpersonal-Attachments-as-a-Fundamental
-Human-Motivation.pdf.

15   Landau, Elizabeth. "How to Understand Extreme Numbers." *Nautilus*, 15 February 2017, https://nautil.us /how-to-understand-extreme-numbers-236443/.

16   Lawler, Moira. "What Are Parasocial Relationships—and Are They Healthy?" *Everyday Health*, 7 May 2024, https:// everydayhealth.com/emotional-health/what-are-parasocial -relationships-and-are-they-healthy.

17   Lindsay, Kate. "The Hard Part of Being a Follower." *Embedded*, 22 May 2023, https://embedded.substack .com/p/the-hard-part-of-being-a-follower.

18   Begley, Sharon. "Why You Click with Certain People." *Greater Good*, 16 August 2018, https://greatergood .berkeley.edu/article/item/why_you_click_with _certain_people.

19   Bowsher-Murray, Claire, et al. "The Components of Interpersonal Synchrony in the Typical Population and in Autism: A Conceptual Analysis." *Frontiers in Psychology*, vol. 13, June 2022, https://doi.org/10.3389 /fpsyg.2022.897015.

20   Yun, Kyongsik, et al. "Interpersonal Body and Neural Synchronization as a Marker of Implicit Social Interaction." *Scientific Reports*, vol. 2, no. 1, December 2012, pp. 1–8, https://doi.org/10.1038/srep00959.

21   Parkinson, Carolyn, et al. "Similar Neural Responses Predict Friendship." *Nature Communications*, vol. 9, no. 1, January 2018, https://doi.org/10.1038/s41467-017-02722-7.

22   Begley, Sharon. "You Had Me at Hello." *Mindful*, 25 June 2018, https://mindful.org/you-had-me-at-hello/.

23 Inagaki, Tristen K., and Naomi I. Eisenberger. "Shared Neural Mechanisms Underlying Social Warmth and Physical Warmth." *Psychological Science*, vol. 24, no. 11, September 2013, pp. 2272–80, https://doi.org/10.1177 /0956797613492773.

24 Williams, Lawrence E., and John A. Bargh. "Experiencing Physical Warmth Promotes Interpersonal Warmth." *Science*, vol. 322, no. 5901, October 2008, pp. 606–7, https:// doi.org/10.1126/science.1162548.

25 Hall, Jeffrey A. "How Many Hours Does It Take to Make a Friend?" *Journal of Social and Personal Relationships*, vol. 36, no. 4, March 2018, pp. 1278–96, https://doi.org/10.1177 /0265407518761225.

5: WHY DO WE GET STUCK IN THE COMPARISON TRAP?

1 Ehrmann, Max, Copyright Claimant, and Bertha Pratt Ehrmann. *Desiderata*. [Between 1920 and 1960] Photograph. Retrieved from the Library of Congress, www.loc.gov/item/2015648050/.

2 TheoryHub. "Social Comparison Theory." Newcastle University, https://open.ncl.ac.uk/academic-theories/34 /social-comparison-theory/.

3 Summerville, Amy, and Neal J. Roese. "Dare to Compare: Fact-Based versus Simulation-Based Comparison in Daily Life." *Journal of Experimental Social Psychology*, vol. 44, no. 3, May 2008, pp. 664–71, https://doi.org/10.1016/j .jesp.2007.04.002.

4 Davidai, Shai, and Sebastian Deri. "The Second Pugilist's Plight: Why People Believe They Are above Average but

Are Not Especially Happy about It." *Journal of Experimental Psychology: General*, vol. 148, no. 3, March 2019, pp. 570–87, https://doi.org/10.1037/xge0000580.

5 Pilat, Dan, and Sekoul Krastev. "Why Do We Feel like We Stand out More than We Really Do?" *The Decision Lab*, https://thedecisionlab.com/biases/spotlight-effect.

6 Gilovich, Thomas, et al. "The Spotlight Effect in Social Judgment: An Egocentric Bias in Estimates of the Salience of One's Own Actions and Appearance." *Journal of Personality and Social Psychology*, vol. 78, no. 2, 2000, pp. 211–22, https://doi.org/10.1037/0022-3514.78.2.211.

7 The Thought Centre. "How to Balance Your Thinking Using CBT." *The Thought Centre*, 18 April 2022, https://thethoughtcentre.ca/blog/balanced-thinking-cbt.

8 Lewis, Michael. "Emotions: Self-Consciouness." Encyclopedia on Early Childhood Development, September 2022, https://child-encyclopedia.com/emotions/according-experts/self-conscious-emotions.

9 Blakeslee, Sandra. "A Small Part of the Brain, and Its Profound Effects." *New York Times*, 6 February 2007, https://nytimes.com/2007/02/06/health/psychology/06brain.html.

10 Rakshit, Devrupa. "The Science behind Why We Blush." *The Swaddle*, 2 September 2020, https://theswaddle.com/the-science-behind-why-we-blush.

11 Dijk, Corine, et al. "The Remedial Value of Blushing in the Context of Transgressions and Mishaps." *Emotion*, vol. 9, no. 2, 2009, pp. 287–91, https://doi.org/10.1037/a0015081.

12   Clance, Pauline Rose, and Suzanne Ament Imes. "The
      Imposter Phenomenon in High Achieving Women:
      Dynamics and Therapeutic Intervention." *Psychotherapy:
      Theory, Research & Practice*, vol. 15, no. 3, 1978, pp. 241–47,
      https://doi.org/10.1037/h0086006.

13   BBC. "Michelle Obama: 'I Still Have Impostor Syndrome.'"
      BBC News, 4 December 2018, https://bbc.co.uk/news
      /uk-46434147.

14   Bravata, Dena M., et al. "Prevalence, Predictors, and
      Treatment of Impostor Syndrome: A Systematic Review."
      Journal of General Internal Medicine, vol. 35, no. 4,
      December 2019, pp. 1252–75, https://doi.org/10.1007
      /s11606-019-05364-1.

15   Cambridge Dictionary. "Syndrome." *Cambridge
      Dictionary*, 13 April 2022, https://dictionary.cambridge.
      org/dictionary/english/syndrome.

16   Tulshyan, Ruchika, and Jodi-Ann Burey. "Stop Telling
      Women They Have Imposter Syndrome." *Harvard Business
      Review*, 11 February 2021, https://hbr.org/2021/02
      /stop-telling-women-they-have-imposter-syndrome.

17   Indeed. "Working on Wellbeing: Mental Health and
      Wellness in the UK Workplace 2022 Report." *Indeed*,
      8 May 2022, https://uk.indeed.com/lead/working-on
      -wellbeing-2022-report.

18   Phan, Janet T. "Apply to a Job, Even If You Don't Meet
      All Criteria." *Harvard Business Review*, 20 July 2022,
      https://hbr.org/2022/07/apply-to-a-job-even-if-you-dont
      -meet-all-criteria.

19 Corbett, Holly. "How to Be an Ally for Black Women in the Workplace." *Forbes*, 2 February 2022, https://forbes .com/sites/hollycorbett/2022/02/22/how-to-be-an-ally-for -black-women-in-the-workplace/. From Forbes. © 2022 Forbes Media LLC. All rights reserved. Used under license.

20 McGregor, Loretta Neal, et al. "I Feel like a Fraud and It Depresses Me: The Relation between the Impostor Phenomenon and Depression." *Social Behavior and Personality: An International Journal*, vol. 36, no. 1, January 2008, pp. 43–48, https://doi.org/10.2224/sbp.2008.36.1.43.

21 Jones, Anna. "The Link between Imposter Syndrome and Burnout." *BBC*, 18 May 2022, https://bbc.com/worklife /article/20220517-the-link-between-imposter-syndrome -and-burnout.

22 Indeed. "Working on Wellbeing: Mental Health and Wellness in the UK Workplace 2022 Report." *Indeed*, 8 May 2022, https://uk.indeed.com/lead/working-on-wellbeing -2022-report.

23 Abramson, Ashley. "How to Overcome Impostor Phenomenon." American Psychological Association, 1 June 2021, www.apa.org/monitor/2021/06/cover -impostor-phenomenon.

6: IS SOCIAL MEDIA CHANGING OUR BRAINS?

1   Tolentino, Jia. "The Age of Instagram Face." *New Yorker*, 12 December 2019, https://newyorker.com/culture/decade -in-review/the-age-of-instagram-face.

2   Yalcinkaya, Günseli. "We Have Entered the Age of TikTok Face." *Dazed*, 22 January 2024, https://dazeddigital.com

/beauty/article/61762/1/the-real-problem-with-pretty
-privilege-and-tiktok-category-trends.

3   Neuroscience News. "Social Media Algorithms Distort
    Social Instincts and Fuel Misinformation." Neuroscience
    News, 3 August 2023, https://neurosciencenews.com
    /social-media-behavior-misinformation-23752/.

4   Brady, William. "Social Media Algorithms Warp How
    People Learn from Each Other." Scientific American,
    25 August 2023, https://scientificamerican.com/article
    /social-media-algorithms-warp-how-people-learn-from
    -each-other/.

5   Vogels, Emily A., and Risa Gelles-Watnick. "Teens and
    Social Media: Key Findings from Pew Research Center
    Surveys." Pew Research Center, 24 April 2023, https://
    pewresearch.org/short-reads/2023/04/24/teens-and-social
    -media-key-findings-from-pew-research-center-surveys/.

6   Amnesty International. "'We Are Totally Exposed': Young
    People Share Concerns about Social Media's Impact on
    Privacy and Mental Health in Global Survey." Amnesty
    International, 7 February 2023, https://amnesty.org/en
    /latest/news/2023/02/children-young-people-social-media
    -survey-2/.

7   Milmo, Dan. "Frances Haugen: 'I Never Wanted to Be a
    Whistleblower. But Lives Were in Danger.'" Guardian,
    24 October 2021, https://theguardian.com/technology
    /2021/oct/24/frances-haugen-i-never-wanted-to-be-a
    -whistleblower-but-lives-were-in-danger.

8   Gayle, Damien. "Facebook Aware of Instagram's Harmful
    Effect on Teenage Girls, Leak Reveals." Guardian, 14

September 2021, https://theguardian.com/technology
/2021/sep/14/facebook-aware-instagram-harmful-effect
-teenage-girls-leak-reveals.

9   Levine, Alexandra S. "Facebook Changes Its Name to
    'Meta' amid Backlash to Whistleblower Revelations."
    POLITICO, 28 October 2021, https://politico.com
    /news/2021/10/28/facebook-meta-whistleblower-517449.

10 Wells, Georgia, et al. "Facebook Knows Instagram Is Toxic
    for Teen Girls, Company Documents Show." *Wall Street
    Journal*, 14 September 2021, https://wsj.com/articles
    /facebook-knows-instagram-is-toxic-for-teen-girls
    -company-documents-show-11631620739.

11 Gayle, Damien. "Facebook Aware of Instagram's Harmful
    Effect on Teenage Girls, Leak Reveals." *Guardian*, 14
    September 2021, https://theguardian.com/technology
    /2021/sep/14/facebook-aware-instagram-harmful-effect
    -teenage-girls-leak-reveals.

12 Cleveland Clinic. "Dopamine." Cleveland Clinic, 23 March
    2022, https://my.clevelandclinic.org/health/articles
    /22581-dopamine.

13 Weinschenk, Susan. "The Dopamine Seeking–Reward
    Loop." *Psychology Today*, 28 February 2018, https://
    psychologytoday.com/gb/blog/brain-wise/201802
    /the-dopamine-seeking-reward-loop.

14 Gantt, Horsley. "Ivan Pavlov—Opposition to Communism."
    Encyclopedia Britannica, 2019, https://britannica.com
    /biography/Ivan-Pavlov/Opposition-to-communism.

15 Sauer, Vera J., et al. "The Phantom in My Pocket:
    Determinants of Phantom Phone Sensations." *Mobile*

Media & Communication, vol. 3, no. 3, January 2015, pp. 293–316, https://doi.org/10.1177/2050157914562656.

16   Marr, Bernard. "Digital Addiction: Should You Be Worried?" *Forbes*, 11 January 2023, https://forbes.com /sites/bernardmarr/2023/01/11/digital-addiction-should -you-be-worried/.

17   Cooper, Anderson. "What Is 'Brain Hacking'? Tech Insiders on Why You Should Care." *CBS News*, 9 April 2017, https://cbsnews.com/news/brain-hacking-tech-insiders -60-minutes/.

18   Blanchflower, David G. "Is Happiness U-Shaped Everywhere? Age and Subjective Well-Being in 145 Countries." *Journal of Population Economics*, vol. 34, September 2020, https://doi.org/10.1007/s00148-020 -00797-z.

19   Haidt, Jon. "Kids Who Get Smartphones Earlier Become Adults with Worse Mental Health." *After Babel*, 15 May 2023, https://afterbabel.com/p/sapien-smartphone-report.

20   Sapien Labs. "Age of First Smartphone/Tablet and Mental Wellbeing Outcomes." Sapien Labs, 2023, https://sapienlabs. org/wp-content/uploads/2023/05/Sapien-Labs-Age-of-First -Smartphone-and-Mental-Wellbeing-Outcomes.pdf.

21   OFCOM. "Children and Parents: Media Use and Attitudes Report 2022." Ofcom, 30 March 2022, https://ofcom.org .uk/__data/assets/pdf_file/0024/234609/childrens-media -use-and-attitudes-report-2022.pdf.

22   Shanmugasundaram, Mathura, and Arunkumar Tamilarasu. "The Impact of Digital Technology, Social Media, and Artificial Intelligence on Cognitive Functions: A Review."

Frontiers in Cognition, vol. 2, Frontiers Media, November 2023, https://doi.org/10.3389/fcogn.2023.1203077.

23 Stone, Linda. "Beyond Simple Multi-Tasking: Continuous Partial Attention." *Linda Stone*, 30 November 2009, https://lindastone.net/2009/11/30/beyond-simple-multi-tasking-continuous-partial-attention/.

24 Andrews, Sally, et al. "Beyond Self-Report: Tools to Compare Estimated and Real-World Smartphone Use." *PLOS ONE*, edited by Jakob Pietschnig, vol. 10, no. 10, October 2015, p. e0139004, https://doi.org/10.1371/journal.pone.0139004.

25 Raichle, M. E., et al. "A Default Mode of Brain Function." *Proceedings of the National Academy of Sciences*, vol. 98, no. 2, Jan. 2001, pp. 676–82, https://doi.org/10.1073/pnas.98.2.676.

26 Killingsworth, M. A., and D. T. Gilbert. "A Wandering Mind Is an Unhappy Mind." *Science*, vol. 330, no. 6006, 2010, p. 932, https://doi.org/10.1126/science.1192439.

27 Sparrow, B., et al. "Google Effects on Memory: Cognitive Consequences of Having Information at Our Fingertips." *Science*, vol. 333, no. 6043, July 2011, pp. 776–78, https://doi.org/10.1126/science.1207745.

28 Stock, Jay T. "Are Humans Still Evolving? Technological Advances and Unique Biological Characteristics Allow Us to Adapt to Environmental Stress. Has This Stopped Genetic Evolution?" *EMBO Reports*, vol. 9, no. S1, July 2008, pp. S51–54, https://doi.org/10.1038/embor.2008.63.

7: WHY CAN'T WE GET ALONG?

1   Ekman, Paul. "Universal Emotions." *Paul Ekman Group*, 2019, https://paulekman.com/universal-emotions/.

2   Turner, Ellen. "Emotion Families: Part 1." *Paul Ekman Group*, 18 June 2019, https://paulekman.com/blog /emotion-families-part-1/.

3   Guy-Evans, Olivia. "Primary and Secondary Emotions." *Simply Psychology*, 17 February 2023, https://simply psychology.org/primary-and-secondary-emotions.html.

4   Frothingham, Mia Belle. "Fight, Flight, Freeze, or Fawn: How We Respond to Threats." *Simply Psychology*, 6 October 2021, https://simplypsychology.org/fight-flight -freeze-fawn.html.

5   Spectrum Gaming. "Masking." *Education Barriers*, 2022, https://barrierstoeducation.co.uk/masking.

6   Shatz, Itamar. "The Empathy Gap: Why People Fail to Understand Different Perspectives—Effectiviology." *Effectiviology*, https://effectiviology.com/empathy-gap/.

7   Loewenstein, George. "Hot-Cold Empathy Gaps and Medical Decision Making." *Health Psychology*, vol. 24, no. 4, Suppl, 2005, pp. S49–56, https://doi.org/10.1037 /0278-6133.24.4.S49.

8   Riess, Helen. "The Science of Empathy." *Journal of Patient Experience*, vol. 4, no. 2, May 2017, pp. 74–77, https://doi .org/10.1177/2374373517699267.

9   Carey, Jason. *Stress & Burnout for Frontline Staff Critical Incident Stress Management (CISM)*. 2017, https:// campusmentalhealth.ca/wp-content/uploads/2018/03 .Stress-and-Burnout-for-Front-line-Staff-presentation.pdf.

10 Kinnick, Katherine N., et al. "Compassion Fatigue:
    Communication and Burnout toward Social Problems."
    Journalism & Mass Communication Quarterly, vol. 73,
    no. 3, Sept. 1996, pp. 687–707, https://doi.org/10.1177
    /107769909607300314.

11 Ducharme, Jamie. "Do You Have 'Compassion Fatigue'?"
    TIME, 8 November 2023, https://time.com/6332107
    /compassion-fatigue-risk/.

12 Roberts, Jessica. "Empathy Cultivation through (Pro)
    Social Media: A Counter to Compassion Fatigue."
    Journalism and Media, vol. 2, no. 4, Dec. 2021, pp. 819–29,
    https://doi.org/10.3390/journalmedia2040047.

13 Humans of New York. (@humansofny). *Instagram*, https://
    www.instagram.com/humansofny/.

14 Maier, Scott R. "Compassion Fatigue and the Elusive Quest
    for Journalistic Impact." *Journalism & Mass Communication
    Quarterly*, vol. 92, no. 3, August 2015, pp. 700–22, https://
    doi.org/10.1177/1077699015599660.

15 Bentley, Paige G. "Compassion Practice as an Antidote for
    Compassion Fatigue in the Era of COVID-19." *Journal of
    Humanistic Counseling*, vol. 61, no. 1, Jan. 2022, https://doi
    .org/10.1002/johc.12172.

16 Moubarak, Bruna. "Navigating Compassion Fatigue in the
    Digital Age." ClearMinds Center for Emotional Health,
    27 December 2023, https://clearmindscenter.com/blog
    /navigating-compassion-fatigue-in-the-digital-age/.

17 Everett, Jim. "Intergroup Contact Theory: Past, Present,
    and Future | Magazine Issue 2/2013—Issue 17 | In-Mind."

The Inquisitive Mind, 2013, https://in-mind.org/article /intergroup-contact-theory-past-present-and-future.

18 Allon, Gad, et al. "Information Inundation on Platforms and Implications." *Operations Research*, vol. 69, no. 6, October 2021, https://doi.org/10.1287/opre.2021.2119.

19 Kubin, Emily, and Christian von Sikorski. "The Role of (Social) Media in Political Polarization: A Systematic Review." *Annals of the International Communication Association*, vol. 45, no. 3, September 2021, pp. 188–206, https://doi.org/10.1080/23808985.2021.1976070.

20 Suk Gersen, Jeannie. "What If Trigger Warnings Don't Work?" *New Yorker*, 28 September 2021, https://newyorker .com/news/our-columnists/what-if-trigger-warnings -dont-work.

21 Tsipursky, Gleb. "Knowing Just Enough to Be Dangerous | Psychology Today." *Psychology Today*, 7 October 2017, https://psychologytoday.com/us/blog/intentional-insights /201710/knowing-just-enough-be-dangerous.

22 Shakespeare, William. *As You like It* (Act 5, Scene 1). *Shakespeare Online*, 10 August 2010, https://shakespeare -online.com/plays/asu_5_1.html.

23 Huff, Charlotte. "Media Overload Is Hurting Our Mental Health. Here Are Ways to Manage Headline Stress." American Psychological Association, 1 November 2022, https://apa.org/monitor/2022/11/strain-media-overload.

24 Hwang, Juwon, et al. "The Relationship among COVID-19 Information Seeking, News Media Use, and Emotional Distress at the Onset of the Pandemic." *International Journal of Environmental Research and Public Health*, vol.

18, no. 24, Dec. 2021, p. 13198, https://doi.org/10.3390
/ijerph182413198.

25 Kahneman, Daniel. *Thinking, Fast and Slow*. New York:
Farrar, Straus and Giroux, 2011.

8: HOW CAN I MAKE A DIFFERENCE?

1 World Health Organization. "Burn-out an 'Occupational
Phenomenon': International Classification of Diseases."
World Health Organization, 2019, https://who.int/news
/item/28-05-2019-burn-out-an-occupational-phenomenon
-international-classification-of-diseases.

2 Future Forum. *Winter 2022/2023 Future Forum Pulse*.
Future Forum, 2023, https://futureforum.com/wp-content
/uploads/2023/02/Future-Forum-Pulse-Report-Winter
-2022-2023.pdf.

3 Scott, Elizabeth. "How to Tell You Have Reached the Point
of Burnout." *Verywell Mind*, 16 October 2022, https://
verywellmind.com/stress-and-burnout-symptoms-and
-causes-3144516.

4 Fryburg, David A. "Kindness as a Stress Reduction—
Health Promotion Intervention: A Review of the
Psychobiology of Caring." *American Journal of Lifestyle
Medicine*, vol. 16, no. 1, January 2021, p. 155982762098826,
https://doi.org/10.1177/1559827620988268.

5 American Psychiatric Association. "The Mental Health
Benefits of Simple Acts of Kindness." American Psychiatric
Association, 17 February 2023, https://psychiatry.org
/news-room/apa-blogs/mental-health-benefits-simple
-acts-of-kindness.

6   Cherry, Kendra. "Why Our Brains Are Hardwired to Focus on the Negative." *Verywell Mind*, 13 November 2023, https://verywellmind.com/negative-bias-4589618.

7   Robertson, Claire E., et al. "Negativity Drives Online News Consumption." *Nature Human Behavior*, vol. 7, March 2023, pp. 1–11, https://doi.org/10.1038/s41562-023-01538-4.

8   OFCOM. "News Consumption in the UK: 2023." OFCOM, 20 July 2023, https://ofcom.org.uk/__data/assets/pdf_file /0024/264651/news-consumption-2023.pdf.

9   Oxford English Dictionary. "Slacktivism, N." *Oxford English Dictionary*, 2016, https://doi.org/10.1093//OED//7955151818.

10 Verhulst, Stefaan. "A new vocabulary for the 21st Century: 'slacktivism.'" *TheGovLab*, Northeastern University, 18 May 2013, https://blog.thegovlab.org/a-new-vocabulary-for-the -21st-century-slacktivism.

11 Coscarelli, Joe. "#BlackoutTuesday: A Music Industry Protest Becomes a Social Media Moment." *The New York Times*, 2 June 2020, https://nytimes.com/2020/06/02/arts /music/what-blackout-tuesday.html.

12 Kalina, Peter. "Performative Allyship." *Technium Social Sciences Journal*, vol. 11, no. 1, August 2020, pp. 478–81, https://doi.org/10.47577/tssj.v11i1.1518.

13 Huff, Charlotte. "Media Overload Is Hurting Our Mental Health. Here Are Ways to Manage Headline Stress." American Psychological Association, 1 November 2022, https://apa.org/monitor/2022/11/strain-media-overload.

14 Psychology Today. "Learned Helplessness | Psychology Today United Kingdom." *Psychology Today*, https:// psychologytoday.com/gb/basics/learned-helplessness.

15 Sneed, Rodlescia S., and Sheldon Cohen. "A Prospective Study of Volunteerism and Hypertension Risk in Older Adults." *Psychology and Aging*, vol. 28, no. 2, June 2013, pp. 578–86, https://doi.org/10.1037/a0032718.

16 Konrath, Sara, et al. "Motives for Volunteering Are Associated with Mortality Risk in Older Adults." *Health Psychology*, vol. 31, no. 1, Jan. 2012, pp. 87–96, https://doi .org/10.1037/a0025226.

17 Creswell, J. David, et al. "Self-Affirmation Improves Problem-Solving under Stress." *PLOS ONE*, edited by José César Perales, vol. 8, no. 5, May 2013, p. e62593, https://doi .org/10.1371/journal.pone.0062593.

18 Lee, Min-Ah, and Ichiro Kawachi. "The Keys to Happiness: Associations between Personal Values Regarding Core Life Domains and Happiness in South Korea." *PLOS ONE*, edited by Shang E. Ha, vol. 14, no. 1, Jan. 2019, p. e0209821, https://doi.org/10.1371/journal.pone.0209821.

19 Selig, Meg. "9 Surprising Superpowers of Knowing Your Core Values." *Psychology Today*, 27 November 2018, https://psychologytoday.com/gb/blog/changepower /201811/9-surprising-superpowers-knowing-your-core -values.

20 Porter, Tenelle, et al. "Predictors and Consequences of Intellectual Humility." *Nature Reviews Psychology*, vol. 1, June 2022, pp. 1–13, https://doi.org/10.1038/s44159-022 -00081-9.

9: CAN I CHANGE MY BRAIN?

1   Cherry, Kendra. "What Is Neuroplasticity?" *Verywell Mind*, 8 November 2022, https://verywellmind.com/what-is-brain -plasticity-2794886.

2   Mateos-Aparicio, Pedro, and Antonio Rodríguez-Moreno. "The Impact of Studying Brain Plasticity." *Frontiers in Cellular Neuroscience*, vol. 13, no. 66, February 2019, https://doi.org/10.3389/fncel.2019.00066.

3   Caire, Michael J., et al. *Physiology, Synapse*. StatPearls, 2024, https://ncbi.nlm.nih.gov/books/NBK526047/.

4   Cafasso, Jacquelyn. "What Is Synaptic Pruning?" *Healthline*, Healthline Media, 3 January 2018, https:// healthline.com/health/synaptic-pruning.

5   University of Cambridge. "Problems with 'Pruning' Brain Connections Linked to Adolescent Mental Health Disorders." University of Cambridge, 24 April 2023, https:// cam.ac.uk/research/news/problems-with-pruning-brain -connections-linked-to-adolescent-mental-health-disorders.

6   Li, Wei, et al. "REM Sleep Selectively Prunes and Maintains New Synapses in Development and Learning." *Nature Neuroscience*, vol. 20, no. 3, January 2017, pp. 427–37, https://doi.org/10.1038/nn.4479.

7   Wang, Lu, et al. "Dysfunctional Synaptic Pruning by Microglia Correlates with Cognitive Impairment in Sleep-Deprived Mice: Involvement of CX3CR1 Signaling." *Neurobiology of Stress*, vol. 25, Elsevier BV, July 2023, https://doi.org/10.1016/j.ynstr.2023.100553.

8   Gonçalves, J. Tiago, et al. "In Vivo Imaging of Dendritic Pruning in Dentate Granule Cells." *Nature Neuroscience*,

vol. 19, no. 6, June 2016, pp. 788–91, https://doi.org/10.1038
/nn.4301. Accessed 16 July 2020.

9   Morizawa, Yosuke M., et al. "Synaptic Pruning through
Glial Synapse Engulfment upon Motor Learning." *Nature
Neuroscience*, vol. 25, no. 11, November 2022, pp. 1458–69,
https://doi.org/10.1038/s41593-022-01184-5.

10 Cherry, Kendra. "What Is Neuroplasticity?" *Verywell Mind*,
8 November 2022, https://verywellmind.com/what-is
-brain-plasticity-2794886.

11 Thompson, Jonathan. "9 Neuroplasticity Exercises to Boost
Productivity." *Work Life*, Atlassian, 9 February 2022,
https://atlassian.com/blog/productivity/neuroplasticity
-train-your-brain.

12 Leisman, Gerry, et al. "The Effects of Music Training and
Production on Functional Brain Organization and Cerebral
Asymmetry." *Art Science and Technology. Proceedings of the
International Conference on Art, Science, and Technology*,
edited by T. Gravchuk, et al., Domus Argenia, 2012, pp.
133–39, https://researchgate.net/publication/292137621_The
_effects_of_music_training_and_production_on_functional
_brain_organization_and_cerebral_asymmetry.

13 Davidson, Richard, and Antoine Lutz. "Buddha's Brain:
Neuroplasticity and Meditation [in the Spotlight]." *IEEE
Signal Processing Magazine*, vol. 25, no. 1, 2008, pp. 176–174,
https://doi.org/10.1109/msp.2008.4431873.

14 Sun, Ying, et al. "Alteration of Faecal Microbiota Balance
Related to Long-Term Deep Meditation." *General
Psychiatry*, vol. 36, no. 1, January 2023, p. e100893, https://
doi.org/10.1136/gpsych-2022-100893.

15 Gard, Tim, et al. "The Potential Effects of Meditation on Age-Related Cognitive Decline: A Systematic Review." *Annals of the New York Academy of Sciences*, vol. 1307, no. 1, January 2014, pp. 89–103, https://doi.org/10.1111/nyas.12348.

16 Luders, Eileen, et al. "Forever Young(er): Potential Age-Defying Effects of Long-Term Meditation on Gray Matter Atrophy." *Frontiers in Psychology*, vol. 5, January 2015, https://doi.org/10.3389/fpsyg.2014.01551.

17 Khalsa, Dharma Singh. "Stress, Meditation, and Alzheimer's Disease Prevention: Where the Evidence Stands." *Journal of Alzheimer's Disease*, edited by J. Wesson Ashford, vol. 48, no. 1, August 2015, pp. 1–12, https://doi.org/10.3233/jad-142766.

18 Asher, Hugh. "The Origins of Forest Bathing." *An Darach Forest Therapy*, 18 June 2023, https://silvotherapy.co.uk/articles/the-origins-of-forest-bathing.

19 Furuyashiki, Akemi, et al. "A Comparative Study of the Physiological and Psychological Effects of Forest Bathing (Shinrin-Yoku) on Working Age People with and without Depressive Tendencies." *Environmental Health and Preventive Medicine*, vol. 24, no. 1, June 2019, https://doi.org/10.1186/s12199-019-0800-1.

20 Havens, Justin. "What Is EMDR? | Types of Therapy." British Association for Counselling and Psychotherapy, https://bacp.co.uk/about-therapy/types-of-therapy/eye-movement-desensitisation-and-reprocessing-emdr.

21 Shapiro, Francine. "Efficacy of the Eye Movement Desensitization Procedure in the Treatment of Traumatic

Memories." *Journal of Traumatic Stress*, vol. 2, no. 2, April 1989, pp. 199–223, https://doi.org/10.1002/jts.2490020207.

22 Pearson, David G., and Tony Craig. "The Great Outdoors? Exploring the Mental Health Benefits of Natural Environments." *Frontiers in Psychology*, vol. 5, no. 1178, October 2014, https://doi.org/10.3389/fpsyg.2014.01178.

23 Piff, Paul K., et al. "Awe, the Small Self, and Prosocial Behavior." *Journal of Personality and Social Psychology*, vol. 108, no. 6, 2015, pp. 883–99, https://doi.org/10.1037/pspi0000018.

24 Keltner, Dacher. *Awe: The New Science of Everyday Wonder and How It Can Transform Your Life*. Penguin, 2023.

25 Dacher Keltner, from the *On Being* with Krista Tippett episode "The Thrilling New Science of Awe", first broadcast 2 February 2023. Reprinted with permission. Hear the full episode at onbeing.org.

26 World Bank. "Urban Development." World Bank, 3 April 2023, https://worldbank.org/en/topic/urbandevelopment/overview.

27 United Nations. "68% of the World Population Projected to Live in Urban Areas by 2050, Says UN." United Nations Department of Economic and Social Affairs, United Nations, 16 May 2018, https://un.org/development/desa/en/news/population/2018-revision-of-world-urbanization-prospects.html.

About the Author

Gemma Styles is a relatable, authentic, and trusted voice online who engages with her ten million Instagram followers to raise awareness about society's most pressing issues. On her award-winning podcast, *Good Influence*, she invites discussion on topics that we should care about, including mental health, sustainability, and feminism. She is also an ambassador for MQ Mental Health Research.